Ignaz Maybaum in his study
Photograph by *Nicholas de Lange*

EUROPEAN JUDAISM

General Editor: Jonathan Magonet
We are pleased to announce a multidisciplinary series of monographs
and essay collections, to be published in conjunction with Leo Baeck
College, exploring contemporary issues in Jewish life and thought.
As with the complementary journal *European Judaism*, it reflects the
wide range of academic, social, historical and theological areas that
are studied at Leo Baeck College with its multinational staff and student body and its unique position as the only progressive Jewish seminary operating in Europe.

Vol. 1: **Jewish Explorations of Sexuality**
Edited by Jonathan Magonet

Vol. 2: **Jewish Identity in Modern Times**
Leo Baeck and German Protestantism
Walter Homolka

Vol. 3: **Ignaz Maybaum: A Reader**
Edited by Nicholas de Lange

Ignaz Maybaum: A Reader

Edited by Nicholas de Lange

Berghahn Books
New York • Oxford

First published in 2001 by

Berghahn Books

www.BerghahnBooks.com

© 2001 Nicholas de Lange

'Ignaz Maybaum: Memories of my Father' © 2001 Alison Jaffa

Extracts from writings of Ignaz Maybaum
© Estate of Ignaz Maybaum

Photograph of Ignaz Maybaum by Nicholas de Lange

Library of Congress Cataloging-in-Publication Data

Maybaum, Ignaz, 1897–
[Essays. Selections]
Ignaz Maybaum : a reader / edited by Nicholas de Lange; with a memo-
rial by Alisa Jaffa.
   p. cm. – (European Judaism; v. 3)
One essay translated from German.
Includes bibliographical references.
ISBN 1-57181-720-4 (alk. paper) – ISBN 1-57181-322-5 (alk. paper)
   1. Judaism – Essence, genius, nature. 2. Judaism – Relations – Islam. 3.
Islam – Relations – Judaism. 4. Christianity and other religions – Judaism.
5. Judaism – Relations – Christianity. 6. Holocaust (Jewish theology). 7.
Zionism. I. De Lange, N. R. M. (Nicholas Robert Michael), 1944– II.
Jaffa, Alisa. III. Title. IV. European Judaism (Providence, R. I.); v. 3.

BM45 M352 2001
296.3–dc21   2001018455

British Library Cataloguing in Publication Data
A catalogue record for this book is available from the British Library.

Printed in the United States on acid-free paper.

ISBN 1 57181 720 4 hardback
       1 57181 520 1 paperback

CONTENTS

PREFACE

The name of Ignaz Maybaum is often cited, particularly in the context of Holocaust theology, but his writings have become inaccessible. The present volume contains a small selection, all taken (with one exception) from his ten English-language books, compiled with the aim of facilitating access to this interesting thinker for students and general readers.

My guiding principle has been to present the characteristic lines of Maybaum's thought. A great deal has had to be omitted, but the main themes of his writing are all represented. These are discussed further in the Introduction. The book is intended only as a small window into Maybaum's ideas, which are rich and complex. It is not offered as a substitute for the reading of his books and articles, and specialist scholars will naturally need to continue to consult the original texts.

With this in mind I have taken it upon myself to edit the excerpts, in some cases fairly radically. With the exception of some sermons, these extracts were not intended to be read as self-contained essays, and so I have tailored them to suit their new setting. I have omitted some sentences, paragraphs and even whole pages to avoid distracting digressions and repetitions. Where footnotes are concerned, I have deleted some references to works which have proved ephemeral; on the other hand I have inserted a few notes of my own where I felt some clarification was needed. These are enclosed within square brackets. I have also revised the language in many places, since although Maybaum was an impressive orator he never fully mastered the intricacies of English style. This is a service I performed for him, at his request, on a number of occasions during his lifetime, and so I believe I have some sense of what interference with his English he would have tolerated.

The transcription of Hebrew and Yiddish words always poses a problem. I have not systematically revised Maybaum's usage, which generally follows a German rather than an English system. Where possible I have opted for familiar and simple spellings, and I have not aimed at philological accuracy. Following Maybaum's German habit, I have retained *ch* for the two Hebrew letters *chet* and *chaf* (in words like *churban* or *chassid*); *ch* is always to be pronounced as in Bach.

I am most grateful to Alisa Jaffa, for the help and encouragement she has given me since the inception of this project, and for kindly agreeing to contribute her own personal memories of her father.

Ignaz Maybaum was my guide and teacher for more than twenty years, and I shall be glad if, with the publication of this Reader, I am able to repay even a small fraction of the great debt of gratitude I owe him.

Cambridge, 31 May 1999

IGNAZ MAYBAUM:
MEMORIES OF MY FATHER

Alisa Jaffa

Born in Vienna under the Austro-Hungarian Empire, my father was the third of four children. His father had a modest tailoring business, and the family lived in an apartment in the Ninth District. Two streets away was the *Gymnasium* (secondary school) he attended, where he received a classical education. One of the school rules obliged the pupils to speak Greek even during breaks between lessons. My father recalled that he was thirteen before the rule was lifted.

During World War I on leaving school he enlisted for army service. As a cavalry officer he gained three medals for bravery, and was decorated in person by 'his' Kaiser, Franz Josef. When as children my brother and I marvelled at a photograph of him in uniform mounted on a horse, my father's laconic response was that the creature proved very useful as it ended up as food for the men when supplies ran out. What saved my father's life was that he was hospitalised with jaundice while on the front at Bolzano. By the time he was released, his company had been virtually wiped out.

I never heard him talk about his army experiences, but it may well have been those searing events that prompted much later pronouncements. In the 1950s and 1960s he was attacked for sermons in which he said that no amount of Israeli territory was worth the life of a single Israeli soldier, referring to them as 'our boys'. I suspect that his own memories of war may have been the reason for such statements.

On release from the army he had decided to study for the rabbinate. He first enrolled at the rabbinical seminary in Vienna. At a dinner given in his honour on his seventieth birthday he described the scene on his first day as a student. On entering the classroom he saw pinned to the wall a large diagram of a cow, divided up into those portions that were kosher and those that were not. Instantly he knew this was not the place for him.

He studied in Berlin at the *Hochschule für die Wissenschaft des Judentums*, living the life familiar to impoverished students, spending hours reading newspapers in a coffee house over one cup of coffee. (Many years later, he urged an embarrassed young man who had arrived early to collect me to join us at the supper table, saying 'You must be hungry, I always was when I was a student'.) Even then his interests ranged beyond his main studies – he also studied history of art as an additional course.

He lodged with his uncle, Sigmund Maybaum, then a distinguished Berlin rabbi famous for his sermons. It was in his uncle's home that he first met my mother. She was sixteen at the time and, in her words, 'a shy and gawky schoolgirl'. She had accompanied her mother to attend a lecture held in the house, and at the time my grandmother was the personality he noticed. My grandmother, an educated woman, was one of nine brothers and sisters all of whom except her were engaged in the arts as painters, musicians and opera singers. (My mother's uncle, Eugen Spiro, was an acclaimed society portrait painter in Berlin, and her childhood playmates included her cousins Balthus, now of world renown, and his brother Pierre.) Five years passed before my parents met again, by which time my mother had blossomed and the situation changed.

They married in 1925, when my father took up his first rabbinical appointment in the small wine-growing community of Bingen-am-Rhein. From there he was called to head the community in Frankfurt-an-der-Oder, where friendships were made with certain families that lasted well beyond their stay there. During this time my brother, Michael, was born in 1929. From Frankfurt my father would travel to Berlin to lecture at the *Hochschule*.

Hitler's seizure of power in 1933 made a rapid impact. As a result of comments critical of Hitler made in the privacy of a closed meeting, and disclosed by a fellow Jew from outside the community, my father was arrested by the Gestapo at the end of 1935, a month after I was born. He spent six weeks in the Columbia Prison in Berlin. At one point he was put in front of a firing squad, which turned out to be for intimidation purposes only.

Pressure from agencies outside Germany mitigated the conditions under which he was kept, giving him the privilege of access to the prison library, and ultimately effecting his release. Many years later, when I was an adolescent, he saw me reading a detective story by Dorothy L. Sayers. 'I never did find out how that ended,' he mused, and went on to tell me that this was the book he had been reading when a prison guard opened his cell door and told him he was free to go. Whereupon he had hesitated, saying, 'But . . . I haven't finished the book'. This was the only time he spoke to me about his imprisonment. The other details were part of the deposition he made in his application for restitution from the German government, which I discovered among his files after his death.

As he left prison, a guard said to him, 'When you get home, make sure you give that man Schoeps a good hiding,' thereby revealing the identity of the Jew who had betrayed him.

My father reached the peak of his professional career in Germany when he was appointed one of the three communal rabbis of Berlin, a position of great distinction in a country that had no Chief Rabbi. He gained wide acclaim for his sermons given in different Berlin synagogues on a peripatetic basis. These should have been his glory years, but by this time conditions for the Jewish community were deteriorating. Jewish students could no longer enter university, as a result of which many youngsters took up Jewish studies as the only form of further education open to them. My father taught classes of these students, in addition to his rabbinical lecturing. As a community leader he was approached by many would-be emigrants, and helped them with their visa applications to leave Germany.

Despite the deteriorating climate my father published two books, wrote articles for the Jewish press, and associated with scholars and academics such as Martin Buber and Leo Baeck, his former teacher.

Under the sponsorship of Chief Rabbi J. H. Hertz of London, my father obtained a visa initially for England, and my parents and I left Germany in March 1939, preceded by my brother who was old enough to travel on a *Kindertransport*. We were reunited as a family some months later, my brother having been lodged in a hostel and then with an English family.

I can remember a conversation between my parents and other refugee friends during the first months in England, when I must have been barely four years old. The issue was whether to have the *lift*, the container with those household belongings that we had been permitted to take out of Germany, transported to London or whether to let them remain in the docks at Rotterdam until such time as we moved on to New York, which was the destination originally intended for both families. In a flash of rare practicality, my father insisted that our belongings should be with us. His prescience was rewarded, because soon after the outbreak of war the Rotterdam

docks were bombed. As well as being surrounded by familiar items
from their former home, my father had his library of books, which
were the tools of his trade.

My father knew no English on arrival in this country. Refugees
from Germany were classified by the British Government as 'enemy
aliens' and men from such families were rounded up for deportation
to the Isle of Man. This was an ironic repetition of the time of the
Gestapo round-ups, when my father had slept at different homes
night after night to avoid arrest, and even spent an entire night in a
car driven round the suburbs of Berlin by a fellow rabbi.

My father's first introduction to the English language came from
entire days spent at the local public library studying English newspapers, in order to avoid being found at home. When officials from
the Home Office called, I remember peering through my brother's
legs as he told them his father was not at home and that he had no
idea where he was. Their attempts to find him failed, and, unlike one
or two of our neighbours, he was not taken away.

For ten years my father was a rabbi without a pulpit. Financially,
the family was initially supported by the Chief Rabbi's Emergency
Council and funds distributed by a refugee organisation based at
Bloomsbury House in central London. During his wilderness years
he wrote three books, the first two written in German and subsequently translated into English for publication. He also officiated
and gave sermons in German at services for German-speaking
refugees held on occasion at the Hampstead synagogue and at over-
flow services during the High Holidays.

Another commitment was travelling on a regular basis to give
lessons to Jewish refugee children at a boarding school in Hindhead
and to individual children lodged with non-Jewish families scattered
outside London, to give them their weekly or monthly 'injection of
Judaism'.

Despite what must have been straitened circumstances for my
parents, my childhood memories of the war years were of a happy
secure home. There were frequent guests at the table: colleagues,
scholars and students. On Saturday afternoons my father would take
me for extended walks, to give my mother the chance of an after-
noon rest. My father had a fine voice and together we would go
through our repertoire of Hebrew, German and other songs as we
walked. On our return he would make coffee for the family and
serve it with home-baked cake.

Wartime Seder nights were memorable. Invited guests brought
contributions of food – and the occasional GI presented unheard of
luxuries from the PX. My father conducted the Seder dressed in his
white kittel, and everyone participated heartily in the singing. This

was during the black-out period, but nevertheless on more than one occasion, at the point when someone went to open the door for Elijah, they would come back saying there were people standing in the street listening to our singing.

A feature of the home were the constant, sometimes heated, political discussions. It surprised me to discover later that this was not the norm in other homes. My father was always receptive to alternative views, and relished the visits of my mother's cousin Peter Spiro, whose political predictions he welcomed. All his life he had a hearty appreciation of topical jokes, and Peter would invariably provide him with new ones.

After the war my father was invited to apply for different rabbinical posts. One was in Stockholm, and my chief memory of this was the presents he brought back to an England starved of all items other than basics. I received my first watch, my mother received nylon stockings, and for my brother there was a ball-point pen (a great novelty). These arrived wrapped in my father's rabbinical gown, to my mother's utter horror when she learned he had not thought to declare them to the Customs. My brother's reaction was to invent a scenario of newspaper headlines: 'Rabbi smuggles contraband in canonicals'.

In 1949 Harold Reinhart, rabbi of West London Synagogue, who had helped install many of the refugee rabbis in Reform synagogues, offered my father the post of congregational rabbi to the Edgware & District Reform Synagogue. I believe my father had always been traditional in terms of religious observance, and moving to Reform practice presumably meant a substantial shift for him. However, Edgware presented an opportunity for him to occupy a pulpit once again and he accepted the post.

The first years in Edgware were a struggle against a cabal of council members who had existed cosily without a rabbi since the inception of the synagogue and rather resented the intrusion of this foreign personality with strong views. It took something akin to a palace revolution, involving the efforts of newcomers, to oust the entrenched leaders of the community.

From then on my father had an easier time and moulded the community into a new and flourishing existence. His warmth, natural charm and empathy won many new members to the congregation. He was frequently called on to conduct the funeral of persons he had never met. Having spoken briefly beforehand to the relatives, he would then give a *hesped* that was as intimate as if he had known the deceased all their life.

Although he seldom leaned on his authority, when the occasion demanded he was quite capable of speaking out with force and expressing vehement criticism. On one occasion he prompted a walk-out by several leading synagogue members when he gave a sermon attacking Jews who joined the Freemasons. In a Friday evening sermon he once slyly referred to 'a family' (his own son) whose regular Saturday morning outing was to go to the launderette. My brother took it to heart and thereafter took his family to synagogue instead. He had a gift for poetic truth, addressing the dissatisfaction of unfulfilled lives with the phrase 'You who sit uneasy in your easy chairs'.

My father was remarkably prophetic in a number of ways. In the 1950s he referred to the 'lost millions' of Jews in the USSR, long before there was any general awareness of their difficulties. Further, in the same period he foresaw the problems that would confront Israel as a result of a governmental system where the religious party held the balance of power. His criticisms were construed as 'anti-Zionist', and he was vilified as a result.

During the 1950s and 1960s he was repeatedly invited to lecture at ecumenical and university conferences in Germany. Lecturing to receptive academic audiences was immensely stimulating and rewarding. He was treated with great respect there, leading to the ironic observation that he never received such recognition on home ground. (When he finally visited Israel in the mid 1960s, after he had retired, he would dearly have loved to lecture at the university but no invitation was forthcoming.)

Alongside conscientious attention to pastoral duties, he continued to write, exchanging ideas with visiting academics from abroad. Professor Talmon and Professor Koebner, both of the Hebrew University, were regular guests in the house. He was also concerned to help struggling fellow refugee scholars who had not found their feet, and was instrumental in securing positions for at least two colleagues at the newly established Leo Baeck College.

Probably the most rewarding period in his later life was as lecturer in homiletics at Leo Baeck College. Generations of student rabbis were exposed to a digest of his current interests. The latest dramatic production in the theatre or on television, art exhibitions, contemporary fiction, and of course political events, all apparently featured in his lectures. He recommended *The Times Literary Supplement* as required reading to his students. He used them as sounding boards for whatever book he happened to be working on and would invite discussion on the topics he was addressing. When the journey to the College became too much for him, the lectures continued in his own home in the form of intimate gatherings, still remembered by the students who came, as much for the tea and cakes served by mother during the break as for the content of the lectures.

My parents' marriage was a true partnership, and my mother's role was pivotal throughout. She was his amanuensis, typing all his manuscripts, which sometimes led to heated argument about the content. She accompanied him on most engagements, pastoral and academic, and in later years attended his needs with devotion and affection. Colleagues still remember her interruptions to give him the eye drops required for treating glaucoma. At a 70th birthday luncheon given by the Assembly of Ministers my father began by saying, 'The fact that I am in the right place, on the right day and at the right time, is entirely due to my wife, who wrapped me up like a parcel and delivered me here'.

On retirement from rabbinical office my father was made Rabbi Emeritus. He continued to write and to lecture at the College, and on occasion he would address the Council for Christians and Jews. He broadcast talks on BBC radio, and his last commitment was an interview with Dutch television, shortly before his death.

My father's younger brother had been in a concentration camp in Austria in 1938. On his release he and his wife emigrated to Palestine where both worked in primitive conditions as doctors. News of his early death from cancer took weeks of wartime postal delays to reach my father. This loss was overshadowed in later years by the torment he felt at the fate of his mother and sisters. After deportation his mother died in Theresienstadt and his sisters in Auschwitz.

When frailty and poor eyesight restricted his outings, his chief delight was having his family around him. He adored his grandchildren and took great pleasure in their jokes and lively antics. To this day remarks made around the table are treasured in the family memory. Perhaps an appropriate note to end on is his reply when asked by his son about how he felt about the future: 'As a Jew, I have to be an optimist'.

I should like to thank Nicholas de Lange for the immense task he undertook in making the selections for this anthology, thereby reviving the contribution my father made to the field of theological studies and making it available to a new generation.

For my part, I have tried to convey to those who did not know him what sort of person my father was, beyond his scholarship and rabbinical achievements. He was a loyal friend and a loving and devoted husband and father with a lively sense of humour and fun, always accessible, however immersed in his work. I am grateful for his life and I miss him to this day.

Zichrono livracha
London, January 1999

INTRODUCTION

Since his death in 1976 the stature of Ignaz Maybaum as a theologian, particularly as a theologian of the Shoah, has grown. At the same time he has been the object of increasing criticism, some of it couched in intemperate terms. As often happens, his critics have generally not taken the trouble to read him at first hand: many of them simply cite each other, not always accurately.

It is my aim in this Reader to set the record straight to some extent by enabling Maybaum, whose writings have long been out of print, to speak out again on a range of relevant issues, not only on the Shoah but on such subjects as the nature and destiny of Judaism, and on the relations between Israel and the Diaspora. It is as a holocaust theologian that Maybaum is best known today, and it is true that almost all his writing is to some extent touched by the Shoah. But what marks it out from the work of other holocaust theologians is the way that, even when the Shoah stands in the foreground of his consciousness, it is always seen within a wider theological context, the foundations of which are in his early work in Germany, but which continued to be developed and modified in the course of his life.

In this introduction I shall first present the books from which the extracts are taken, and then briefly introduce the extracts themselves, drawing attention to some features that might otherwise elude or confuse contemporary readers. I have not included a biographical sketch, as this has been admirably done in the foregoing memoir by his daughter, Alisa Jaffa.

The direction of Maybaum's ideas was in a sense directed by his life. Born a Jew in German-speaking Central Europe in the year of the first Zionist Congress he was, inevitably perhaps, fascinated by the place of the Jews in the Europe of his day, a war-torn Europe where enlightenment had given way to romantic nationalism and Jewish emancipation was being challenged by antisemitism, and where a marriage of romantic nationalism and antisemitism had in their turn given birth to Zionism. Having grown up in Vienna and studied in Germany he was imbued with a deep love of German culture, but he was also, as a witness and victim of German antisemitism, compelled to recognise that this culture concealed unforeseen dangers. Called upon to minister to the Jews of Berlin in their twilight hours, and later to interpret the German Jewish experience in its glory and its catastrophe to an often uncomprehending British public, Maybaum never ceased, throughout a long career as a rabbi and theologian, to scrutinise the formative events and influential writings of his own and the preceding generation with the aim of discovering what had gone wrong and what lessons could be learned for the future.

In the course of a long working life Maybaum wrote twelve books and many articles.[1] The excerpts in this reader are, with one exception, taken from the ten books published in English. They have been chosen to convey the essential lines of Maybaum's thought, but they do not represent the particular argument of each book. Consequently, by way of introduction, I shall run through these ten books in chronological order, drawing attention to the salient points of each.

The first English book, *Man and Catastrophe* (1941), is a collection of sermons delivered in German to refugee congregations in various London synagogues, under the auspices of the United Synagogue, between 1939 and 1941. They are naturally preoccupied with the situation in Germany and the War, and they attempt to hold out a message of hope to his Jewish hearers. The book was published, however, with a Christian readership in mind as well, and it has a preface by William Temple, at that time still Archbishop of York. Temple commends the book to a Christian readership with the words: 'Thus we may all go to school with this Rabbi and learn from him a better understanding, not only of the Jewish people, but of that which for us as for him is the Word of God'.

Synagogue and Society (1944), dedicated to Leo Baeck, is subtitled *Jewish–Christian Collaboration in the Defence of Western Civilisation,* and is also addressed to Christian as well as Jewish readers. Although the book is concerned most immediately with Hitler and his challenge to

---

1. There is a full bibliography of Maybaum's writings to the time of his death in Marmur, ed., *A Genuine Search,* pp. 16–25. His last book, *Happiness Outside the State,* was published posthumously in 1980.

Judaeo-Christian civilisation, Maybaum begins with the Christian origins of synagogue-burning. 'The words "Burn down the Synagogues" occur in the writings of Martin Luther,' and therefore the book is not only about Hitler, but about Jewish-Christian relations. As Maybaum puts it, in the modern world 'the Jew . . . is faced by a problem he did not know in the Middle Ages. His problem is the Christian.' Maybaum aims to initiate a dialogue by investigating the distinctive and different character of Judaism and Christianity. 'Mutual understanding between Jews and Christians is possible only when we do not try to obscure the differences.' All the major themes of Maybaum's subsequent work are foreshadowed in this book, and particularly the implication for Jews and Christians of enlightenment and Jewish emancipation, political liberalism and progress, and the dangers stemming from nationalism, socialism and secularism.

The Jewish Home (1945) is a cross between a text-book and a theological tract. There is clearly a therapeutic element in its writing. 'I have seen Jews in happiness. In these times of martyrdom of the Jewish people I wish to tell of this happiness . . . I shall not describe happiness or define it. I shall describe family life.' (p.9) Outwardly a description of the life of a Jewish home, the book is heavily charged with theological reflection, beginning with the praise of the *ba'al habayith* ('master of the house' or paterfamilias), which is a recurrent theme in Maybaum's work from his Berlin days on. The Jewish home, with the patriarchal figure of the *ba'al habayith* at its head, offers permanent, stable and human values in the face of inhuman chaos. The state is the enemy of the family; it begets revolutions and wars. 'The father is the priest in the family, creating a sanctuary of God's atonement'. Rebellion is the natural role of sons, but sons must learn to become fathers. Maybaum is worried that this development is under threat: 'Our generation is not only a fatherless generation because so many sons are losing their fathers on the battlefields, but because the new generation does not know how to be a father towards wife and child' (p. 28).

In *The Jewish Mission* (1949) Maybaum uses for the first time his well-known designation of the Holocaust as the 'third *Churban*', the third destruction in Jewish history, after the destruction of the first and second Temple. He calls on Jews to respond by being faithful to the God of Israel, and rejecting all false gods – including the false god of political Zionism. What is the 'Jewish mission'? Maybaum builds on ideas long established in German Jewish liberalism. The Jews are chosen to be God's witnesses in the world. They bear witness not necessarily by what they say, but very often simply by their existence.

Jewish Existence (1960) begins with a study of the relationship between Judaism and bourgeoisie. Jewish life is equated with family life, which is constantly threatened by the power of the state. Maybaum proceeds to consider the image of the tragic hero, an image at the heart of Christianity that is also at the centre of political idealism. He makes use of a Biblical example which became very dear to him, and to which he reverted again and again, the *Akedah*, or (as Christians call it) the Sacrifice of Isaac. In a Jewish reading, this story has a happy ending: Isaac is not sacrificed, but finds a wife and founds a Jewish home. A Christian reading sees this story as a type of the crucifixion, and the political idealist, too, identifies the destruction as noble: 'Innumerable are the altars in world-history on which man of all ages laid his sacrifice as soldier and politician, as thinker and artist' (p. 90).

The next book was a collection of sermons, *The Faith of the Jewish Diaspora* (1962). These sermons, delivered on Sabbaths and Festivals in his Outer London synagogue, provide the best introduction to Maybaum as a Biblical theologian. He was clearly comfortable preaching in the time-honoured manner on a text (the texts, provided by the Jewish lectionary, come from the Pentateuch and the Prophets). Many of the sermons engage in one way or another with the problem of the Holocaust. Few, however, tackle it head-on; such sermons were held back for use in the book that followed.

The Face of God After Auschwitz (1965), dedicated 'In loving Memory of my Mother and my two Sisters, three of the six million', is the book which really enlarged Maybaum's reputation outside a narrow circle. The book consists of seven separate sections. 'The Human Imagination after Auschwitz' is an introduction tracing the outlines of the book. The emphasis is on the future, not the past, and Maybaum writes with a sense of almost prophetic urgency. 'We deceive ourselves when we plan for the future without admitting that it leads away from all our yesterdays . . . After Auschwitz and Hiroshima we must face a hitherto unknown element of human existence . . . The globe itself, populated with numerous races, must become our concern. Only the Biblical view of the world as the creation of God and every human being as created in the image of God can save us from the catastrophe looming on the horizon' (pp. 38–9). 'Preaching to Jews after Auschwitz' is a collection of 18 sermons. The themes are the by now familiar ones of Maybaum's preaching, but a new image makes its appearance: Auschwitz as the Golgotha of the twentieth century. Maybaum addresses the Christian image of the crucifixion as applied to the Jewish victims of the *Churban*, and refuses to see anything noble in their 'sacrifice'. On the contrary, the *Churban* represents the triumph of paganism over the Jewish element in Christianity. The triumph of paganism over true Christianity does not, however, diminish, but rather highlights, the Christian responsibility for what happened: 'Auschwitz is the pagan Golgotha of our time. A Christianity withdrawn from the responsibilities of history shares the responsibility for the twentieth century Golgotha of six million Jews' (p. 80).

The third section, 'Leo Baeck in Terezin: religious humanism tested' is an appreciation of Baeck that underlines how he brought to his scholarship certain perennial Jewish values. The assertion of such values, in the face of an unfeeling, self-destructive world, came to be very important to Maybaum. A short essay on Walter Rathenau (the foreign minister of Germany who was assassinated in 1922) entitled 'The Jewish intellectual in politics' has a similar theme, insisting that Rathenau in no way turned his back on the Jewish ethical tradition but that, on the contrary, his political commitment was motivated by the same faith in justice that inspired the Biblical prophets. A short meditation on the Biblical Book of Esther leads into the two most substantial sections of the book: 'Farewell to the Middle Ages' and 'The Forward March of Western Civilisation'. Although some of the themes of these two chapters (the characterisation of the Jew as a quintessential bourgeois, the engagement with Christian theology and with the German intellectual tradition) have already been encountered in previous books, there is also a more specific and explicit focus than before on the concept of progress, which takes its starting point from a familiar topos, the 'Sacrifice of Isaac'. The message of the *Akedah*, that God does not require human sacrifice, points to a peaceful and optimistic model of progress. Another theory 'says that progress is the way from catastrophe to catastrophe. At Golgotha Isaac is sacrificed.' It is when Christianity is cut off from its Old Testament roots that Auschwitz becomes inevitable (p. 197). Even after Auschwitz, however, the first kind of progress can continue, and Maybaum seeks for hints that will make sense of this idea in reality. He finds a clue in the strange realisation that the Holocaust wiped away the 'medieval' Jewish civilisation of eastern Europe and left the whole Jewish people in the 'Western camp' (p. 201).

> My interpretation of the post-*churban* era sees the Jewish people now, by the will of God, a Westernised people, because Western civilisation can be the mediating agency which brings to mankind what God has planned for mankind: justice, kindness, freedom and peace (p. 200).

Auschwitz thus completed the process of emancipation, 'the movement in which we progress from the civilisation of medieval Islamic despotism towards the civilisation of Western democracy' (p. 220). 'Islam' for Maybaum is a sort of symbolic keyword that indicates what was wrong with 'medieval' Judaism: submission before a law seen as a 'book from heaven', with the accompanying loss of liberty, and particularly the oppression and degradation of women. This part of the argument can be read as an apologia for Reform Judaism in the face of a dominant and rigorist Orthodoxy, but it also becomes part of the larger argument about Auschwitz and progress.

Four years after the *Face of God* Maybaum published *Creation and Guilt*, subtitled *A Theological Assessment of Freud's Father–Son Conflict*. In many ways this is Maybaum's most accessible and attractive book, even though it has some very hard things to say, to Jews, to Christians and to Muslims. Taking his cue from Freud, Maybaum looks at the relationship between sons and fathers, and he identifies a strong patricidal tendency in a generation of university-educated Jews in Austria who, like Freud, for essentially social reasons rejected their forebears who had been catapulted by the partition of Poland from the ghetto to Austrian emancipation. To establish their own credentials they had to reject and kill their own fathers. The portrait of Freud's Vienna in this book is painted critically but with familiarity and affection. If these brilliant Viennese intellectuals, men like Otto Weininger, Karl Kraus, Franz Werfel and even Ludwig Wittgenstein, rejected their Jewish heritage because of the pressure of antisemitism, and paid a heavy price in the process, the search for the roots of that antisemitism take us back to an analogous father-hatred in the early Church. The early Christians had to deny their Jewish origins so as to establish their own credentials, and in a sense the figure on the Cross is not the Son, it is the Father.

Trialogue between Jew, Christian, and Muslim was published in 1973, and Maybaum states in the Preface, 'I regard this book as a kind of commentary on Franz Rosenzweig's *The Star of Redemption*. He describes Rosenzweig's *magnum opus* as a *Guide for the Perplexed* of contemporary Jewry. What Maybaum does in this book is to single out some key themes in the *Star* and read them in such a way as to make explicit his own debt to Rosenzweig and at the same time to invoke Rosenzweig's authority in support of his own ideas.

Rosenzweig, in a famous phrase, describes the Jew 'striding through history without a sideways glance'. This is of obvious relevance to Maybaum's warnings about the betrayal involved when Jews espouse the values of the state and political movements, or the pursuit of culture as an end in itself. Standing outside the currents of history, the Jew enjoys a foretaste, as it were, of eternity, even though the final redemption, the full liberation from the shackles of history, is still to come. Redemption, one of the three pillars of Rosenzweig's work (together with creation and revelation), is a relatively minor theme in Maybaum, but the sense of eternity in the here and now pervades Maybaum's writing about Judaism.

The title of the book, *Trialogue between Jew, Christian, and Muslim*, indicates an argument that Maybaum had never before pointed up so explicitly. When we make a careful comparison of Judaism with Christianity and Islam we find that it shares some features with each, but is different from both. Judaism treads its own individual path: sometimes it walks between the other two monotheistic traditions, sometimes it may side with one or the other, but its insights are always capable of enriching both.

This same line of reasoning characterises the short posthumous book *Happiness Outside the State* (1980), which repeats and summarises views Maybaum had expressed previously, but does not, I believe, add anything substantially new.

Surveying Maybaum's writing as a whole, it is remarkably consistent from beginning to end. Despite the huge upheavals in his own life and in the Jewish society he lived in, he did not fundamentally change his views. The key ideas are already found in the two books he published in Germany in the 1930s and in his wartime sermons preached in London. This is quite important to understand if we try to assess his theology of the Holocaust. Although Maybaum spent half his life meditating on this tragic and cataclysmic disaster in the story of German Jewry which was also his own story, in a sense what he was doing was to fit it into pre-existing structures rather than reacting to the events as to some new discovery, as some other Holocaust theologians have done. Reading the successive books one sometimes has an impression of someone moving the pieces of a puzzle around, perhaps getting a tiny bit closer to a solution each time, but at the end it seems as far off as ever. At each stage Maybaum incorporates different insights, often drawn from his reading, sometimes from conversations or from current events. There are changes of view, but there is no radical shift.

Ignaz Maybaum was first and foremost a German Jew, and his points of reference, outside the Bible, are German: Goethe, Lessing, Mendelssohn and Heine, Hegel, Nietzsche, Karl Marx and Hermann Cohen. Judaism, for him, came of age in nineteenth-century Germany, and he devotes long passages to the two great pioneering German rabbis, the Liberal Abraham Geiger and the Orthodox Samson Raphael Hirsch, insisting on their similarities rather more than their differences. The modern world, he liked to say, was the product of three German-speaking Jews: Marx, Freud and Einstein.

It is important in considering his interpretation of the Holocaust to understand that he sees it from a German Jewish perspective. In a sense the key question raised by the Holocaust was not so much 'Why did God allow it?' as 'What did the [German] Jews get wrong?'

Hence the constant preoccupation with the might and violence of the state and its tendency to corrupt and paganise Christianity, and indeed Judaism too, and with the false values associated with the worship of culture.

Another important point is that Maybaum the theologian is never divorced from Maybaum the congregational rabbi and preacher. Sermons make up a large part of his published oeuvre, and it was in writing a new sermon each week, around a Biblical text, that he refined and reworked his theological ideas.

This helps us to understand the place of the Bible in Maybaum's thought. The Bible is never far in the background: often it is in the foreground. He is the most Biblical of contemporary Jewish theologians, not just in the way he weaves Biblical allusions and citations into his text, but also in his commitment to what he sees as Biblical values. The Bible for Maybaum is the word of God in a very real sense. He does not feel called on to justify or explain this, but it is perfectly clear from the way he quotes the Bible. It carries supreme authority for him, and he assumes his hearers will share this commitment. The Bible here means the Bible as read and interpreted by the Rabbis. Jacob and Esau, for example, stand for Jews and Gentiles, and the Suffering Servant signifies the people of Israel.

Yet he is never *merely* an interpreter of the Bible. The text speaks to him and through him out of the contemporary situation; it speaks of contemporary concerns; and it is inseparable from the complex and sophisticated interpretation of European civilisation which underlies his theology of the Shoah.

This book is divided into four parts, corresponding to the four main interests attested in Maybaums writing. These are not, however, watertight compartments. Inevitably he touches on various themes in the course of a single passage. The Nazi Holocaust recurs again and again, and the final section, on Zion, has been deliberately kept short because many statements on this subject have already been quoted in the other sections.

The first part is concerned with Judaism, and it reveals both Maybaum's deep attachment to Jewish tradition and his deep commitment to the modernist reforms initiated by the German Reformers, among whom he numbers, paradoxically, the arch-conservative S. R. Hirsch. He situates his own Judaism firmly within this modernist tradition, which aims at a marriage of essential Jewish and post-Enlightenment European values. It will be seen that Maybaum has a strong belief in what he calls 'Western civilisation', but at the same time he is wary of its errors and excesses, which in his view help to explain why Germany fell under the power of Nazism. He is also concerned to separate the perennial values of Judaism from those which, however deeply entrenched in the popular mind, are outmoded or even dangerous.

The first extract, 'Friday Evening', conveys something of the didactic yet poetic and strangely passionate flavour of the book *The Jewish Home*, which is both a primer and a personal theological statement. The emphasis on Sabbath peace is poignant in a book written so soon after the end of the war, while the emphasis on the priestly role of the father within the home contains more than a hint of the priestly role of the Jews within the wider world (which is made explicit in a later extract in this first section, 'Jewish Migration'). The clear stress on the distinct roles of the 'father' and the 'lady of the house' is not accident. As the extracts in this Reader make plain, Maybaum was far from being a male chauvinist, but in the face of war-torn Europe he was a firm believer in the primordial value of the family, and in the role of the father as its head.

The next two extracts are concerned with German Jewish modernism, and they illustrate Maybaum's insistence on the importance of S. R. Hirsch, commonly thought of as the founder of Modern Orthodoxy, as a reformer at the side of the father of Liberal Judaism, Abraham Geiger. By showing their points of difference as well as those things that united them he explains his conclusion that neither can be dispensed with.

In writing about Sigmund Freud Maybaum was brought back to the Vienna in which he was born and grew up. Like Martin Buber, who receives a more positive mention here than elsewhere in Maybaum's books (notably in *Trialogue*), Maybaum had made the move from Vienna to Germany, and his book about Freud indicates clearly the value that he placed on this move. Freud's (and Hitler's) Vienna comes across as a spectacularly brilliant yet fatally ineffectual place, dominated by the pale and distant father-figure of the emperor, and with the hordes already at the door. Freud's attitude to Judaism is explained against this background, which also leads into a parallel onslaught on Christianity, similarly beset with a preoccupation with a paradoxical father-figure and with the pagan hordes at the door. These extracts make plain what happens when the father of 'Friday Evening', who makes a cameo appearance here as Freud's own father, is overthrown by the excessively self-confident sons. Yet at the end Maybaum reclaims Freud, and with him Marx, for Judaism: they may not have been good Jews, but they pose a 'Jewish challenge' to Christianity.

Maybaum considered himself to be a disciple and interpreter of Franz Rosenzweig, but he was also a pupil of Leo Baeck, and in 'Leo Baeck in Terezin' he permits himself a critical, if sympathetic, account of his teacher. Baeck's essay on Paul had stressed the

complexity of the Jewish relationship to Hellenism; both Baeck and
Maybaum were accustomed to a coded language in which 'Hellenism' stood for German culture. For all its inherent dangers, 'Hellenistic wisdom' has its place at the heart of rabbinic Judaism, and it
is a fatal error for Jews to turn their back on it. The consequences of
this error are spelt out in 'Prophetic Judaism and the *Halachah*'. Nineteenth-century scholarship rescued rabbinic Judaism from the
opprobrious (and inherently antisemitic) designation of 'Pharisaic
legalism'. The rabbis were concerned with law, but they were the
true heirs of the Biblical prophets. Contemporary Orthodox rabbis,
by emphasising practice above the prophetic spirit, have fallen into
a heresy which Maybaum associates, rightly or wrongly, with Islam.

The relationship between Judaism and Islam is the subject of the
second part. It must be said right away that, keen though Maybaum
is to engage in a dialogue with Christianity, and indeed to broaden
it into what he pioneeringly termed 'Trialogue' by bringing in Islam,
he is more often concerned to define the other two religions over
and against Judaism. He reminds us more than once that an awareness of differences is a necessary prerequisite to dialogue, but
although he speaks at times with appreciation, and even warmth, of
the heritage of Islam and Christianity, he is apt to represent Islam in
particular in somewhat stereotyped and dismissive terms. There are
several reasons for this. In the first place, he was far better
acquainted with Christianity than with Islam. Secondly, as has
already been remarked, he regularly exploited the example of Islam
in his polemic against the over-rigid and all-encompassing legalism
(as he saw it) of Jewish Orthodoxy, so that when he writes of Islam
one sometimes has the impression that he is really writing about
Orthodoxy. That said, however, he is consistently at pains to stress
that Christianity, Islam and Judaism are intimately related to one
another within the 'monotheistic family', and in some respects he
favours Islam above Christianity, notably in its historic treatment of
religious minorities.

It is impossible to extricate Christianity from the quest for the
roots of Nazi antisemitism, and this is an aspect of Jewish–Christian
relations that preoccupied Maybaum throughout his adult life. On a
personal level he laboured for a better Jewish understanding of
Christianity as well as for a better Christian understanding of
Judaism. He was one of two Jewish representatives on the Prepara-
tory Committee that led to the founding of the Council of Christians
and Jews after the War, and he strongly supported the work of the
Council. Yet he did not shrink from speaking and writing of
'Christian antisemitism', of two thousand years of Christian hatred
for the Jews. He was interested in investigating the theological roots

of this hatred, and in laying bare its consequences. It is impossible to do justice to his arguments in a few words, but it is important to underline one aspect of his thinking on this subject. The relationship between Christianity and Judaism is a very close one: Christianity was born out of Judaism and has a great deal of Judaism within it; but it is always open to being infected by pagan values, and herein lies the danger. Maybaum does not say that without the pagan elements there would be no Christian antisemitism, but in writing of Christian responsibility for the Holocaust he insists that it was a paganised Christianity that was partly to blame.

The Biblical story of the *Akedah*, the trial of Abraham in Genesis 22, furnishes a neat paradigm for Maybaum illustrating the differences between the three religions. For a Jewish reader father Abraham is a type of Jewish trust in God, while for a Muslim he embodies the cardinal virtue of submission (the meaning of *islam*). The Jewish reader makes a direct connection between the trial of chapter 22 and the sequel in chapter 24, where Isaac marries a wife, and thereby takes his place as one of the ancestors of the holy people. A Christian, however, cannot resist reading Genesis 22 through the lens of the Gospel story, in which the Father offers his Son as a sacrifice for the sins of the world. As Maybaum points out, in giving the story the title 'the Sacrifice of Isaac' Christians betray the fact that in their reading Isaac is not spared. The Christian Isaac will never marry and have children. This Christian Isaac, like the Isaac in Wilfred Owen's poem which was set to music by Benjamin Britten in his *War Requiem*, stands for all the young men offered up on the altar of European nationalism in the Great War, and in so many other wars. Maybaum contemplates with horror the thought that Israel, too, might become the sort of state which makes such inhuman demands of its young citizens. He was no doubt unaware that dozens of poems have been written in Israel likening fallen soldiers to Isaac.

Maybaum's comparative treatment of Judaism, Christianity and Islam relies very heavily on that of Franz Rosenzweig in the *Star of Redemption*. This is evident in the essay on 'The Year One', 'Islamic Submission to the Law' and 'The Islamic Gown of Jewish Orthodoxy'. But Rosenzweig is only a starting point, and Maybaum endeavours to enlarge upon and develop his treatment of these topics. On occasion (not very often) he is even prepared to criticise his master, or at least to rebuke him mildly, as when he finds him speaking of an 'immutable law'. This is a disturbing discovery for a Maybaum who is concerned to reclaim Rosenzweig, sometimes cited as a proponent of Orthodoxy, for Liberal Judaism. However he manages to show that Rosenzweig soon retracts this 'Islamic' statement, and that in fact his attitude to the Jewish law was entirely consonant with Liberalism.

In 'The Holy Seed' Maybaum pursues Rosenzweig's remarks about blood as a vehicle of Judaism, revealing a certain ambivalence on the question of whether a proselyte can be an authentic Jew. Rosenzweig is not an easy writer to read. A younger generation of Jewish thinkers has recently begun to revisit Rosenzweig and to expound him in terms of contemporary concerns. There is much to be learned also by reading him through the mediation of an older generation – not only Maybaum, but men such as Nahum Glatzer and Ernst Simon – who were closer to the source.

Maybaum was a voracious and critical reader, but he also took a lively interest in other media, and was well able to spin a lecture or sermon from a visit to the theatre or from watching television (as can be seen from 'The Medieval Passion Play'). Nowhere is his interest in the theatre more apparent than in the long essay 'Shylock, the Tragic Champion of the Law', from the book *Trialogue*. In the course of a penetrating exposition of Shakespeare's Jew in the context of the contrast between Christian, Jewish and Muslim attitudes to law and love Maybaum refers to several actual productions of the *Merchant of Venice*, some of which he had seen himself and others he had read of. Purely visual elements of a production are as important to him as textual ones, and the response of the audience is as material to his argument as the intentions of the playwright. This essay gives a voice to a side of Ignaz Maybaum that was familiar enough to those who knew him but that in his writings usually comes out only in an occasional aside.

The third part concerns the Holocaust. Most of Maybaum's writing relates to this theme in some form or another; the eight extracts collected in this section contain some of his most important statements on the subject, but other insights can be found elsewhere in this book. 'The Third *Churban*' was, as I have already said, Maybaum's own distinctive way of referring to the Holocaust, coined at a time when there was still no accepted terminology. The term *churban* is not chosen at random: it is intended to conjure up the destruction of the first and second temple, and Maybaum's contention is that these three destructions are singled out uniquely in the Jewish experience, and set aside from other catastrophes such as the destruction of Spanish Jewry during the Christian *Reconquista* or the Chmielnicki massacres in seventeenth-century eastern Europe, which have also left a deep wound in the collective psyche. The two great acts of destruction, by the Babylonians and the Romans, were blows struck at the heart of the Jewish people and their religion; the extraordinary fact is that not only did neither spell the end of

Judaism, but both, in a real sense, led to momentous progress, converting Judaism from a local cult based on animal sacrifice to a worldwide religion expressed through bloodless worship. In coining the phrase 'the third *Churban*', Maybaum asserts his confidence that this event, too, will be powerless to destroy the Jewish people or its spirit, but that, on the contrary, in some mysterious way it will lead to momentous progress. Maybaum is neither entirely explicit nor consistent about what this progress consists in, but the essence of his message is that with Auschwitz an era in world history comes to an end, and for the Jews in particular this means the end of a medieval, feudal age. Externally, the process of emancipation that began in the eighteenth century is completed, and Jews have now regained political responsibility and self-reliance within a democratic political system; internally the process of reform that began with the emancipation movement is completed, and the domination of powerful but blinkered rabbis is at an end. Maybaum laments the loss of Eastern European Jewry, yet he insists that there is a glorious future ahead, even if it demands a struggle.

It is precisely his Biblical faith that allows him to look so confidently towards the future. Maybaum is not a fundamentalist, in the sense of endowing the text with oracular value because it is in some supernatural way the word of God. He fully accept the fruits of modern Biblical scholarship. Indeed, his strongly developed sense of the historical background of the text heightens its impact. His interpretation is thoroughly historical. The argument goes something like this: after the first *Churban* – the Babylonian destruction – the leaders of the Jews could easily have shrugged their shoulders and said 'too bad, we lost', or they could have protested about the injustice of what had happened. But they did neither. They attributed the power to God and as a corollary they cast the blame on the sins of the people. This was a daring and no doubt unpopular move, but its effects were immeasurable, and splendid: the survival of the Jews as a people under God during the long years of Babylonian captivity, with confidence in their God, whose power had not been shattered or diminished by the razing of his temple but in fact, paradoxically, magnified so that his home became the whole world. It is the judgment of history that vindicates the prophets' response, and Maybaum's identification with that prophetic response is therefore grounded less in a reverence for the 'word of God' than in awe at the effectiveness of their unexpected ploy. Confidence begets confidence, and his reaction therefore to post-*churban* bewilderment was to assert firmly that God is still in command of history.

Maybaum's Biblical theology of the Holocaust has been misunderstood in some quarters, particularly by philosophers who are concerned with the question of theodicy: how could a good and all-powerful God have allowed such a terrible thing to happen? The logic of the question leads to only one answer: he could not. Maybaum, with his Biblical faith, is not concerned with the philosophical riddle. The Holocaust *did* happen: that much is certain. The responsibility, however, lies not with God but with man. Like the Biblical prophets, Maybaum insists that catastrophe is the result of human failure. The prophet Jeremiah went so far as to call Nebuchadnezzar, the destroyer of Jerusalem, 'my [i.e. God's] servant', and Maybaum, in a sermon delivered in 1963, comments: 'Would it shock you if I were to imitate this prophetic style and formulate the phrase "Hitler, My servant"?' This isolated remark has provoked a horrified reaction among students of theodicy.[2] It has been cited out of context as if it were the sum of all Maybaum's teaching on the Holocaust. None of his critics, to my knowledge, has come up with a convincing solution to the question of theodicy, whereas Maybaum's approach at least has the virtue of safeguarding the Bible as holy scripture, which his critics seem unable to do.

The last section of this Reader concerns Zionism. As a young rabbi in Germany Maybaum had been a member of Zionist KJV (*Kartell jüdischer Verbindungen*, 'Federation of Jewish Fraternities'), that was committed to the renewal of a Jewish nationalism [*Volkstum*] worthy of the Jewish past. But he was not an uncritical Zionist; we should bear in mind that Zionism was unfashionable in Germany before 1933, and to some extent his attachment to it reflects his own independence. After 1933, when Zionism was espoused by more Jews, his criticisms of it multiplied (particularly his criticisms of what he saw as misrepresentations of true Zionist ideology) and he came to be a spokesman for Diaspora existence. His first books, *Parteibefreites Judentum* (1935) and *Neue Jugend und Alter Glaube* (1936), reflect this shift of political outlook and hint at the later development of his ideas. They set out his conviction that there are eternal Jewish values that are more readily embodied in the stable family life of the bourgeois *baal habayith* than in the fervour of the pioneer (*chalutz*), even if the latter's Jewish spirit enables him to avoid the inhumanity often associated with world reformers.

Maybaum was often castigated as an anti-Zionist, but he was certainly not an anti-Zionist in the sense of opposing the existence of the Jewish state (except in a purely theological sense). In his view, once Israel had come into being in 1948, Zionism belonged to the past. The creation of Israel delivered God's verdict on anti-Zionism: the state could never have come into being had God not willed it.

2. See particularly Katz, *Post-Holocaust Dialogues*, pp. 248–67, and Rubenstein, *After Auschwitz* (second edition), pp. 163–8.

Equally, history delivered its verdict on the apocalyptic Zionist claim that with the establishment of a Jewish homeland the Diaspora would be liquidated. The Diaspora has refused to die, and this too must be seen as a mark of God's will. A Jewish state, in Maybaum's view, is a contradiction. The Jews are a priestly people, and like the priests of old they have no share in the distribution of territory. Their destiny is to be God's ministers to all nations. 'The State of Israel is not outside, but part of, the Diaspora.' Nevertheless, Maybaum admired and supported Israel, and as the final excerpt testifies, he encouraged others to support it.

Ignaz Maybaum belongs to an earlier generation, but his concerns are still of contemporary relevance, and many of his pronouncements seem prophetic. Although some of his views may provoke an adverse reaction, or even cause offence, they are always well considered, and they are solidly grounded in a profound knowledge of the sources of Judaism and of the Western intellectual tradition. Even those who do not fully agree with him are able to learn a lot from him. Part of Maybaum's significance lies in his pivotal position between pre-war Jewish theology, which was couched mainly in German, and its post-war, English-language successor. Contemporary Jewish theology in North America and Britain has to build on Continental foundations, and in this enterprise Maybaum is a valuable resource.

Part I

JUDAISM IN THE MODERN AGE

Chapter 1

FRIDAY EVENING

It is Friday evening. Let us go to a Jewish house, a home where people eat, sleep, cook, wash and work and spend their leisure time. Is it possible to find in such surroundings the atmosphere of the House of God? Can the sanctity which reigns in places where a religious community prays pervade a home where there are beds, where marriage, birth and death, the crying of children and the moans of the sick are associated with the rooms? Can there be sanctity in the midst of the commonplace? Yes, it is possible. Let us see what it looks like in a Jewish house on Sabbath and holy days. Let us enter a Jewish house on Friday night.

In a Jewish house on Friday evening our attention is directed to a centre just as in a Christian Church the eye is drawn towards the altar. This centre is a table which has been laid and on which two candlesticks have been placed. Usually, even in very poor Jewish homes, the candlesticks are of silver.

While the Temple stood, so it is said in the Talmud,[1] the altar atoned for Israel's sin; since its destruction the table in Jewish homes has this power of atonement. The festive table on Friday night merely demonstrates the function which this family table fulfils during the whole week. The table unites the family and has the power, which formerly the altar of the Temple possessed, to bestow sanctity.

Beside the Sabbath candles a glass of wine and two white loaves are to be found on Jewish tables on Friday evenings. These are the sole accessories of the simple ceremonial. The Sabbath candles are lit by the lady of the house. She lifts her hands in front of them so as not

1. Babylonian Talmud, *Sukkah* 55b.

to see them before they have been blessed and then says the Hebrew blessing: 'Blessed art thou, O Lord, our God, King of the Universe, who hast sanctified us by thy commandments and hast commanded us to light the Sabbath candles'. The candles are lit, the father and the other members of the family take their seats round the table, but the meal does not begin yet. The most solemn act of Friday night, the 'sanctification of the Sabbath' (in Hebrew, *Kiddush)* first takes place. It is, however, customary in many Jewish homes to begin with a short song which contains a variation of these words in four lines: 'Peace be with you, you angels of peace' and to follow it with Proverbs 31: 10–31. When the father sings or speaks these lines of the Proverbs, the Jewish wife hears something that is, although not literally, yet factually contained in them: the ancient and yet new Jewish declaration of love, freshly repeated every Friday evening: 'She looketh well to the ways of her household, and eateth not the bread of idleness. Her children rise up and call her happy; her husband also, and he praiseth her, saying: Many daughters have done virtuously, but thou excellest them all. Favour is deceitful, and beauty is vain, but a woman that feareth the Lord, she shall be praised. Give her of the fruit of her hands; and let her works praise her in the gates'.

After these last words the father rises and lifts the glass, filled to the brim with wine, and sings the words of the *Kiddush* according to the melody familiar to him from the Synagogue. These words, in their intellectual content, are extremely important for an understanding of the atmosphere of sanctity which the Sabbath brings into the Jewish home. However, there is something else on which we shall have to dwell. It is the fact that here a man, be he banker or tailor, businessman or intellectual, young or old, rises to fulfil a priestly function in his private home. He is surrounded by his family, who know him as one knows a person with whom one lives, and they do not see before them the idealised person, such as might be created by a priestly robe. The man who says *Kiddush* is dressed in his best clothes, but he wears no robe. And in this setting he is a priest.

After saying the blessing, the father and the other members of the family drink from the glass of wine which is on the table for the celebration of the Sabbath. In this way the glass is passed round till it reaches the youngest person present. This has nothing to do with mystical symbolism, as is well demonstrated by the history of the origin of the rite. The synagogue, the house of prayer, was formerly also the place where strangers were given hospitality. The ritual serves only as a simple thanksgiving for the gift of God. The blessing over the fruit of the vine which, as *Kiddush,* is said in the synagogue and in the home, is a thanksgiving to God for the magnificent gift of wine. And this is followed by the blessing over the bread.

Bread and wine on the Sabbath table stand for all the gifts of God to the earth. The Sabbath is the festival of creation. This is the name given it in the *Kiddush.* Bread and wine under the shining Sabbath candles prove the heavenly origin of all earthly things. The world is not only the subject of astronomy, the earth not only a star among stars, the solar system is more than merely a problem for mathematicians. World is creation. God created the heaven and the earth. Bread and wine under the glow of the Sabbath candles proclaim the wonderful greatness of God who has created the heaven and the earth, and man, and all that grows and lives on this earth. Bread and wine can better testify to the creation of the earth by God because they are no more than refined products of the earth. 'Bread and wine are the most perfect works of man, works that cannot be surpassed. They cannot, however, be compared to his other works in which his inventive mind artfully combines the gifts of nature, and in the act of combining goads itself on to greater and greater artfulness. Bread and wine are nothing but the ennobled gifts of earth, one is the basis of all the strength of life, the other of all its joy. Both were perfected in the youth of the world and of the people thereon, and neither can ever grow old. Every mouthful of bread, and every sip of wine tastes just as wonderful as the first we ever savoured, and certainly no less wonderful than in time immemorial they tasted to those who for the first time harvested the grain for bread and gathered the fruits of the vine'.[2]

Neither the glass of wine which is solemnly raised to celebrate the Sabbath nor the two loaves of bread on the table is a mystical symbol. The 'natural' explanation of the duality goes back to the time of the wanderings in the desert. Then the Israelites were forbidden to desecrate the seventh day by gathering food. They must provide for the Sabbath on the sixth day so as to be free from gathering, cooking and baking. For this reason the double loaf (Exodus 16:22) which they brought home on the sixth day kept wonderfully fresh, while at other times any supply of bread beyond the needs of the current day went stale. By reminding us of those times, the two loaves of bread make us realise how old is the command to celebrate the Sabbath. The observance of the Sabbath is always emphasised as the foundation stone of the whole teaching.

Every Sabbath which punctuates our working days tells us that the world is the outcome of creation. Sabbath is the commemorative festival of creation. Thus the blessing of the *Kiddush* clearly and unequivocally defines it. This blessing attributes two commemorations to the Sabbath: that of creation and of the exodus from Egypt. Both these commemorations concern the same fact, although from

---

2. Franz Rosenzweig, *The Star of Redemption,* p. 312.

different angles. The exodus from Egypt, the overthrow of slavery, the entry into the realm of freedom, form the beginning of the history of the Jewish people. History, however, is not outside the range of creation. No prophet discovers in his vision anything which has not been set there by the kindness and wisdom of almighty God. No heroic action for the good of mankind can add to the world anything which has not been made possible by God, the creator of the world, by the way in which he created the world.

History alters the surface of the earth. This must be considered a great achievement, particularly in these days of technical progress, which changes whole landscapes. But this feat is not creation. Man is not a creator. The history of mankind shows man as a builder, but even as such he remains a being created by God. Man can merely take the paths, obediently and in humility, which the world as created enables him to take. But he may go on his way confidently, in spite of the terrors of night and storm, war and revolution, illness and death. Creation is the creation of God. It is not chaos. The great and wonderful deeds of the history of mankind do not make the world any better, but fulfil its destiny. The world is as glorious as on the first day of creation. The Sabbath, by its peace, stillness and calm, brings the glory of creation into the life of men. We come closer to the perfection of creation, the sanctity of God, through peace, quietness and calm. What is peace? It is the peace of God.

God created the world. But the most precious thing in the world is peace. It is also the holiest thing. For it is peace that God intended for himself at the end of his creative work. 'And there was evening and there was morning, the sixth day. And the heaven and the earth were finished and all their host. And on the seventh day God had finished his work which he had made; and he rested on the seventh day from all his work which he had made. And God blessed the seventh day, and he hallowed it, because he rested thereon from all his work which God had created and made' (Genesis 1: 31–2: 3).

With these words the Jewish father, lifting the glass of wine, begins to fulfil the ritual of the sanctification of the Sabbath. He continues, and, after the blessing over the wine, says the second part of the *Kiddush*, which unites the creation and the exodus from Egypt into one identical set of facts. 'Blessed art thou, O Lord our God, king of the universe, who hast sanctified us by thy commandments and hast taken pleasure in us, and in love and favour hast given us the holy Sabbath as an inheritance, a memorial of the creation, that day being also the first of the holy convocations, in remembrance of the departure from Egypt. For thou hast chosen us and sanctified us above all nations, and in love and in favour hast given us thy holy Sabbath as an inheritance. Blessed art thou, O Lord, who hallowest the Sabbath'.

Then the third part of the *Kiddush* follows, the blessing of the bread. It is one sentence only, usually the first Hebrew sentence that a Jewish child has to learn by heart, and which later he learns to see as the great thanksgiving prayer of life: 'Blessed art thou, O Lord, king of the universe, who bringest forth bread from the earth'.

The recitation of the *Kiddush* takes less than five minutes. If it is not sung but spoken in the form of a litany, it takes still less. But the dramatic division makes it appear as a concrete event before the eyes of the people assembled at the table. They not only hear the words, but see the different stages of these events and take part in them. They drink the wine and they eat the bread with salt. All this makes the *Kiddush* before the meal a solemn festival. An outsider may not be able to grasp that in a private house something takes place which does not yield in solemnity to a ceremony in the House of God.

For our Sabbath peace on this earth we have the example of the holiest peace: God. He rested on the seventh day. Manifold, profound and great things are said by the prophets in the name of God, but the most profound thing that prophetic statements report is their message of peace. What is peace? Let us not misinterpret it in the mystical attempt to spiritualise it. Peace is quiet, stillness, rest from work. It is remoteness from the profanity of the week, dwelling in sanctity. This holy peace – why continue to search for further attributes? – is the Sabbath. The Sabbath as a remembrance of the creation is the festival of peace. For creation culminates in peace.

But just as the creation was not exhausted by the act of making the world, but finds complete fulfilment only in its daily renewal, so the Sabbath, the festival of creation, must not be a single, annual festival. It must recur weekly in the same way, and yet differ every week, in that different portions of the Law are read from the Torah. Thus the Sabbath must repeat itself throughout the course of the year. The Sabbaths of the year form the spiritual year – the Jewish year, as it is called. For by living the cycle which is formed by the regularly recurring Sabbaths, the Jew lives in a special territory set apart from the profane. Through the Jewish year we have a Jewish world. If we call the Jewish year our own, we also possess a Jewish atmosphere wherever we may live. The Jew who goes to the synagogue on the Sabbath finds the same order of service and the same prayers as on the preceding Sabbath. Only the portions of the Law are different for every Sabbath, until in the course of a year the entire Pentateuch has been read and the cycle begins again with the first portion of the Law. This is the realm which the Jew enters when he goes to the synagogue.

Prayer is not meditation, but the atmosphere of meditation has to pervade the prayer. This atmosphere is not revealed to Jews in

material form. The effect of majestic surroundings, which in themselves may be the beginning of meditation and prayer, becomes
apparent to us in the mediaeval Gothic cathedrals. But it is not the
surroundings which create for the Jew a world fit for his service. The
Jewish world is created by the system of the Jewish year, arranged on
the basis of the Sabbaths. The Jewish calendar, the *Luach*, guides the
steps of the Jew through the spiritual year, and it is the succession of
Sabbaths which forms the structure of the Jewish year.

In the synagogues, on Friday night, the Sabbath is heralded by the
salutation: 'Come, my friend, to meet the bride; let us welcome the
presence of the Sabbath'. Israel is the bridegroom, Sabbath the
bride. At home, after the meal and before the prayer, other songs are
sung. Then follows, as an introduction to the thanksgiving for the
meal, the one hundred and twenty-sixth Psalm, which may be
described as 'Hallelujah in tears', but which, for the Jew, is simply
the 'psalm of the Sabbath'. The Jew who celebrates the Sabbath is a
royal priest. This royal priest in pre-Messianic times is also the suffering servant. The psalm gives wonderful expression to both ideas:
the strength of the Jew who is capable of grasping holiness, who is
able to celebrate the Sabbath, and also the world which today, on a
Sabbath, lies far off, and in which the Jewish people have to live.
'When the Lord turned again the captivity of Zion, then were we like
unto men that dream. Then was our mouth filled with laughter, and
our tongue with joy. Then said they among the heathen, the Lord
hath done great things for them. The Lord hath done great things for
us already, whereof we rejoice. Turn again our captivity, O Lord, as
the rivers in the south. They that sow in tears shall reap in joy. He
who now goeth weeping and beareth forth good seed shall likewise
come again, rejoicing, bearing his sheaves with him'. This psalm is
followed by the grace. The Sabbath candles, which may not be
extinguished, still gleam, grow smaller and fade out. But the Sabbath
continues to shine into the morning.

Chapter 2

LIBERAL AND REFORM JUDAISM

The Jews of Germany were the first Jews to experience westernisation, and they had to adjust their religious life to this new situation. There was no controversy over Jewish law: the relevance of Jewish law to social and commercial life became obsolete, and the change was hardly noticed by the bulk of German Jewry. The German Jews translated *Torah* not as law but as teaching (*Lehre*), and from the beginning all intellectual efforts were concentrated not on law but on doctrine. Besides the reinterpretation of Judaism as doctrine, the minds of the Reformers were occupied with liturgical problems. The German Jews wanted their divine service to harmonise with their determination to remain faithful Jews and with their westernised approach to cultural life. In the hasty compilation of a hymn book for one of the Reform synagogues, the printer, or the publishing committee, blundered and retained the word Jesus from the Christian original. Dubnow[1] duly reports this mishap and draws conclusions which are unfair to the true motives of the handful of men who stood at the cradle of the Reform Movement, which eventually led to Franz Rosenzweig. An ancestor of this greatest of German Jews was Meir Ehrenberg (1773–1853), one of the earliest Reformers. These men did not intend to defect to Christianity; as mere beginners, they made the 'mistake' of regarding Judaism as a religion of reason, a mistake made also by Maimonides and Hermann Cohen.

The non-Orthodox section of German Jewry – representing the vast majority – was first known as Reform Judaism and later as

---

1. [Simon Dubnow (1860–1941) was the author of a ten-volume *World History of the Jewish People* (Berlin, 1925–29). This extract is from an article about the section of the *World History* dealing with the German Reform movement.]

Liberal Judaism. To understand these two terms we must not think of
any of the various meanings which the words 'Reform' and 'Liberal'
have subsequently acquired in Anglo-Jewry and in American Jewry.
In Germany, the first creative impulse of Progressive Judaism was
known as the Reform Movement. Dubnow regards the Reform
Movement as being more radical than the later Liberal Judaism.
Here Dubnow adopts the conventional opinion current among German Jews after the First World War. The facts are different. The original progressive movement, the Reform Movement, was truly
religious; it was not a political movement dictated by expediency.
The word 'ideology', with which Dubnow summarises the views of
the German Reformers, is entirely out of place. It was only later,
after the *Richtlinien zu einem Programm für das liberale Judentum* (Directives for a Programme for Liberal Judaism) had been formulated by
the *Vereinigung der liberalen Rabbiner* (Berlin and Frankfurt am Main,
1912) and had been accepted by the *Hauptversammlung des liberalen
Judentums,* that the progressive synagogues, with their objection to
Zionism, often possessed nothing but an ideology, a liberal ideology
which opposed Jewish nationalism. The endorsement of the *Richtlinien,* which from then on were always quoted, led to a period when
the controversy between Liberal Jews and Zionists dominated the
Gemeindestuben. It is true that only one insignificant congregation,
that of the Johannisstrasse in Berlin, retained the name *Reform-
Gemeinde.* All the other progressive congregations called themselves
Liberal. But the replacement of the term 'Reform' by the name 'Liberal' is one of those accidents of history which prove nothing. In the
earlier Reform Movement there was a truly creative and religious
spirit which, like early Hasidism and the Haskalah, bestowed a blessing on Jewry.

Dubnow does not realise that historically western Orthodoxy is a
product of the Reform Movement. This seems paradoxical only to
those – and they are many – who have a distorted picture of this
movement. The founder of western Orthodoxy was Isaak Bernays
(1792–1849). Samson Raphael Hirsch (1806–88) was his pupil. Their
orthodoxy was entirely different from the Orthodoxy of today,
which is nothing but fundamentalism and traditionalism rooted in
the memories of the *shtetl,* the little Polish town. Dubnow sees too
much in Bernays' opposition to the Hamburg Jews who built their
Tempel. No questions of Jewish doctrine or Jewish law played any
role in the whole *Tempel-Streit.* Bernays' objections were of a liturgical nature and his reasons are accepted today by many Progressive
rabbis. Dubnow's portrait of Bernays is drawn entirely from his role
in the *Tempel-Streit.*

The true character of Bernays emerges from two instances: firstly, from his contempt for the old-time rabbis still existing in his time, secondly, from his reasons for adhering to ritual. They were reasons of his own, as we shall see, not founded on obedience to Jewish law. When Isaak Bernays accepted rabbinical office in Hamburg, he had stipulated a strange condition: he was not to be a 'rabbi'. He assumed the title 'Chacham'. He deemed the Judaism of his time so debased that he would not accept the title of Chief Rabbi of Hamburg. In this respect he resembled Zunz, who called the contemporary pre-Reform rabbis *Pfaffen,* a word much more derogatory than its translation, 'parsons', implies. Bernays and Zunz represented the *esprit laïque.* In rebelling against religious professionals they opened the door to a new era. The rabbi was no longer to be an ecclesiastical official, but a man equal to his coreligionists whom he guided not by reason of his special degree of priesthood, but because of his greater knowledge of the Holy Scriptures. The true Jew must not be a layman; he must be a lay priest. The Jewish principle of the kingdom of priests makes the rabbi himself a lay priest insofar as his authority is not conferred on him by a religious institution. His authority is that of a scholar. Abraham Geiger (1810–74) liked to call himself a theologian rather than a rabbi. The Reform Movement created the type of rabbi who led his congregation by preaching and teaching. A Berlin rabbi I visited in 1924 had a nameplate outside his flat. On it was his name and – according to the German middle class custom – his profession. The profession was: *Prediger und Lehrer der jüdischen Gemeinde Berlin* (Preacher and Teacher of the Jewish Community of Berlin). Bernays, the founder of western Orthodoxy, had the same negative attitude to the pre-Reform rabbis as the Reform rabbis had towards their medieval colleagues. The German Reform Movement re-created rabbinical leadership in the true image of the rabbi of the classical age of rabbinical Judaism, as he stands before us in the second century CE. The Reform Movement gave the rabbi a place in westernised Jewry.

Bernays' passionate advocacy of Jewish ritual was not in itself a reason for calling him an Orthodox rabbi. He did not plead for ritual on the grounds that the Jewish law commanded it. He was deeply impressed by Schelling, whose greatness Dubnow underestimated. Whatever Dubnow may think, it is no reflection on Bernays that he was influenced by Schelling. It was Schelling's philosophy of Christian symbols that led Bernays to an appreciation of Jewish ritual and symbolism. The way in which people sometimes have to work their way back to religious life may seem odd to the uninformed, but the difference between the western Orthodoxy of Bernays and present-day Orthodoxy is obvious. Bernays did not demand the performance of Jewish ritual out of obedience to Jewish law, the *din,* but out of convictions acquired in a personal religious struggle.

This distinctive feature of western Orthodoxy as a product of the Jewish Reform Movement becomes even more apparent in Samson Raphael Hirsch, Bernays' pupil. Dubnow is aware that Hirsch's programme *Torah vederech erets* (Torah plus the way of the land) was the door through which he, also an Orthodox rabbi, allowed modern life to enter Judaism. But Dubnow's portrait of Hirsch does not make the main point clear. He fails to see that Hirsch was a liberal, who firmly believed that the liberal state would solve what Herzl later called the 'Jewish problem'. In that Hirsch was in full agreement with Abraham Geiger.

Shibud malchiot is a Talmudic term meaning bondage under heathen government. The liberals of the schools of Geiger and Hirsch said, following Maimonides, 'Only *shibud malchiot* separates us from the Kingdom of God'. They did not know how right they were. What they meant was that the liberal state was lagging behind over the question of Jewish emancipation and that the expansion of liberalism in the world was still incomplete. They did not understand that any rule not of the Kingdom of God, including the rule of the liberal state, is *shibud malchiot.*

Those who concur with Dubnow and fail to see the common ground on which Abraham Geiger and Samson Raphael Hirsch stood will derive a wholesome lesson from the strong criticism which Hirsch encountered in his post as rabbi in Nikolsburg (Moravia) in the years 1847–51. Hirsch, whom a later generation celebrated as the great representative of Orthodoxy, was looked upon as a Reformer by the defenders of the old ways of life. In his synagogue service decorum was demanded and everything was regulated down to the minutest detail. Was that not Reform? And what a strange innovation was introduced for the marriage ceremony! Hirsch stopped the customary weddings in the open air; he performed the ceremony in the synagogue and gave an address to the bridal couple. Was this not Reform? It was also a strange innovation when Hirsch came to the synagogue on the Sabbath in a frock-coat and a white tie! Was that how a *Landesrabbiner* should appear in public? They still remembered Rabbi Mordechai Benet,[2] a predecessor of Hirsch in Nikolsburg, who used to walk through the streets in a long silk kaftan and a tall fur hat. One cannot say that the contemporary critics who branded Samson Raphael Hirsch a Reform rabbi were superficial. They were well aware that a major change was taking place in religious life. Both Abraham Geiger and S. R. Hirsch put the Bible, the world of prophetic Judaism, at the root of their message.

The critics of S. R. Hirsch in Nikolsburg were surprised by his

2. [Also known as Markus Benedict, 1753–1829.]

ways of teaching in the *Beth-hamidrash*. He lectured on the psalms. What head of a *Beth-hamidrash* before Hirsch had ever before troubled to introduce psalms into the studies of his adult students? They had learned them as children. The *Tehillim* (psalms) were said in the form of a litany by pious men and women on all occasions, hence the expression *tillim sogen,* the reciting of the psalms. They were 'said' as prayers were said, not studied. Now S. R. Hirsch, the new rabbi, treated the psalms with the seriousness due to a rabbinical code or the Talmud. The *Dayanim* sighed: 'In our days we learned *Gemara* (Talmud) and said *Tehillim* (psalms); now they learn *Tehillim* and say *Gemara*'. They saw clearly that a change had taken place and that it was having an effect on the study of the Talmud.

Dubnow treats Isaak Bernays and S. R. Hirsch as opponents of the Reform Movement. This indeed they were. But at the same time, they were themselves the product of this Reform Movement, although as children of their age they were unaware of the fact.

Chapter 3

SAMSON RAPHAEL HIRSCH AND ABRAHAM GEIGER

Judaism is messianism, which sees history as a stage where the plan of God will unfold itself, where his promise, given through his prophets, will be fulfilled. God's kingdom will come: with this hope in his heart, man struggles on, detached from all solutions and achievements which are celebrated in the victories and festive days of history, and remaining firm and courageous in the catastrophes, frustrations and sufferings with which history may beset him.

But Judaism is not only messianism. Both prophet and priest are the eternal prototypes of the Jewish man. Side by side with the prophet, who teaches hope for the promised time, stands the priest. The priest does not look towards the future: he faces God here and now, on the very day of his present life and in the very place where he lives his life.

The liberal and the national ideologies brought modern Jewry back to the stage of history and awakened Jewish messianism. Liberalism believed in progress, humanity and mankind; Zionism turned this belief towards Zion. The Socialist ideology followed soon, adjusting its programme to the existing liberal or national framework. These ideologies prevented western Jewry from becoming static.

But besides messianism the Jewish people must understand and achieve priestly peace. Samson Raphael Hirsch discovered priestly Judaism for his generation. He discovered the Judaism of the *mitsvot*, the holy commandments.

Hirsch did not teach anything new; he taught what the two thousand Rabbis who speak to us in the Talmud taught. Zacharias

Frankel, who demanded 'Historic Judaism', not Orthodoxy, has the same aim as Samson Raphael Hirsch. But Hirsch, as a child of the liberal age, speaking the ideological language of this time, preached this Judaism of the *mitsvot* with a new passion.

Zacharias Frankel and Samson Raphael Hirsch seem very much the same, both conservative types. But there is a difference. Frankel is the noble conservative, still rooted in the past and loftily unaffected by the loud voices of a new generation. But Samson Raphael Hirsch belongs to this new generation. The founder of Orthodoxy is a liberal, an optimistic believer in the chances of history.

The Eastern European rabbis struggled with the alternative of Europe or Judaism. Hirsch's programme was Europe *and* Judaism. To those who doubt whether the western world provides any fertile ground for the growth of Judaism, the work of S. R. Hirsch can successfully dispel such doubt. He is a typical German Jew, and a Rav, a *hasid*. Hasidism can flourish in western Jewry, too.

It is stimulating and inspiring to compare S. R. Hirsch with his friend of student days and later opponent, Abraham Geiger. Orthodoxy, of which S. R. Hirsch is the founder, is a western formula. It is a new approach, as new as the approach of Geiger. Hirsch was unable to see that the Jewish life which he lived and taught others to live was no longer the life of our forefathers. The modern Jew became a citizen of a western state. Hirsch, as a son of the liberal era, was enthusiastic about this change which – how could it be otherwise – he fully accepted. Of the inroads and transformations which this change brought about he was not aware.

Both Geiger and Hirsch were liberals and therefore optimistic about secular history. Hirsch made his peace with secular history in his principle *Torah vederech erets* (Torah plus the way of the land); Geiger made the same peace in his 'law of development' showing that the Torah had both its eternal essence and its changing appearance in the various epochs of history.

Geiger and Hirsch were not merely sons of the liberal age. In Hirsch the priestly Jew was a driving force, in Geiger the messianic Jew. Geiger's great interest was the 'solution of the Jewish question', which he believed was possible through liberalism. For this aim he worked not as a politician but as a scholar. The political emancipation of the Jews, it seemed to him, cannot be achieved as long as the non-Jewish world has a wrong view of the Jewish religion. A scientific study of Judaism might bring home to the Christian world what Jewish religion is and what the world owes to the Jewish religion.

Geiger drew the attention of the Protestant universities and theological seminaries to his scholarly work, and forced the Christian world to accept the Jewish point of view. His *Urschrift* inspired

Travers Herford in his work on the Pharisees, to give only one example of Geiger's importance.

Hirsch had a different audience: he was concerned about the *kehillah*, the Jewish religious community, which he created anew. He spoke to the *baal habayit*, to the people who stood in the midst of life, whom he brought back to the holiness of Jewish home life and to the Jewish year with its centre, the synagogue. His commentary on the Pentateuch is not a scientific work, but it made German Jews good Jews. This book brought the atmosphere which hasidic books and the Musar literature spread in Eastern Europe into many Jewish homes in Germany.

Geiger drew his congregation to the synagogue as a preacher. He preached Judaism. He was more inclined to plant Jewish conviction in the hearts of his fellow Jews than demand from them loyalty to Jewish practices. He put the religious heritage of Jewry before the westernised Jew as a system of doctrines and as a history. This westernised Jew, with his dual loyalty to the western world and to Judaism, had to be convinced of the truth of Jewish doctrine and had to be exhorted to remain faithful to his past. That was the reason why Geiger stressed the preacher in the rabbinical office. In this he set the pattern for the Rabbinate in the western world, both Orthodox and Reform. As a lecturer at the *Lehranstalt für die Wissenschaft des Judentums* in Berlin, he himself educated the new type of rabbi who is both theologian and preacher.

Geiger, like Hirsch, fostered Hasidism in the western world. But his Hasidism is of another kind than that of Hirsch: it is the Hasidism of the Synagogue-goer. Hirsch, in the midst of the success of his synagogue, became doubtful whether the western synagogue was capable of preserving Judaism. He hoped more from the Jew who had a Jewish home. But Geiger and the school of rabbis who were his pupils made the modern Jew go to synagogue for the sake of worship, sermon and communal song.

After Abraham Geiger and S. R. Hirsch, rabbis trained in the rabbinical seminaries of the western world, no matter whether Orthodox or Reform, are no longer halachic authorities like Eastern European rabbis trained at a Talmudic high school of any of the famous centres of Talmudic learning. This fact, obvious as it is, has been hushed up by western Orthodoxy.

Abraham Geiger and S. R. Hirsch reacted differently to the fact that Talmudic law had gone out of use in the West. Before we look into their different reactions, it is necessary to underline that they both stand on the ground created by the Emancipation which made the Jew a citizen of the state and charged him with loyalty to the law of the state.

In his attitude to the Talmud and to Talmudic law, Abraham Geiger drew the only consequence which remained possible. The Talmud became to him a historical source which he investigated with all the means of modern scientific research. His interest was that of the theologian who has the burning desire to make Judaism as a faith clear to himself, to his fellow Jews and to the world. But he was not given the chance to work as a theologian. The field was not yet prepared. He had to prepare it himself. He worked as the historian of the Jewish religion and gave the next generation the material on which the theologian could work.

Geiger stands before us as the new type of the learned rabbi. Jewish law as far as it was civil and criminal law had no application in the reality of a western Jew. Geiger continued to cultivate the field of the Talmud with the same devotion as was done in the Talmudic high schools of the East. But he had another aim.

The Talmudic laws, the rabbinical texts in Mishnah, Talmud and Midrash, had to reveal to Geiger the way of the Jewish people through history. He had stepped out of the rabbinic tradition, but he preserved this very tradition as a scholar. He gave the profession of the rabbi a new scope, that of the modern scholar. The learned rabbi of the West, with Abraham Geiger as his example, speaks about the Torah with the authority of the historian, the philosopher or the theologian, whereas his colleague in Eastern Europe spoke with the authority of the lawyer.

With Abraham Geiger, Jewish learning emancipated itself from the old methods. Specialisation was the great principle. The vast expanse of Jewish learning became accessible through a chart which divided the whole area into different parts: language, history, philosophy, theology, law, and so on. The rabbis who fashioned their studies before they took office, with Abraham Geiger as their example, and working in their congregations as he did, remained spiritual leaders and did not become experts lacking real contact with the men, women and children of their congregations. They invited every member of the congregation to take an interest in the findings of the scholarly studies that shed light on Jewish history and Jewish thought. Jewish learning adjusted itself to the democratic age. With the great possibilities of the pulpit, with historical societies springing up all over the country, with lecturers who visited the smallest congregation, with the help of books and journals, the modern Jew is given the opportunity of learning as his forbears did, and of becoming a citizen of the truly Jewish home of Jewish learning.

Hirsch, no less than Geiger, had to find a new method to preserve Jewish learning. He could not transfer the yeshivah to the western world. The yeshivah flourished in a world in which a few privileged people had the leisure, with a slaving army of unprivileged at their command, to build Gothic cathedrals. The cathedral reached heaven, and on the ground where it stood lived medieval man, ignorant, haunted by superstitions and cursed by the primitive civilisation of the Middle Ages in which drunkenness and lechery were as much part of the social life as were the Holy Mass and bishops. The background of the Eastern European yeshivah is medieval civilisation.

The yeshivah is a Gothic university in the midst of the rural Polish, Lithuanian and Russian civilisation in which Jews lived as a third estate between a neolithic peasantry and a feudal caste. We admire the great rabbis who were the products of this yeshivah; in romantic exaggeration we consider ourselves small and unworthy in comparison with these intellectual giants and saints. We do not see the multitude broken by the inhuman pedagogics of the *cheder*: a boy had to learn to read when he was three and study legal treatises when he was six, and there was no provision for girls, who grew up illiterate.

In two great poems ('*Ha-Matmid*' and '*Al Saph Beth-hamidrash*') H. N. Bialik convinced us that his emancipation from the yeshivah was a necessity. So far, looking back over the last 200 years, it has not been possible to transplant the East European yeshivah to a country of the West in this age of democracy and industrial civilisation. The will to preserve the great spiritual heritage of the yeshivah had to find new means and create new institutions.

That was the position which Hirsch had to face as head of a yeshivah in Nikolsburg and of a Jewish secondary school in Frankfurt, just as it was the position of Geiger in Breslau and Berlin. Both had to go new ways. But they went different ways.

The way S. R. Hirsch took is illuminated as in a flash by the complaint of the dayanim at Nikolsburg that Hirsch put the Talmud on the same level as the Psalms.[1] To Hirsch, the Talmud had become a religious book in a new sense. To the Jew who, until Mendelssohn, really lived under an order created by Jewish law, the law was holy, and the books which recorded it were the necessary means to its study. The Jew who studied it remained in the world like any man who performed a job that was necessary in daily life. It was in daily life that the law was needed, interpreted and obeyed. But when Hirsch studied the Talmud he was no longer connected with daily life where, in fact, the Jewish law was no longer in use; he was in the world of religious uplift, saying prayers, reading the psalms or the prophets.

For Geiger the history from our father Abraham to Joseph Caro,

---

1. [See above, p. 13.]

the author of the *Shulchan Aruch*, was a period stretching over three thousand years. But to Hirsch, studying the rabbinic Scriptures, this history was one period in which time was eliminated. He entered a world in which he sat together with the two thousand rabbis of the Talmud, with the Geonim and rabbinic commentators. Our father Abraham, King David, the prophets, the rabbis of the Talmud and the Arab world, of Spain, Poland and Russia, were all his contemporaries.

Hirsch opened a volume of the Talmud in the religious mood in which a man enters a house of worship. This was a new approach. The rabbinic colleagues of S. R. Hirsch in Eastern Europe studied the Talmud because the legal guidance which it provided was needed in their daily lives. In the Talmud *shiur* (lecture) which Hirsch introduced to his congregation, Jewish law, as a matter of living interest, was as absent as in any Reform Synagogue. In the hundred years of its existence western Orthodoxy has not produced a single Talmudic scholar capable of training rabbinical students. They always had to be imported from Eastern Europe. The Talmud *shiur* of S. R. Hirsch served the same purpose which Geiger had at heart: to make Jewish history come to life. But it did it in another way.

European historians write history as the history of great individuals and of outstanding facts. The history inherent in the Talmud and other rabbinical writings is concerned with the impact of eternity on history; it is the history of redemption from history, the history of the coming of the kingdom of God into history. Neither S. R. Hirsch nor Abraham Geiger could afford to neglect history. The kingdom of God is not yet ; it will come, and its coming in the future forms our present. Hirsch, the priestly Jew, rejoiced in the splendour of the kingdom to come, visible before his eyes in the history which he read in the biblical and rabbinical writings. Geiger, the messianic Jew, watched the stations through which the kingdom of God passed in history, giving him the blissful hope of the final chapter at hand. We cannot do without either of them as our guide and teacher.

Chapter 4

JEWISH SELF-HATRED
(ON SIGMUND FREUD)

There was hatred in everything Freud felt and said concerning the religion of his father, and also concerning Christianity. He could not even enjoy the paintings of the great masters, because they so often dealt with religion. He fought a battle with his relatives about his wedding, which he wanted to be without the Jewish religious ceremonies. He was determined that his wife should give up her 'religious prejudices'. There is some disagreement between Freud's biographer Ernest Jones and Freud's family. Jones is inclined to regard Freud's father as an Orthodox Jew; the Freud family denies this and speaks of him as a freethinker. But it is not necessary to emphasise the tension between Orthodox Jew and freethinker in order to arrive at the subconscious hatred in the father–son relationship which an analysis of Freud would discover. The tension between westernised son and not yet westernised father justifies the analyst in speaking of such subconscious hatred.

Had Freud submitted himself to psychoanalysis, he might have been told that he hated his father. Subconsciously he did. He hated his father when he made *Kiddush*.[1] As a child Freud must have seen this ceremony with which the eve of Sabbath and Festival is sanctified at the family table of a Jewish home. Freud hated his father when he said Grace and perhaps mumbled it in the lax manner of a Jew who still observes the custom of saying this long prayer after the meal but no longer observes it with the respect of the convinced adherent. Freud hated his father when he observed the Sabbath rest, and he

1. [See above, p. 4.]

hated him when he presided at the *Seder* table on the Passover nights. This posthumous analysis is borne out by a sociological study by Theodor Lessing which describes not Freud himself, but the whole set of Freud's Jewish circle. Lessing's book is entitled *Jewish Self-Hatred.*

The westernised Freud, struggling for emancipation from the past, hated religion. In everything connected with religion an exclusive reduction to an impersonal scientific approach is impossible. In matters of religion you either love or you hate. Where God is concerned, man cannot be neutral. Man is by nature a worshipper: he worships either God or Moloch. Freud with his hate turned to the stories of primitive tribes and found there the story of a patricide[2], believed to be the event causing the subsequent salvation of the tribe. According to the story of the primitive tribe the sons gained their freedom through the murder of their father. With this tale Freud undertook to explain religion. All the ethnologists call it nonsense and a fairy tale, but Freud adhered to it with stubbornness in the face of scientific contradiction. He rationalised his own hatred of his father by using – or rather misusing – material from primitive ages.

Freud rationalised the historical situation as it existed all over Europe. There was a fatherless generation, a generation which did not experience sonship because the old age and the new age were turned against each other in hostility. 'Fatherless generation' has become a sociological term which can be applied even where the fathers are alive. The question is, do the fathers understand their role as fathers, and can they successfully play this role? Since 1914, so many fathers have died in the wars, and owing to political and economic changes so many children have not experienced home life. We call God Father, and we call religion 'trust', *bitachon.* Trust, security and peace are experienced in the home. The young who grow up with the protection of father and mother have trust. A fatherless generation is without security, is therefore without trust, and is therefore agnostic or atheistic.

Our prayer book, our psalms, our *midrashim,* in fact our whole religious literature speaks of God as Father. *Avinu, Malkeinu*: 'our Father, our King!' This may be called symbolic language, but it concerns the reality of God. It is in his obedience to and his trust in his father in heaven that the Jew is a Jew. The Jew, as a father obeyed and trusted by a son, by his children, has a priestly role. In England a priest is called 'Father', in France 'père', in other Latin countries 'padre'. Only the Germans do not give their priests the attribute 'Father'. With the expression *'Herr* Pfarrer' the Germans see the

2. [As some reviewers pointed out, the correct English term is 'parricide'. Since, however, Maybaum uses the form 'patricide' repeatedly and gives it such prominence in his argument, it has been left unchanged here.]

priest as a member of the ruling class. The Germans were the nation which more than any other became a fatherless generation and which in autogenesis substituted the *Führer* for the father. Where the family is dissolved and the role of the true father is taken over by a political father-figure society is sick. A father-figure is like the cruel god of the Greek myth who devours his own children.

Freud spent the first four years of his life in Freiburg (Bohemia). There the Jews lived in their still unbroken medieval piety, and there was no Jewish household into which the Day of Atonement with its atmosphere of a *mysterium tremendum* did not penetrate. Freud had the same childhood surroundings in the Jewish districts of the Vienna of the 1860s. Whatever the Freud family may have told Ernest Jones about Freud's freethinking father, even the most assimilated Jew of those days did not and could not free himself from the great power of the Day of Atonement. Even if it was only the solemn tune in which a cantor sang or a layman hummed the prayer *Avinu Malkeinu,* 'Our Father, our King', as a child Sigmund Freud was reached by this prayer, and even if he forgot it later it rested in his subconscious mind.

'Our Father, our King'. But where was there for Freud a father whom he could respect? His father was of the Micawber type, always expecting that something would turn up, and always unable to save his family from grinding poverty. At the age of ten or twelve Freud was walking with his father when the latter told him of an incident of the past. The incident should prove that Jews were now living in happier days. As a young man Freud senior had been walking along the streets in Freiburg. He was well dressed and wore a fur cap. A Christian came along, knocked his cap into the mud and shouted: 'Jew, get off the pavement'. Anxiously the son asked the father: 'And what did you do?' He never forgot the calm reply: 'I went into the road and picked up the cap'. Sigmund Freud's future hero was the Semitic general Hannibal, who hated Rome and almost destroyed it. Rome represents both political and religious authority, the authority of the Caesar and the authority of the popes. But this reminiscence also throws some light on Freud's relationship with his father. Did he, could he respect him? 'Our Father, our King' – was there fatherhood, either in his own family, or in his generation, which could be revered according to the commandment 'Honour thy father and thy mother, that thy days may be long upon the land which the Lord thy God giveth thee'?

And was there in Freud's days a king to be revered as the holder of the office of David, the saviour of his people? There was the Emperor Franz Josef. The Viennese sang:

Draussen im Schönbrunner Park sitzt ein alter Herr – sorgenschwer.
Guter, lieber, alter Herr, mach' dir doch das Herz nicht schwer!

(Yonder in the Park of Schönbrunn sits an old man, beset with sorrows. Kind, good old man, shrug off your cares.) Here we have the blueprint of the myth-maker Freud. He had a vision – 'I would rather say vision, not hypothesis', he himself says – 'that "in the beginning" people lived in hordes under the domination of a single powerful male . . . One day, however, the sons came together and united to overwhelm, kill, and devour their father'.[3]

The prophets of old announced the coming of a day, a day of judgement, a *dies irae,* a terrible day still in the future but visible to them in the present. Freud also spoke of 'a day', a terrible day, the day of patricide. The 'day' of which he spoke as the primeval beginning of all history was in fact his own present. The weak king assaulted by the young sons of the 'hordes' was there in contemporary history. Freud saw and heard the 'hordes' from the window of his flat in the Berggasse. The nationalism of the intellectuals had in his days become mass nationalism. The intellectuals, as historians, philologists and romantics, had discovered the new nationalities, but they had lost the leadership of the nations to the politicians of the mass age. From his window Freud saw the Czechs demonstrating and demanding Czech schools in Vienna, he saw the demonstrations of German-speaking Austrians demanding that Vienna remain German, he saw the demonstrations of the antisemites occupying the entrance to the university – situated only five minutes away from his flat – and preventing any Jew, or, as the case might be, any member of the non-German nationalities – from entering the building. Finally he saw the marching columns of workers, led either by Social Democrats or by Christian Socialists.

Freud would not dismiss his myth of the primeval hordes despite all the scholars who told him that he was talking nonsense. He saw what he saw and he wrote about it. He wrote about the primeval hordes. He saw them from his window. And the father to be killed by his sons? In Schönbrunn sits an old man, troubled by his sorrows. A quarter of an hour's walk from him sat a Russian, a tenant in his single room, studying Marx. His name was Stalin. A tramp by the name of Adolf Hitler walked through the streets. Freud's 'vision' of a prehistoric past with wandering hordes and with a rebellion of sons who killed their father was a vision not of the past but of a future which he saw advancing upon him and his generation. It was the future of a Europe where people had ceased to pray 'Our Father, our King'. Freud was haunted by the vision of a fatherless generation. He had the vision, but he did not understand his own vision.

3. *Autobiographical Study* (London, 1935), pp. 124–5.

Freud was not a prophet, because his vision did not place him outside the multitude for which it would have been a saving message.
He was himself a part of this multitude, part of a fatherless generation. A fatherless generation dissolves itself into warring groups:
brothers become enemies, nation fights against nation, and
ploughshares are forged into swords. As he was a Jew, this confla-
gration outside took place in his own heart. The hated father was
everybody who belonged to the decadent establishment represented
by 'the old man in Schönbrunn', his own father included. In his subconscious life Freud was assailed by self-hatred. Jewish self-hatred
became common in a Jewish generation at the historical juncture
when the westernised group of the Jewish people had to overcome
the medieval form of life of the group that was not yet westernised.
Jews also became 'hordes' who hated their fathers.

Freud was in the grip of what is now called by a freer Jewish generation 'Jewish self-hatred'. Only when we cease, when speaking of
Jewish self-hatred, to imply that it is nothing but the neurotic and
ignominious approach of the Jew to himself shall we have achieved
mental freedom. We shall then have truly emancipated ourselves from
our fascination with progress which is blind to the past, and from the
psychological evils of persecution. History is not an organic process.
It does not move on with the innocence and inevitability of the
growth which takes place in nature. History is often a chain of tragic
events. The past does not fall away from us like the skin sloughed off
by a snake. A struggle has to be fought to bring forth a desired future
or to prevent an unwanted one. Nothing happens organically in history, everything in it is brought into being by love or by hatred, by justice or by anarchy, by mercy or by cruelty, by truth or by folly.

The move away from the Middle Ages which had their sunset in
Austria-Hungary was passionately desired by new-born nations and
was stubbornly opposed by the old establishment, especially by the
Roman Catholic Church. The Jews who were attacked from the pulpit by the Roman Catholic priests of the Christian Socialist party
were themselves weighed down by the Middle Ages in their outmoded way of life. The split into progressives and conservatives,
which was affecting Christian society, took place within each Jew.
The Jew, progressing from a past age into a new one, was a man who
both hated and loved a part of his own life. Longingly looking
towards a future which emancipation and westernisation held out for
him, he could not but hate everything which prevented him from
reaching the New Dawn. But his hatred concerned his own Jewish
past and was therefore self-hatred, because his past had formed him
in his mother's womb (Jeremiah 1: 5). This was all the more the case
the less he understood his past.

It was Zionism which cured the Jews of Austria-Hungary of Jewish self-hatred. They had never had the benefit of a Jewish Reform movement, which mostly flourished among the German Jews, enabling them to reach inner human freedom in the times of transition. The Zionists' achievement of emancipating Jews from an inferiority complex leading to self-hatred may one day be regarded as equally important with their political success. Looking back to Freud's Vienna we must not speak with contempt of these Jewish writers and intellectuals who were in the grip of Jewish self-hatred. The road to freedom is a long one. There are many pilgrims who become sick along the way and many do not reach the goal. The final word about Jewish self-hatred has to come from an understanding of the modern Jew, swayed by an inner struggle: two civilisations, the medieval and the modern, oppose each other in the very self of the Jew. The conflict between westernised Jews and Eastern European Jews has nothing to do with the East–West conflict of today which is a conflict between Asia and the West. The Eastern European Jew was himself a Westerner. His language was western – Yiddish is Middle High German. The secular part of his Polish culture was also western. Poland was as Roman Catholic as any Latin nation. The Eastern European Jew was a western Jew, but on a medieval pattern. His fellow Jews in Germany had emancipated themselves from the Middle Ages, and the Austrian Jews were in the middle of this process. Torn between two worlds, the modern Jew, outwardly diseased by self-hatred, was again Jacob, the man who had to fight with God and man, and even when achieving blessing in the end left the scene of his struggle limping. The conflict between the Middle Ages and the modern era was raging in the hearts of individual Jews. The fate of the Jew and the fate of mankind are always interrelated. It was in Austria, among the sick of a civilisation in travail, that the merciful healer Sigmund Freud learnt his profession of psychoanalysis.

Chapter 5

FREUD'S VIENNA

The suicide in 1903 of the young Viennese Jew Otto Weininger at the age of twenty-three illustrates the severity of the conflict between the not yet westernised father and his westernised son. Weininger's personality sheds light on Jewish writers like Karl Kraus and Franz Werfel and many others of this group around Freud. Ludwig Wittgenstein, although different from them, belongs to them in more than one respect. Truly different from all of them is Franz Kafka. Freud wrote with admiration in his last book, *Moses*, of the Pharaoh Akhnaton. The Egyptologists think little of this particular pharaoh and call his age a 'butterfly age'. The Vienna of Freud, with most of the Jewish writers, artists and philosophising physicians crowding round him, was the home of a 'butterfly civilisation'. Rilke, not a Jew, was more representative of this civilisation than his Jewish fellow writers and artists. He identified art with religion.

The Viennese Jewish *jeunesse dorée* did not go into the businesses of their successful fathers. They loathed the trades which provided the money which gave them independence and allowed them, if they wished, to live as playboys. Siegfried Trebitsch, later famous as the translator of G. B. Shaw's entire literary output, cut a ridiculous figure as a young man. He nearly died after a duel. The swords used in the duel were not lethal weapons. Under the code of the duel they could do no more than possibly give a martial appearance to a boyish face. But Trebitsch's opponent's sword was rusty, and our hero was laid up for weeks with blood-poisoning. During this time he was visited daily by the other young man, whose offence 'could only be washed away with blood'.

The non-Jewish, well-to-do sons of imperial Vienna had the

opportunities of the army, the higher civil service, and the Church. For the Jewish youth who had talent, character and ambition, art and science provided the way away from the reality in which they were born and bred. The Viennese medical faculty became world famous and was *verjudet,* full of Jews. Freud never considered baptism, which would have made his university career easier. He was an uprooted Jew. The Jewish scientists, artists and writers were reminded by the antisemites that they, who cared little or not at all about their Jewish faith, were still Jews. Their Jewish origin became their hated past. Some emphasised their Jewish existence as a national characteristic and became Zionists, some suppressed it and became what the new terminology called 'assimilationists'. To Freud Jewish religion was a non-rational component of his life, unacknowledged, no longer understood, suppressed, but unpleasantly interfering with his daily existence.

Otto Weininger committed suicide because he hated his human existence as a Jew with the fierceness of an antisemite. He saw the two worlds, the Jewish world and the world which he admired, the ideal world created by artists and great politicians. The approaching end of the decaying Austrian Empire was not visible to him. In the Vienna Opera he revelled in the works of Wagner, he revered Beethoven. The works of Goethe and Shakespeare were his Holy Scripture. The officers of the Hapsburgs in their impressive uniforms appeared to be heroes. An ideal world was not an illusion, it was there in contemporary history. Reality, as far as it was not affected by the ideal superstructure, was contemptible. Reality could be called, in line with Schopenhauer's idealism, 'Jewish' – the attribute used with the venom of the antisemite. Schopenhauer's indictment 'reality – a Jewish conception' hit out against Christianity, too. He saw in the existence of the Jews a Christian meaning: the Christian saint represents the homeless Jew, the talmudic scholar studying his huge volumes represents 'Jerome in his cell'. Superficial comparative religion does not reveal much.

Weininger, although an expert in modern science, was a medievalist. In medieval society two kinds of human beings had no place: women and Jews. They were regarded as contemptible. Weininger wrote a book called *Sex and Character* in which he accepted the medieval scale of values. He proves the inferiority of women 'scientifically', and draws the same conclusion about the Jews. He went to an exhibition of Beethoven manuscripts, and there, in a place exalted in his eyes through the relics of the great master, he shot himself. There were many candidates for a suicide with Weininger's motive, but they lived to old age. Freud was one of them. He never repudiated Judaism. He can even be called a 'proud

Jew'. But he was not free from the Jewish self-hatred which also tor-
mented Marx and Lassalle. When he was fourteen years old Lassalle
wrote in his diary: 'Two types I hate – the Jews and the journalists'.
And yet he also wrote: 'I would risk my life in order to save the Jews
from their present oppressed situation. I would not even be frightened by the guillotine, if I could make the Jews a respected nation.
Following up the trend of my childish dreams, it is my dearest wish
to lead the Jewish people, with a weapon in my hand, towards independence'.

Marx and Freud throughout their lives were different from Lassalle. They have been called 'two of the most terrifying antisemites'.
They desired to be 'ultra-Greeks', and they succeeded in this
endeavour to a surprisingly high degree. Marx called Lassalle a
Judenjunge (a Jew boy); but Bismarck said that any squire could be
happy to have Lassalle as his neighbour. 'In the Jewish antisemite,' it
has been said, 'antisemitism becomes a religious power. The Jewish
antisemite wrestles with himself'. Freud 'killed' his own father by
inventing the myth of patricide, the father of the horde murdered by
his sons. His last publication could have been written by any antisemitic Old Testament scholar.

Otto Weininger would have liked to be an ultra-Greek. History
was to him the glittering world of the sons, but not of Jewish sons.
The Austrian officer-class, gay and idle, as they appear in Lehar's
operettas, the Court, the Wagnerian theatrical Middle Ages of Parsifal, the music of Beethoven and Schubert, art and heroism – this was
history, a world of gods and heroes. The Jewish world, as Anton
Kuh, a gifted writer of the Viennese circle around Freud, describes it,
is a world of 'old men with patriarchal caps, of parents, uncles and
aunts'. It is a life lived in the family, centred round a table on which
food is offered and where ceremonies are performed. A Jew, says
Kuh, sees in the Jew 'a fellow eater and a fellow worshipper'.

The table at which the family in a Jewish home sits is indeed an
altar. Jews do not have their altar in the synagogue, they have it in
their home. When he talks about the totem meal, Freud refers to the
Holy Communion of Christian worship, but he had no personal
experience of the Christian Holy Communion. Kuh's formula 'fellow eater and fellow worshipper', on the other hand, describes
exactly Freud's childhood experience in which a father or a grandfather – Freud's grandfather had the title rabbi – sanctified a Sabbath
or festival meal in the ceremony of the *Kiddush.* A Jewish code of ceremonial has the title *Shulchan Aruch,* which means 'the properly laid
table'. Even the most assimilated Jew knows these two Hebrew
words They may occur in the daily talk of a Jew who does not know
any Hebrew. Freud, without any doubt, knew this expression. It

meant to him something crude and primitive. How could he, the Jew ignorant of Judaism, know that the expression 'the laid table' is a quotation from Psalm 23: 'Thou preparest a table before me in the presence of mine enemies'? Eating and worshipping together meant something primitive to the author of *Totem and Taboo*. Had he really read the Bible, as he claimed, he would have known that the numerous sacrifices in the Hebrew Bible create communion with God during a meal: God is our host, and we are his guests. Freud leaves God out and sees a primitive custom. When God is seen as present, is invoked as present at the meal, the custom even of a primeval clan is not primitive, but is, in all its simplicity, sublime.

A great Viennese rabbinic scholar, whom Freud's father would have had the knowledge to appreciate, is called by Freud the son 'a very hard, bad, and uncouth man'.[1] It is worth while looking more closely to find out who was this man who seemed so despicable to Freud. He was a lecturer at the Viennese Rabbinic Seminary, the author of a standard work on the oral rabbinic tradition. His name was Isaac Hirsch Weiss. On his retirement, at the age of eighty, he concluded his manifold scholarly publications with an autobiography which remains an important source book for the talmudic education in the yeshivot of Bohemia during the time of his youth. This autobiography also gives us a description of the life of Freud's ancestors. We read there, indirectly but with cogent details, of the life of Freud's grandfather and great-grandfather. Of I. H. Weiss Sigmund Freud's letter speaks in a most disrespectful way: 'In his home there was no love but bitter poverty, no culture but numerous duties'. All the sons had to study 'in order to satisfy the great vanity of the father'. In fact, none of the sons had a successful life – Freud's letter tells us – and two of them committed suicide. One of these unhappy sons was a medical colleague of Freud, and Freud went to his funeral. The education of sons according to outdated methods in the country of the *Kleine Nachtmusik* could only have disastrous results. But Freud did not learn the lesson which his observation of the tragedies in the family of I. H. Weiss could have taught him. He merely reacted to I. H. Weiss the father with the hatred which he, as a son, unknown to himself, felt against his own father and which many westernised sons in Vienna, also unknown to themselves, felt against their own fathers.

Can a Jew get away from his Judaism? Weininger said no and shot himself. Freud did not shoot himself but found relief in another way. He rationalised his self-hatred by showing that it is a primitive sphere where fathers rule over sons. If the rule of the father was the

1. *Briefe 1873–1939* (Frankfurt, 1960), no. 58.

order of the primitive sphere, he, the westernised, the emancipated son no longer had anything to do with it. The son had emancipated himself from the father. The Jew was no longer a Jew.

When Otto Weininger committed suicide, Karl Kraus was twenty-nine. He defended Weininger's death as a meaningful action which, he pleaded, the contemporary historical situation could not afford to ignore. Kraus was the greatest figure of the Viennese circle around Freud. From Freud's psychoanalysis Kraus kept aloof: 'I do not want to meddle in my private affairs'. Kraus acknowledges that man's mind has its inner experience which should remain his 'private affair'. This made him the creator of profound poems and essays. As editor of *Die Fackel*, Kraus was as well known in Vienna as Socrates was in Athens. Socrates said 'know thyself'. So did Freud. Kraus also said it, but he said it as a satirist, as a relentless critic, as a pamphleteer.

His *Fackel*, like Maximilian Harden's *Die Zukunft* in Berlin, followed the example of Henri Rochefort's *La Lanterne*. Rochefort, the formidable opponent of Napoleon III, had chosen the title *La Lanterne* for his journal because he wanted to remind his fellow citizens that during the French Revolution the aristocrats were hanged on lanterns. With his title *Die Fackel* ('the Torch') Kraus followed no such programme. Politically, he was a conservative. He did not attack a system but men, especially servile journalists whom he termed, regarding their sloppy language as a sin against the Holy Ghost, 'these *journaille*' (from the word *canaille*, 'rabble'). Today we know the journalist as a reporter, whose opportunities of making policy are strictly limited. It was different in Karl Kraus's days. Journalism was a part of literature, and the journalists had access to the corridors of power. It was said that in the office of the mighty editor of the *Neue Freie Presse*, Moritz Benedict, Balkan kingdoms were created and brought to nought. As the *journaille* contained a high percentage of Jews, Kraus's crusade against them was made passionate through his own Jewish self-hatred.

The Spanish inquisitors, investigating cases of Marranos, newly and superficially baptised Jews, found criminal *opiniones Judaicae* in remarks which seemed of no importance to the victims. Like these inquisitors Karl Kraus persecuted his Jewish fellow writers and found Yiddish hidden in their German, and even exaggerated their style by repeating it in Yiddish diction like a gutter antisemite. Often he had a case. The antisemitic journalist Stapel found that Jews wrote either better or worse than German writers, but never like them. Buber, who in his old age called himself a Polish Jew, wrote in a German style which was both famous and peculiar. Franz Rosenzweig, like no other German writer, could still write German after World War I which was the German of Goethe. But an age consists of the few who are great and the many who are not great, even if they have their place and their function in contemporary literature. Those who were not great are forgotten today, and one wonders whether Karl Kraus's crusade against them was worthwhile. Why did they annoy him so much? The answer is clear. They were Jews, and he, the baptised Jew, had remained a Jew. His Jewish self-hatred was alive, or shall we say creative, in his literary criticism. Karl Kraus was the most typical representative of Jewish antisemitism, and he was also its most typical victim. He was forced to write daily from morning till evening. When a newspaper reprinted an essay of his but put a comma in the wrong place he took the paper to court. (He won his case.) Is this greatness or madness, or both? Kraus wrote in self-defence against anybody who might have said, not even in words but with a look, in an innocent remark: 'You are a Jew'. This remark was offensive, to one who knew nothing of the holy glory of being a Jew.

One thing was common to the *Lanterne* and the *Fackel*: both journals refused to accept advertisements, in order to preserve their independence. Rochefort, however, was not interested in what was Karl Kraus's main purpose. Kraus wanted to save the language from becoming soulless, dishonest and dead. This concern puts him side by side with the linguistic philosophers Ferdinand Ebner, Franz Rosenzweig, Ludwig Wittgenstein and Martin Heidegger. Freud also belongs to this group. He, too, was deeply concerned with the human word. Its subconscious meaning should be discovered, made conscious and become fit for communication.

There are two sentences in Franz Rosenzweig's *Star of Redemption* which provide the creative vision for the various forms of linguistic philosophy, however different they eventually became. Rosenzweig writes: 'The ways of God are different from the ways of man, but the word of God and the word of man are the same . . . What man hears in his heart as his own human speech is the very word which comes out of God's mouth'.[2] Here the Jew Franz Rosenzweig and the Roman Catholic Ferdinand Ebner are in full agreement. Wittgenstein would have understood Rosenzweig, whose linguistic philosophy I venture to sum up in the words: 'Listen, O man: listen to what a husband says to his wife, a wife says to her husband, to what parents say to their children and children say to their parents, what the bridegroom says to his bride, and the bride says to her bridegroom. Listen to what a man says to his fellow man. Listen to the words once spoken and afterwards written down in Holy Scripture. Listen, and you will hear the word of God spoken by man'.

2. Rosenzweig, *Star of Redemption*, p. 151.

Rosenzweig turns to the private language of man and to the Hebrew Bible. In these two instances he finds the word which is still human because it is unaffected by the language of the advertisements and the bellowing of the puppets of the totalitarian age. Rosenzweig began to translate the Hebrew Bible into German. He was convinced, as the authors of the Septuagint were before him, that the Hebrew Bible can be translated into the language of western man. In this way decayed language can be regenerated, and can announce a message beginning with the words 'Thus says the Lord'. The biblical prophet speaks his own word, and it is the word of God. The prophet, being not merely the mouthpiece of his own civilisation, speaks a word that is valid for all civilisations. In this he is not a superman but truly human.

Both Freud and Karl Kraus turned to words spoken by man. To Freud words were important because of their roots in the unconscious, to Karl Kraus they were important as the currency of culture. It can be argued that Freud made an important contribution to linguistic philosophy (of which he had no concept). He did so as the prophetic interpreter of words which cannot be understood if taken only as coming from the rational level of mind. Freud is more Jewish than Kraus, who is mainly concerned with the cultural superstructure above reality.

The Empire is decaying because people write bad German: this is Karl Kraus's linguistic philosophy in a nutshell. Kraus remained a worshipper of culture, of great works of art, of poetry. He remained chained to aesthetic values. He was an uprooted Jew. He, who did not understand the biblical prophets, could not understand that in speech – as in love – the difference between transcendence and immanence disappears. Love and speech are immanent in man, and at the same time they transcend man. A word spoken by man, understood as the word of God, made the biblical prophet a man to whom the people of Jerusalem listened.

The people of Vienna in the years of their 'butterfly civilisation' had no prophets, nor were they men of the kind which listens to prophets. This gap was filled by apostate Jews who, if they were not prophets, preached like Karl Kraus. He preached as a satirist, as a critic, and as the evangelist of what is called today 'the new morality', of which he was the first immature pioneer.

Solitude was praised by Schopenhauer and Nietzsche, by Oscar Wilde, Baudelaire and Flaubert. It was recommended to youth as a situation offering creative possibilities. But which solitude, we must ask these men of the *fin de siècle*. To be alone is every man's predicament. It must be endured, and can be endured, without bitterness, and in a spirit which always looks for and finds human contacts. To be alone in the sense of being cut off is dangerous and has to be avoided. Boys who cut themselves off from their fathers and teachers when they have their first sexual awakening, and remain 'fixed' in this solitude, are condemned to remain boys for their whole lives. They may become poets and writers of a sort, even creators of great books, but men, adults, they will not become. Otto Weininger and Karl Kraus were helped financially by their loving Jewish fathers who were still alive when the two were boys. But the difference between westernised sons and not yet westernised fathers made the two 'fatherless'. Being fatherless they were not qualified to write about marriage and love. They wrote a lot about the emancipation of sexuality from prejudice. They could not help others, because they themselves were in need of help. They were without help from their fathers when they were boys, and this condemned them to a long drawn out adolescence for life.

Freud – like the playwright and novelist Arthur Schnitzler – remained aloof from Karl Kraus's propaganda for 'healthy sexuality'. Karl Kraus never realised that he was fighting a crusade against the Christian heresy of Manichaeism. Manichaeism equates sex and sin. Freud remained a physician. He grew into mature manhood, where others remained boys until their death in old age. Kraus remained an unmarried man, and made the Viennese *Kaffeehaus* his home. His 'affairs' were many, as his poems, some of lasting beauty, reveal. Freud lived as a *paterfamilias*. Karl Kraus entered the Roman Catholic Church. In 1920 the Salzburg Cathedral and the Franciscan Church were allowed to be used as the backcloth for a performance of Hofmannsthal's *Jedermann* (Everyman). This enraged Kraus and he rejoined the Jewish community. He had aesthetic reasons for joining the Church and aesthetic reasons for leaving it. Christian faith has nothing to do with this kind of baptism. Nor is baptism as breakdown a true conversion to Christianity. Nietzsche wrote of Wagner: 'He broke down at the Cross'. Parsifal's faith, the faith of Wagner's Parsifal, is the end of a journey of despair and not the victory over despair. It is the same in Orwell's novel *1984*, where the poor victim of cruel totalitarianism looks at Big Brother and imagines that he loves him.

About the baptism of Franz Werfel only rumours exist. In America he was often visited by a Roman Catholic priest who showed his kindness to the sick and down-and-out refugee in various ways. Werfel's baptism, of which no reliable record exists, would have been a deathbed conversion, another case of one who 'broke down at the Cross'. More to the point is Werfel's approach to the Christian setting which he often chose in his writings. There is no real commitment to Christianity in his many references to the Christian faith, but this lack of commitment is not made explicit. His *Christozentrik* as 'source of rejoicing in existence' must be traced to Goethe, not to the New Testament. The worst example is his novel *The Song of Bernadette*. The reader is left to assume that the author shares Bernadette's belief in the miracle. But does he? If he does not, we must say that a Jewish author unable to accept the Christian faith wrote a book with the aim of edifying a Roman Catholic public. On the whole it is more his lack of proper knowledge in matters of Jewish and Christian theology than lack of character for which Werfel has to be blamed.

Henri Bergson and Edmund Husserl died as faithful Jews. The scraps of utterances to the contrary collected by Christians interested in missionary work to Jews prove nothing. The two great philosophers died in a world echoing the victories of Hitler. They did not die as Christians, but they felt they had to die like the Christ of the New Testament. This is what they said in one way or another to the Roman Catholic nursing sister and to the few friends who dared to come and visit them. One died in Paris, the other in Germany, both deserted by former disciples and friends, cut off from the world in which the heathen Caesar had triumphed. Both refused to give in, and died as Jews.

We cannot say anything so noble about Werfel. But we can defend him. In 1937, in *Höret die Stimme* (Listen to the Voice) he spoke against the times, whereas the Churches in Austria went with the times. He was a novelist, a poet, and a pamphleteer with a moral cause. Writing about the relationship between the Jewish and the Christian faith, he was misinformed and muddled. It is strange that his *Paulus unter den Juden* (Paul among the Jews) appeared in 1926, seven years after Franz Rosenzweig had finished his *Star of Redemption* and six years after its publication, and twenty years after Albert Schweitzer's *The Quest for the Historical Jesus*. But Werfel, like Freud, clung to the views of the Victorian scholars who ignored the Jewish roots of Christianity in the ages before Paul.

Simone Weil wrestled with Christianity and died a Jewess. She did not become baptised. There was no Simone Weil in Freud's Vienna. What Freud and Werfel wrote about Paul – let everyone who studies Freud be warned – is historical and theological nonsense. The Church in Austria was not in a position to give an impressive account of herself and so challenge Jews to respond with a profound testimony to Judaism. Buber, who originally belonged to the Vienna of Freud and Karl Kraus, left it, settled near Frankfurt, studied philosophy, which Freud as a positivist avoided like the plague, joined Franz Rosenzweig and saved his soul. Yet in the fine art of his short essays Buber is a pupil of Kraus. All his life Buber adhered to his belief in the concept of a 'Jewish culture'. Culture, the aesthetic substitute for Church, religion and, indeed, God, was the centre of Viennese humanism. Against this humanism Grillparzer, with whom Karl Kraus is often compared as a writer, had warned his fellow Austrians with the words: 'From humanism to nationalism, from nationalism to barbarism'. With his message of Jewish culture, preached in various forms, Buber remained a man of the Vienna Circle.

A generous postscript has to be written about the sad chapter of the wave of baptisms in the Jewish bourgeoisie and among the Jewish intellectuals. First of all, it happened among a small minority. The Viennese Jewish population turned away from these individual cases with contempt. They regarded them as cowards. Not a single case can be shown of a Jew conspicuous as a leading personality in the public or literary life of Vienna becoming a Christian out of conviction. But numerous cases are known in which Jews at the universities, in the civil service, in the army, threw away advantages which baptism, explained to them as a formality, would have granted.

The generous postscript to all this has to point out that the Vienna of 1900 had become an island of positivism and psychology, of the natural sciences and of music. Philosophy, epistemology, critical thinking about thinking, was out, and the enlightenment, not that of the great Voltaire but of the little schoolmasters, was in. Freud was a typical example. He wrote: 'Even when I have moved away from observation, I have carefully avoided any contact with philosophy proper. This avoidance has been greatly facilitated by constitutional incapacity'.[3]

Franz Werfel's play *Paulus unter den Juden* is written on the basis of the erroneous contrast between Judaism as law and Christianity as love. By Werfel's time Geiger and other German Jewish scholars had rehabilitated Pharisaic Judaism, so that the theological antithesis between law and love was relegated to the armoury of a backward Christian theology. Hermann Cohen and Franz Rosenzweig had published their works. Nothing of this penetrated Austrian Jewry. The Orthodox rabbis objected to German-Jewish influence as being 'Neology' or 'Reform'; the intellectuals without contact with rabbis had read Buber's immature *Reden über das Judentum* (Lectures about Judaism) and discussed Zionism. Religious Judaism interpreted in the language of the new age was not available to those Jews who would have liked to enter into a Jewish–Christian dialogue. Nowhere in Austria was there an opportunity for such a dialogue. The confrontation was not between Jew and Christian, but between Jew and antisemite. The Christian priest was as a rule an antisemite. In this

3. *An Autobiographical Study*, p. 109.

insincere, hateful, in fact godless atmosphere Jewish baptism was a formality. The baptised Jew left his Jewish faith, of which he did not know anything, and entered Christianity, of which, still being a Jew under his skin, he did not think much. Max Brod wrote a poem about the baptised Jews in which he ends with the self-accusation: 'We have not loved you enough'.

The baptism of Karl Kraus and Otto Weininger was not a real conversion. And yet, in their aesthetic preference for history, for the superstructure above reality, rather than reality itself, they were more Christians than Jews. In this respect Freud had nothing to do with the Vienna Circle. His *Future of an Illusion* can be ignored as an attack on belief in God but must be carefully read as a criticism of established religion and of culture and civilisation.

Freud, as the discoverer of the non-rational structure of the human mind, drew a metaphysical conclusion about the nature of the universe. The world appeared to him in a way which man's visible and accountable history did not reveal. To speak in theological terms, Freud defended the superiority of creation against history. He stands where Marx stood before him, Marx who rehabilitated the material world which was ignored and neglected by the spiritualistic Hegel. Simone Weil speaks the right word on behalf of Marx and Freud: 'The substance of matter is obedience'. The sentence of this Jewish girl leads into the post-Marxist and post-Freudian age. The economic fate of man – the way our daily bread is providentially provided – and elements of our thinking – the conditions of our belief in God – are mysteriously directed by the material world itself, by the subconscious layer of the human mind, in short by creation. Marx and Freud unmasked history. They were both Jews, and their contribution to mankind has to be gratefully acknowledged as a Jewish one. What the Marxists and the Freudians did with the revelation which the two pioneers were chosen to receive is not their fault. They were misunderstood, and they themselves, as can happen with prophets, did not clearly understand the consequences of their own vision.

Marx and Freud looked into history without illusion. They, and we, the generation after them, saw the face of Medusa. The face of a Saviour did not appear. This is the challenge of Marx and Freud to Christianity. Their materialistic metaphysics may be dead, but the challenge of Marx and Freud remains: it is a Jewish challenge, and Christianity has to answer it. We Jews wait for this answer which must come forward, if a Judaeo-Christian civilisation is to come again.

The Vienna Circle, with its aesthetic belief in history, was a last pre-Marxist and pre-Freudian attempt to give history a meaning by proclaiming that art offers redemption. This claim is not true, although it has been naively believed in Europe since the Renaissance and, as hope against hope, alleged for the last time by such writers of despair as Stendhal, Flaubert and Nietzsche. The dying imperial Vienna gave the artist the function of entertaining a public certain of the coming end and too feeble to master a tragic situation. The Viennese were fond of saying that their situation was 'desperate but not serious'.

The Jewish writers of the Vienna Circle believed in art. When the catastrophe came they had nothing to say. Karl Kraus stopped publishing the *Fackel* in 1933. Hitler occupied Austria in 1938. Kraus, who died in 1936, would have had three years to find the right word against Hitler. His friends urged him to continue to publish his journal. He refused. He did not want to speak in the apocalyptic hour. His unwillingness was inability. It turned out he was, in the words of Nietzsche, 'only a fool, only a poet'. He had nothing of the prophet. He admitted *Mir fällt auf Hitler nichts ein* ('I can think of nothing to say with regard to Hitler'). He published, though, one heart-rending poem, *Letztes Gedicht* (Last Poem) in which millions who lived through the Hitler era will find their own mournful mood expressed:

> . . . *No word is right*
> *One speaks only in one's sleep* . . .

It ends with the line:

> *The word went to sleep* [or died – *entschlief*]
> *when that world awakened.*

In Germany, Leo Baeck, Martin Buber and many rabbis could find words which reached their fellow Jews and the world under the very noses of the Gestapo. 'The word' did not go to sleep in German Jewry from 1933 to 1939. It may be that some of Buber's writings will one day become dated. What he wrote in Germany from 1933 to 1938 will last. In these writings Buber appears fully emancipated from his aesthetic Viennese beginnings. But Karl Kraus's silence must not only be judged as a negative attitude. The poet Kraus saw more clearly than did the psychoanalyst Freud. Freud had developed his psychoanalytical therapy into a psychoanalytical totalitarianism. This psychoanalytical totalitarianism, as it has been called, is no longer confined to psychology but makes metaphysical statements about man and his world. No wonder that Freud misjudged his time. The victory of Hitler in Germany in 1933 did not open Freud's eyes to the real situation. What he said in those years to his biographer Ernest Jones testifies to the shallowness of a bourgeois preoccupied with his own position and pushing the thought of mankind away from his own conscience. Karl Kraus at least 'spoke' through his silence – though not by the spoken word – and impressively told of the imminence of the human catastrophe.

Vienna did not die when Hitler marched into the imperial city. But many Jews died, or were marked out for a death soon to come. They lived, when they were poor – and the majority were poor – in the district called Leopoldstadt. Those who could save themselves are now dispersed all over the world. What is Vienna today? It is the city of Freud even more than anything else. It is the city of the *Donauwalzer*. A friendly city? The neolithic peasants of the Alpine villages which surround Vienna, the prototypes of Freud's 'hordes', who were held at bay during the reign of Franz Josef, conquered through Nazism the city of writers, artists, musicians, scientists and humanists. The waltzing stopped, the lights of the ballroom went out. Nazism is more of Austrian than of German origin. The Austrian peasant population led by Roman Catholic clergy of peasant stock did not defend the city against the onslaught of the barbarians. Freud's vision of 'hordes' was a reality. But the guilt of the worshippers of beauty must not be overlooked. As Grillparzer, a great Austrian, said, the way from the worship of beauty leads to the Beast of the Apocalypse.

Vienna was not Brecht's city of Mahagonny nor was it an innocent Nineveh, which deserved the mercy of God. It was a city in which Jews were killed, and in that respect it was a city like others. Why do Christian people kill Jews? Why do sons kill their fathers, as Freud tells us they do in the myth which he invented. Has the mythmaker Freud given his Jewish answer to the question, 'What is Christian history?'

Vienna was a city of ordinary people, Christians and Jews, wrongly portrayed by Lehar and in *La Ronde*. Jerusalem, when it was destroyed by Rome, was also a city inhabited by ordinary people. Holy events take place among ordinary people. To contemplate these holy events, to interpret them, gives us survivors consolation, guidance and the strength to hope again. There was Dr Johnson's London, Tolstoy's Moscow, Balzac's Paris, Fontane's Berlin, Joyce's Dublin. There was also Freud's Vienna. It died in 1938.

Chapter 6

Jewish Migration

'These are the stations of the journeys of the children of Israel, which went forth out of the land of Egypt . . . And Moses wrote the places of their goings out according to the stations of their journeys, by the commandment of the Lord' (Numbers 33: 1–2). We shall hear in tomorrow's reading of the Law the geographical names of each of the many stations connected with the Jewish wanderings. We shall hear a travel account read as sacred history.

Today we travel by train, boat or air. But nothing has changed. It is the same sacred road, as sacred today as it was then, because it is our lot, imposed by our faith, to wander forth from the places where barbaric paganism rules, and to seek new places, places of peace and justice.

'And they departed from . . .', 'And they pitched in . . .', 'And they went forth . . .', 'And they encamped at...'. Over and over again the same words echo in our ears as we read. It is the rhythmic beat of Jewish destiny. Jewish history, which is sacred history, is the history of the stations of Jewish wandering.

The science that studies the different forms of human society differentiates between two basic types of mankind: nomads and peasants. The nomad wanders from place to place. Arab Bedouin and seafaring Vikings both have this itch to wander far off into strange and distant places, to take warlike possession of them. The peasant is settled, bound to the soil, and the law of the earth is his law. The gods of the earth are his gods. Woven into the woof and warp of the fateful procession of spring, summer, autumn and winter, bound to the vital laws of earth, plant and beast, the unchristianised peasant is himself a clod, an Adam, pre-Revelation man. He is 'soil-bound', as they say today in Germany, where deliberate paganism is the order of the day. The spirit of man is free, and to be 'soil-bound' can only mean, as it does mean in present-day Germany, an unwillingness to waken to the realisation of the nature of the spirit. For the spirit of man is not bound to any locality, it is universal. It has liberated itself from the earth, in so far as it is not just nature. But the nomad and the peasant are a bit of nature. The nomad is a bit of dynamic nature, the unchristianised peasant is a bit of static nature, heavy, lumpish, patiently persistent and enduring.

What is a Jew? He is neither a nomad, though he wanders, nor a peasant, though he certainly loves peace and the idea of a settled life. We do not wander because we like wandering, but because it is our destiny.

What is a Jew? We are not nomadic warriors, lured into distant places by the thought of adventure. We are forced to wander by cruel necessity, held up against us by the pagan world like a menacing fist. But there is also another force that makes our wandering intelligible. It is not the lure of adventure, but the call of God, who leads us from station to station.

What is a Jew? Though the science that deals with the different forms of human society tells us that the nomad and the peasant are the two basic types of man, it also knows a third type, the priest. The priests are the founders of cities. The urban character of the Jew is not merely external. The citizen is as much settled as the peasant, but his settledness is determined by the spirit and is more free from the law of the earth. The priest too wanders, but not like the nomads and the warriors. The priest wanders without the sword, and his wandering is linked with the fate of the man who serves God. But he who serves God does not always enjoy the peace of a settled life as his lot on earth.

What is a Jew? This is our answer, given with our eyes fixed upon actual reality and rigorously eschewing all suspicion of the mere romantic. A Jew is a wandering priest. Jewish wandering is the road of the priest. We must and we can see what is holy in our present fate. For what has happened? We have been persecuted and robbed. Then we were able to get a permit or an affidavit, and through a narrow door we came out of our inferno of persecution into a free land, but we are aliens there. We encounter new difficulties when we try to adjust ourselves to the life and culture of this country that has saved us. All these are brutal facts. What is there holy about it, people ask. There are fools and wise men among us, ordinary, simple, prosaic people, and inspired enthusiasts, mercenary, self-seeking people and noble generous folk, good and indifferent, all the various types of mankind imaginable. Yet we are *all of us* fought against by a pagan world and have been ejected from this pagan world, because we did not belong to it. There is the proof that we stand on a higher plane.

We were happy where we were, in Germany, Austria, Czechoslovakia. We were happy there, we had been there for generations, and it is a hard and cruel fate to be driven from one's home. Yet here is our patent, like a patent of nobility: that there is no room for us in a world returning to paganism. That we are aliens is our priestly destiny. Whoever will not or cannot see holiness when it shows itself in the streets and market-places of the world will never see it, will never be able to comprehend it. Look at the humanity of the Jew, we can say to the world, and behold holiness visible to all eyes.

People in ancient times could not have regarded the wanderings of the Jewish people as anything strange, because in those days they were nothing unique. For side by side with the Jewish wandering there was another, that of the Greeks. Just as there was a constant flow of people emigrating from Jerusalem, from Palestine, to all parts of the Mediterranean basin – and the Mediterranean basin in ancient times was the world – so there was a similar flow of people emigrating from Athens, from Greece, and in every town and island of the old Mediterranean world the Greek was as much in evidence as the Jew. Historians have pointed out that the routes and centres of the Jewish Diaspora and the routes and centres of the Greek Diaspora were identical. Wherever the Greeks came they brought culture and enlightenment with them, and afterwards, together with the Romans, civilisation. One was either a Greek or a barbarian. Wherever the Jews came they brought with them the belief in the One God. One was either a Jew or a pagan.

One might indeed ask which of the two it was that formed this ancient world, this Mediterranean world, into a historic unity, into an organic world, the Greek or the Jew, the forces of culture and civilisation or the force of faith. But the question is badly put. It is not a simple one either. The Jew stands just as much for culture and civilisation as the Greek.

Jewish messianism, the faith that God's cause will win, is at the same time the faith that culture, progress, humanity and civilisation should not be merely the possession of a privileged class but must ultimately become the possession of all mankind. Only Judaism is also committed to the certainty that culture, progress, humanity and civilisation always revert to barbarism unless they are bound up with belief in God.

Just as the Jewish wanderings as a pilgrimage of faith and the Greek wanderings as a mission to spread culture and civilisation proceeded along a common road and in contact with each other in the ancient world, so they still do today. The Jew, being the carrier of faith, is also the carrier of contemporary cultural values. If all that was once honoured throughout the world under the name of German culture is to be completely destroyed in Germany by the Nazis, it may well happen that the noble spirit of Germany's great poets and thinkers, annihilated in Germany itself, will be preserved for the world by Jews. Judaism has its justification as the Judaism of civilisation. The Judaism of faith and the Judaism of civilisation, which should never be separated from each other, are in union the great opportunity of Judaism.

Zionism goes to show how important Jewish wandering is as a civilising factor. Think of what Zionism has made of Palestine. Just as the Greeks once came to Palestine as the pioneers of western civilisation, so the Zionist youth have come there today. They have converted marshes into fertile land, they have built new towns and created new life. The word *chaluts*, which has been adopted to designate the Jewish worker in Palestine, means pioneer. It is a Hebrew word that occurs in the Bible. But in modern Hebrew the Biblical Hebrew word has acquired the Greek spirit, it has re-embodied the spirit of the old colonising, civilising Greeks. Judaism is capable of combining the spirit of the *chaluts* and that of the prophet. Two spirits can form a unity only when there is an inward relationship between them. When God says, 'Whom shall I send, and who will go for us?' the prophet answers, 'Here am I, send me ' (Isaiah 6: 8). This call and this answer can both be applied to the *chaluts* youth.

We shall not do justice to the *chaluts* if we consider him only as a political figure, to be understood in terms of European idealism. The idealism of the *chaluts* has its roots in the world of Jewish religious faith, even though those who represent the *chaluts* to the outside world as his leaders rarely realise this. The ideology of the *chaluts* is the ideology of the European political parties, from Left to Right, but the heart of the *chaluts* is a Jewish heart. And this heart of his burns with the sacred flame of the love of Zion. There are forces in *chaluts* Judaism that are akin to those of prophetic Judaism, so that the unity of *chaluts* Judaism and prophetic Judaism definitely becomes a Jewish possibility.

The port of Tel Aviv and the University of Jerusalem demonstrate the range and scope of Zionism. The *chaluts* in Palestine is the Jewish agricultural worker with his spade, and he is equally the chemist in his laboratory experimenting to find a cure for malaria, a way to deal with the malaria-carrying mosquito, and he is the professor at the Jerusalem University, whether he is at work in the Institute of Jewish Studies, throwing new light on the literary monuments of the Jewish past, or whether he holds an advance post on behalf of the European spirit within the Islamic world, and is in this way creating the basis for the renewal of that Jewish–Arab collaboration that constituted such a valuable and fertile chapter in the history of their relations in the Middle Ages.

But this great positive value in matters of culture and civilisation that is bound up with Jewish wandering does not only affect the Jewish wandering into Palestine. After all, in every discussion of the Jewish emigration problem by non-Jews we find stress laid on the fact that wherever Jews come they act as a stimulating element in raising the economic and cultural standard of the countries to which they have emigrated. Nevertheless, the most profound and final reason for Jewish self-realisation is not merely the fact that Jews in their wanderings, like the Greeks in ancient times, have carried spiritual values, culture and civilisation from land to land.

It is completely and entirely in accord with Jewish destiny that Jewish professors are being hunted out of German, Austrian and Czech universities, that Jewish writers, doctors and intellectuals are driven from their homes and must look all over the world for new places in which to settle and continue their activity and earn their living. It is the Jewish destiny. But the full depth and sacredness of Jewish destiny will be understood only if we realise that every small businessman and every petty official from Germany, Austria and Czechoslovakia who has been deprived of his livelihood is not merely a dispossessed citizen, but a man who is suffering for the sake of God. The man who suffers for the sake of God has a priestly destiny. Jewish wandering is the priestly road. For let us consider: the Jew lives in one or another country of this earth. How does he secure his rights? The warrior has his sword to defend his rights. The priest has no sword. The Jew is powerless and demands justice. In barbaric pagan lands this is hopeless. Justice without the power to enforce it, the prophet has promised us, is the essence of the messianic era. Thus the Jew beats at the doors of the world and his enquiry 'Can I come to live here?' coincides with the priestly query to mankind: have you heard the message that the kingdom of God will be on earth, the kingdom of justice and peace?

Every place where this message is unknown or is actually repudiated, he must leave and go further. This is the fate of the Jew. It is a holy fate.

'And they departed from . . .', 'And they pitched in . . .', 'And they went forth . . .', 'And they encamped at . . .', That is what we read in our portion of the Torah. It is the rhythm of a sublime and sacred destiny. It is the rhythm of Jewish destiny. And since voices of hatred are lifted up against us in our sacred wandering, we shall emphasise proudly the glory of the Jewish fate. The words of our portion, 'And Moses wrote the places of their goings out according to the stations

of their journeys, by the commandment of the Lord', are words that
the nations of the world should not fail to hear. The divine commandment means writing down the names of the various countries
from the point of view of whether they provide resting places for
Israel or not.

I have been saying all along in these sermons which I have been
delivering in London, as a refugee to Jewish refugees: take the consolation that our religion offers us. We are, indeed, sufferers in need
of consolation. I have urged you to trust and hope. We are all indeed
poor weak mortals, and we need trust and hope. But today I call
upon you also to be proud. The pride which is self-satisfaction or
complacency is a fault. Jewish pride is something quite different. The
soldier shows his wounds – see, this is how I fought. I was at the
front. God will bless these scars as he blesses all that is brave and
true. The Jew too is always at the front. The Jew shows his road
through the world and God sees the stations of his journeys of suffering. Our suffering is endured for the sake of God. That is our
pride, our consolation and our hope.

Chapter 7

LEO BAECK IN TEREZIN

Among Leo Baeck's activities in London (1945–1956) the publication of his book *The Faith of Paul* (1952) deserves the closest attention. The importance of this small volume lies in its interpretation of the Book of Daniel; it is not, like other works of Baeck, a translation from a previous German publication; it was directly published in English. The man who had survived Terezin had something to say to the world, something which he had not said before. Terezin was a transit camp leading to Auschwitz. With its humiliation, starvation and constant nearness to death, Terezin still made the pretence of not being one of the various German 'death factories'; it granted short moments to the inmates in which they could think of themselves as human beings.

Baeck, a scholar who would have graced the most famous university, and who was a personality imbued with everything with which European culture can ennoble a man, has been seen by admirers as a humanist. But Dr Baeck was also Rabbi Baeck. Surely his humanism, if it was humanism, must have been rooted in Judaism; it was therefore, different from the humanism of an Erasmus. Scholars, scions of the world of letters and politicians made their pilgrimage to Baeck to converse with him. Was he one of them? Or was he the man to whom *shul*-goers could look as their rabbi? His exegesis of the Book of Daniel in his *The Faith of Paul* answers the question. This book, written after Terezin, shows him as a Jew who sojourned in the 'tent of Yavan', in the land of Plato and Aristotle, but who succeeded in remaining always the man 'from rabbinical stock' *(mi-geza rabbanim)* – the words he chose himself for the inscription on his tombstone.

Nineteenth-century humanism had its aesthetic tinge. The humanists of his period were not yet fascinated by the natural sciences but were under the spell of the *belles lettres,* of art, of culture. The intellectuals confessing humanism were often Jews and were also Christians. But humanism should never have become identified with Judaism, or with Christianity. Westernised Jews were inclined to see European humanism as a rightful offspring of Judaism, and non-Christian anti-intellectuals, in the heated battle of ideas, gave humanism the attribute 'Jewish'. Heine said of the Germans, 'Goethe is their Bible', and he warned them that this 'Bible' does not avail against the rise of barbarians. After 1933 German booksellers complained that the market was swamped with the works of Goethe, Schiller, and the other classics: they all came from the dissolved households of German Jews.

The ancestor of the European humanists, these highly cultured people who never consciously betrayed their Christian or Jewish origin, was Erasmus of Rotterdam. Of him his biographer, Huizinga, says that 'his voice hardly ever had the sound of coming *de profundis'.* The time came when we heard Baeck's voice speaking *de profundis.* This voice said: humanists cannot remain what they have been up to now.

When Baeck arrived in London from Terezin, his friends quickly – alas, too quickly – arranged a lecture for him. The place of this memorable occasion was the Embassy Theatre, Swiss Cottage, in a part of London in which great numbers of German Jews lived. The theatre was packed with continental Jews, relatives of people who, before they had perished in the gas-chambers of Auschwitz, had been together with Baeck in the concentration camp of Terezin. The afflicted relatives came to hear the man who had been in the Nazi hell and who had come out alive to tell the tale. Baeck always had much to give to those who came to hear him as a preacher or as a lecturer. But on that day Baeck must have disappointed his Jewish audience at the Embassy Theatre. A kind man stood there in calm greatness, and spoke about progress, which he no longer explained with the metaphor of the straight line leading forward. He spoke instead of a spiral leading onward in spite of setbacks. But after Auschwitz a philosophy of progress expressed in the metaphor of a spiral did not give comfort.

It took time before Baeck found the strength to speak on and give his answer to the events through which he had passed. In the exegesis of the Book of Daniel of the London essay, the rabbi who brought with him his message from Terezin speaks. It is the message that progress, redeeming change, exists in history because he who 'changeth the times and the seasons' (Daniel 2:21) exists. Progress is not achieved by power immanent in history. Progress is assured, but it comes 'from another place' (Esther 4: 14), a place which the humanists in their philosophy of history ignore. Hope is vision and power, it transcends time and place and reaches the realm beyond the historic situation existing at the moment. When Mordecai, in the Book of Esther, surveys the barren and hopeless situation in which he stands, dangerously defenceless, he says: 'Relief and deliverance will arise to the Jews from another place'.

Franz Rosenzweig emancipated himself from Hegel's philosophy of progress three decades before Baeck. In his London essay Baeck settled his account with the philosophical belief in progress and with historicism. Hegel had given historicism its mythology in the statement that truth develops. I doubt whether Rabbi Dr Israel Mattuck, the eminent theologian of Liberal Judaism, ever realised that with his concept of a 'progressive revelation' he was a follower of Hegel. We must look at Hegel's statement today as we look at the most fanciful mythologies of Semitic and Greek antiquity. The philosophy of Hegel, and after him that of Comte and Marx, had within it a modern mythology telling modern man that truth develops. The philosophy of immanence, alleging that truth is to be found in man himself and in man alone, and therefore in history understood as the handiwork of man, needed this myth to explain the baffling variety and change in history. The way out of the dilemma was to say, in history there is truth, but it develops. 'Truth in ourselves' wrote Rosenzweig 'is a philosophy of blasphemy; ourselves in the truth is the human situation'. Revelation is witnessed by man in his own mind and heart but it is not produced by man. Moral commandment and love, both constituting revelation, are experienced in the consciousness of man but they transcend it. Truth – like the world – is the creation of God. So is love. Love is never merely human love, it is always heavenly love, and the moral sense is not merely human consciousness but the voice of God speaking in man. Truth, morality and love are the creation of God.

Progress is no illusion as long as it is progress towards the Kingdom of God. But those who walk forward towards the Kingdom of God are not taught by philosophers to do so; they are sent on this journey by God. The directives of history guide us, if at all, to the next crossroad and no further. We cannot expect revelation to arise from history itself, from a culture manufactured by creative man who forgets that he is the creature of God. In an historic period which denies the realm that transcends history, men carry on for a while living on capital borrowed from a former, healthier age. When the day comes that this capital is exhausted, there will be no reserves to face the hunger which is not for bread and the thirst which is not for water. Man without God does not live in an historic process which 'develops' either according to the pattern of Hegel or that of Comte or that of Marx; this process develops like a cancer. Development exists in the field of biology. Truth does not develop. It is there, it is with us, from the day 'in the beginning'; with this word Genesis opens its story of the creation of the world.

Pursuing truth we obey the moral law and the commandment to love. It is not in the least paradoxical to say: thou *shalt* love. The loving 'I' cannot say anything else to the beloved 'thou' except: thou *shalt* love me. The call to act justly and to love God and man is heard; an image is seen. In history we face images. We must gratefully acknowledge and accept the peace which civilisation offers, but we must see that there is a peace which is beyond the beauty of music, poetry, colour, and form. Baeck, returning from Terezin, taught his pupils this lesson which he himself had acquired in the exegesis of the Book of Daniel.

Jewish messianism sees time in its linear progress towards 'the end' when the goal of history will be reached and God's kingdom, the realm of truth, justice and love, will have arrived. The Jew is messianic man, obeying the commandment 'Go thou thy way till the end be' (Daniel 12: 13). With this commandment the Jew receives direction for his way and is content. Can his way, walking with God, be anything else but progress? 'Happy is he that waiteth' (ibid.): he is happy because he waits for the future, and future is what has not been before and which has its window to eternity. The philosophic belief in progress never concerns eternity but only an infinite dragging on along the road of time, never transcending the route of an unredeemed history. The Jewish benediction which thanks God 'who has planted eternity into our midst', cannot be spoken by philosophers like Hegel, Comte, or Marx who project the vision of their own time into the future.

History in the Hebrew Bible is not separated from the universe, the creation of God. The division between nature and history is unknown in the Old Testament. There is no Hebrew word for nature in the Bible, neither does the Old Testament have a concept of what in the last hundred and fifty years has been called history, a realm cut out from the world and administered by men who see themselves as the only creators. Implicit in biblical messianic hope is a concept of progress, but this biblical concept of progress is different from the modern belief in history which the Italian philosopher Benedetto Croce called the 'last religion of the educated'. 'Educated' here stands for the German word *Gebildete*: they are those who believe that refinement springing from culture brings the redemption of man. With this belief the humanist stands outside the

Synagogue and outside the Church. How will Jewish messianism, the faith of the prophets in the progress towards the Kingdom of God, react to what the Book of Daniel calls 'the time of trouble'? What happens to those who do not live to see 'the time of the end' (11: 40)? In 'a time of trouble such as never was since there was a gentile nation' (12: 1), what hope have those who do not live to see that end, the end within history which brings liberation? The messianic redemption 'belongeth to the time of the end' (8: 17), to 'what shall be in the end of the days' (2: 28). What about those who suffer death in the days before 'the end of days'? What about those who die before Antiochus is defeated, asks the author the Book of Daniel. What about those who die before Terezin is liberated, Leo Baeck must have asked.

Baeck's answer, given with his exegesis of the Book Daniel, distinguishes between horizontal and vertical messianism. Baeck had no need to borrow the phrase 'vertical ascent' from Karl Barth. What he found in the Book of Daniel prompted him to speak of vertical messianism. Vertical messianism, displayed in the Book of Daniel, gained a permanent place in Judaism. Alexandrian philosophers, who were often Greek Jews, had changed the concept of biblical messianism. Progress in time was replaced by a 'progress' away from time. Progress forward was replaced by progress upward. *Olam hazeh* (the present world) was seen as world below, and *olam haba* (the world to come) was seen as the world above. The hope of man looks, indeed, both forward and upward. Baeck agreed, and spoke of the two forms of messianism which, he said, can live side by side.

In the Book of Daniel vertical messianism springs forth as consolation for the victims of 'the time of trouble', for those who die before the time of persecution ends. They 'that sleep in the dust of the earth shall awake' (12: 2). We do not die into the grave, we die into the eternity of God: the man who cherishes this hope is not a humanist. Death is the test case; at this point the humanist is a man with a shallow philosophy or with despair or stoic calm. But we can have another point of view. God is the creator of the world, a world so perfect that death is not a limitation but part of this perfection. Hope that looks forward to the 'end' need not be abandoned in the face of death; hope looking forward remains valid beyond the grave because this hope is justified from 'the beginning'.

There are two 'historic' facts: the beginning and the end, creation and messianic goal. Between them stretches human history, meaningful only through its origin and its goal and not, as the humanist thinks, with a meaning in itself. In horizontal messianism vertical messianism is implicit. The author of the Book of Daniel has not made a discovery of a faith unknown to the prophets and to the

Psalmist. The man who trusts in the creator of the world and looks forward to redemption will also look upwards, he will also be hopeful that the end of his way is not the end. More the Book of Daniel does not say. More the Old Testament does not say. It is not necessary to say more. But Christianity says more. Christianity adds to the God-created world and to the God-directed way of man in the world a third realm – the realm of spirit.

In his exegesis of the Book of Daniel, Baeck arrives where Franz Rosenzweig had arrived in his *Star of Redemption;* in the modern interpretation of Judaism, Baeck – if we forget for the moment his exegesis of Daniel – represents like nobody else the westernised Jewish generation before World War I. True, Baeck was an Army Chaplain from 1914 to 1918. But Franz Rosenzweig was a soldier in the trenches and therefore nearer to death. As a soldier Rosenzweig wrote in letters to his parents what turned out to be the first outline of the *Star of Redemption.* This work begins with an indictment against the philosophy which ignores the fact that man is destined to die one day.

Both Baeck and Rosenzweig state that a split between secular and spiritual realms is not a concept of Jewish Scripture. 'Judaism is not marred by this split', Baeck had said thirty years before he formulated the phrase 'vertical messianism'.[1] Is this vertical messianism an ascension to a world of the spirit? Has Baeck now himself accepted this category for which the Bible provides no Hebrew word? In the Old Testament, the Hebrew word *ruah* (for which the Greek translation is *pneuma)* means the power of God getting hold of the word of the prophet; owing to this power, the word which the prophet speaks is not the prophet's word but God's. Has Baeck now gone beyond the biblical use of the word spirit and accepted the Hellenistic meaning of the word, which points to a world beyond our world? Here we must turn to Rosenzweig for our defence of the Jewish character of Baeck's vertical messianism. Rosenzweig states that the reference to a spiritual world is not to be found in our Hebrew Bible; but it is the Hebrew Bible which has created it. The point is so important that it is appropriate to quote Rosenzweig's own words: 'The Bible itself does not contain the discrepancy between this world and the world to come which arose everywhere, even in Judaism under its influence; and it is therefore a guarantee that the discrepancy which it has created is no ultimate division, and that both worlds are destined to meet again in eternity'.[2]

The decisive difference between Judaism and Christianity, of

---

1. *Judaism and Christianity*, p. 174.
2. *Jehuda Halevi*, p. 211.

which Baeck rightly says they can exist 'side by side', remains, and
Rosenzweig elucidates this difference most satisfactorily: 'The Christian is the better visionary of the eternity beyond life; the Jew is the
better banner bearer of mankind's messianic goal; the Christian
stresses the seriousness of the transition from the old to the new, from
this world to the world to come, the Jew with his trust in the "eternity
in our midst" can ignore the radical change implied in this transition'.

Since this world as the creation of God has itself eternity in its
midst, there can be no urgent reason to speak of transition to the
world beyond our world. A preoccupation with death is not characteristic of Jews. Whither does the way lead after death? The Jewish
answer is: into life. Life *(hayim)* is the Hebrew word of the Bible for
eternity. The inscription on a Jewish tombstone after the name of the
deceased reads: 'May his soul be bound up in the bond of life'. The
Jew calls the cemetery 'the good place'. Anne Frank writes in her
diary: 'I so much want to live on, even after my death'. We fear
death. Everyone does. But the Jew does not tremble at the thought of
a world beyond, and therefore, does not ponder much about it. Why
should he? When death in the last hour removes his mask, he will
say: Don't you know me? I am your brother.

While confessing vertical messianism with Baeck, we can remain
rooted in Judaism. From the Book of Daniel and from the Book of
Job and from the many Psalms there is a path which leads to the
Pharisaic doctrine that God is Lord 'who quickens the dead in great
mercy', a doctrine expressed not in the form of dogma, but as praise
in the daily liturgy. This liturgy brings home the meaning of Job
19: 25–27 to every worshipper, simple or learned:

> But as for me, I know that my redeemer liveth,
> And that he will witness at the last upon the dust;
> And when after my skin this is destroyed,
> Then without my flesh shall I see God;
> Whom I, even I, shall see for myself,
> And mine eyes shall behold, and not another's.

It can happen that vertical messianism loses its roots in Judaism
and becomes separated from horizontal messianism. It happened
and led to the rise of Christianity, which rose, to use Yehuda Hallevi's parable, as a tree, the seed of which was in Judaism, in the
Book of Daniel, for instance.

Judaism and Christianity are, and remain, different, as different as
the seed is from the tree. In telling us that horizontal and vertical
messianism can live 'side by side', Baeck, as a Jew, has acknowledged Christianity, not out of mere tolerance, but out of his understanding of Judaism. He has never blurred the difference.

Baeck's 'side by side' comes from a man who has painfully

experienced the failure of Christianity in the hour of Jewry's greatest catastrophe. It is a prophetic statement, whose theological implication must be worked out. But first of all we must heed what Baeck in his prophetic commandment says to our generation.

In Terezin baptised Jews, mostly Roman Catholics from Austria, came to Baeck in their distress: they were Christians without the consolation of a Christian pastor, they were Christians among Jews from whom they or their parents had cut themselves off, they were Christians among Jews who suffered from the hands of baptised gentiles. Baeck spoke kindly to them. The rabbi became their pastor.

Baeck lectured in London in the years which were spared to him after coming from Terezin. Friends of his had revived *the Montags vorlesungen* (Monday Lectures) for which the Berlin *Hochschule für die Wissenschaft des Judentums* was once famous. Thus the old sage had his regular audience of German Jewish intellectuals, German rabbis, the few who were left and resided in London also came. But young students who came, attracted by what they had heard about Baeck, were quick with their judgement; they quoted in one way or another Benedetto Croce's 'religion of the educated', and soon stayed away. Baeck's lectures could not be summarised as historicism, as these critics thought. Historicism remains immanent in the historic process with no window open to a trans-historic, transcendent world. The hope of modern historicism that historical relativism will cure itself is indeed futile. But Baeck's lectures on history did not look for a revelation within history or for an absolute within history. With his hope for what is the goal of history and for what is above history, with his horizontal and vertical messianism, Baeck could say profound things about history from his viewpoint outside history. As a Jew, Baeck has his roots outside history. The whole Book of Genesis deals with man outside history. Rooted in the life outside history, the prophet is equipped to speak about history.

The critical visitors to Baeck's *Montagsvorlesungen* could have learned something which is peculiar to Baeck and which the new generation will have to learn to appreciate. It was wisdom, *chochmah,* which lived in these lectures. *Chochmah* is biblical Hebrew, and a great part of post-biblical Hellenistic literature is *chochmah* literature, in many instances genuinely identical with the biblical wisdom literature. It is true, the Hellenistic *chochmah* literature led away from Judaism, but it also led into Pharisaic Judaism and always remained characteristic of Judaism.

A term corresponding to *chochmah* is *derech erets,* the way of mankind. The Jewish people is loyal to mankind. Speaking of the various Jewish schools of 'wisdom' in the Hellenistic era, Baeck writes: 'No Jew could reject such aspects of "Hellenism" without renouncing a part of his own self. One was, indeed, prepared to ascribe to Hellenistic teachers the "wisdom" of which the Bible spoke. A Jew, on meeting such a teacher, had to praise God for "having given of his wisdom to a human being"'.[3] For 'wisdom' read humanism, learning, refinement through civilised life, culture – not necessarily 'Jewish' culture but culture uniting the book reading part of mankind. The fundamentalist rejection of 'wisdom' must not be tolerated. In the exhaustion and perplexity of our post-Auschwitz era the rabbi as fundamentalist has unexpectedly become a considerable danger to our Jewish way of life. Jewish religious leadership which does not try to emulate the example of Baeck is not to be trusted.

3. *The Faith of Paul*, in *Judaism and Christianity*, p. 153.

Chapter 8

PROPHETIC JUDAISM AND THE HALACHAH

Halachah and Sunna

No word of the Jewish vocabulary has been used as often recently as the word *halachah*. It is understood as a legal term. Because of the central place given to this term in the discussion between the Orthodox and Progressive sections of modern Jewry, the whole mass of arguments elaborated by Progressive Jewish thinkers shifted into the background, and their achievements were forgotten. What had been made articulate through doctrinal formulation was forgotten. Forgotten, too, was the successful Jewish formulation of Judaism through doctrine. Now, after the breakdown of Progressive Jewish learning owing to the cataclysmic end of the German-Jewish renaissance in the nineteenth century, Jews ignored the access to Judaism through doctrine and spoke only of *halachah,* wrongly understood as an exclusively legal term. Arguments about the Torah became arguments about a Jewish law. The dialogue between Progressives and Orthodox left the philosophical or at least the theoretical level and became instead a controversy between two or more schools of law. Even the Progressives, who could have argued with the clarified ideas and with the historical achievements of the German-Jewish past, ignored the rich treasures of that past and defended their non-Orthodox Judaism as if pleading before judges who had all the answers in their codes of law. An unthinking dogmatic use of the word *halachah* transformed our prophetic and classical rabbinic Judaism, the Judaism of Yavneh, the Judaism of Yohanan ben

Zakkai, into a kind of Islam. A revived understanding of the term *halachah* and a rejection of the post-holocaust use of this term will again make Judaism the Judaism of the prophets and the tannaitic rabbis. Where this is done – and it must be done, especially in Israel – the rabbis will be rabbis and not *ulema,* not officials dispensing law with religious authority.

God demands justice. This is his law. It is absolute law, eternally valid. The laws regulating social and political life are relative laws, changeable according to circumstances.

It may seem as though Jewish and Islamic religious concepts are nowhere as near to each other as in the concept of the Hebrew word *halachah.* This assumed nearness is a mistake which has to be rejected. *Halachah* is a noun derived from the verb *haloch,* walk. It may seem furthermore as though this word *halachah* belongs more to the vocabulary of rabbinic than of prophetic Judaism. This is doubtful. The linguistic history of the word *halachah* begins with Micah 6: 8, where it says:

> God has told you, O man, what is good;
> and what is it that the Lord asks of you?
> Only to act justly, to love loyalty,
> to walk humbly before your God.

In Micah's 'to walk' we have the verb *haloch.* The linguistic origin of the word *halachah* clearly points to prophetic language. What does God ask from man? The answer is that he asks man to walk in a certain way. *Halachah* means 'walking'. What in Hebrew is called *halachah* is called in Arabic *sunna,* 'path', a path trodden as it has always been trodden. We must think of the camel in the caravan. If it walks on the trodden path, it will arrive at the oasis with palm trees and life-giving water. If the trodden path is left, the way leads to death in the waterless desert. *Halachah* can be misinterpreted as being what the Muslim's *sunna* is; this misinterpretation is avoided when the prophetic meaning of *halachah* remains alive.

Man walking with God, walking before God – the translation may vary, but not the meaning – this is the Jew. To put the same point in a different way, the Jew is a man like everybody else, a man in his ordinary full humanity, but a man walking with God. The Jew is a man walking in the path of the *halachah.* A *halachah,* derived from Micah 6: 8 or from any other prophet, demands a specific deed which is always guided by only one motive: to walk with God.

The Jew walking the path of the *halachah* – *halachah* understood not as *sunna* but in its original meaning in the prophetic speech – is a man in his unchanged humanity. The Christian, on the other hand, is not merely a man in his ordinary human state, he is a 'changed man', a man who has had his encounter on the Damascus Road.

Damascus makes the Christian a 'new man', 'a new Adam'. Mere humanity does not make a man a Christian.

The Jew walks a certain way, the Christian believes. *Halachah* versus faith, this is the difference between Jew and Christian. The Jew walks the way through history, and history has its various oases of peace and its chain of catastrophes, but the Jew walks on. The Jew walks the way before God, with God, that is to say he walks in hope. His walking before God, with God, makes his way in history a way leading to the Kingdom of God. For the Jew the Kingdom of God is not merely a doctrine. The Jew walking with God makes the Kingdom of God a reality, both to himself and to everyone who beholds him walking on. There is no solution for the Jewish question: neither assimilationist theology nor Zionism can offer one. The Jew, walking with God through history, walks on without relying on an historical solution. His way is meaningful to him as *halachah,* as a way leading to the Kingdom of God. The pessimism of those who stop walking on as Jews and see no solution for the Jewish predicament of a life in the midst of the gentiles cannot be contradicted. Those who go on walking through history as Jews claim only one reason: their hope in history's progress to the Kingdom of God.

Judaism is inseparably connected with the conviction of the holiness of the moral law. The *halachah* leads the Jew into the realm of the moral law, but it can also lead into the realm of ritual, or into the socio-political order into which history places the Jew. Where *halachah* contradicts the moral law, we reject it as a misinterpreted directive and insist on a reform of the *halachah.* Jewish history is the history of a *halachah* continuously changing, continuously reformed, continuously rejected as out of date. The history of the *halachah* is a history in which it was faithfully kept and was also rigorously rejected. This rejection took place without a revolution; some *halachah* was simply forgotten and in this way deleted from tradition.

Most Jewish benedictions start with the formula: 'Blessed art thou, O Lord our God, king of the universe, who hast sanctified us with thy commandments.'. This is the general introduction, after which the specific benediction follows. Judaism, we say, is not constituted by doctrines, like Christianity, it is constituted by commandments, *mitsvot.* Islam is constituted, as the Muslim would say, by the *sunna,* by the *hadith,* by tradition leading back to the Koran.

In numerous cases our Bible thunders imperatives. The Jew hears again and again the words 'thou shalt'. Yet the Bible is a document of antiquity, and we must not expect in it an orderly separation of moral laws from laws concerning rituals or regulating the social life of the individual and the group. With the laws of the latter type historical relativity creeps into the text of our Holy Writ, in which we rightly search for and read of the eternal, unchangeable moral law. When we obey the moral law in the many instances of our life, we are in agreement with the prophetic *halachah,* with Micah's 'God has told you, O man, what is good . . .' and with similar prophetic injunctions.

In distinguishing between a prophetic and a rabbinic *halachah* we are not saying that the rabbinic *halachah* is cut off from the spirit of the prophets. The rabbinic *halachah* too, must be in harmony with prophetic teaching. The rabbinic *halachah* differs from that of the prophets in that the rabbis added the practical details of Jewish life to the admonition of the prophets. Only in this is there a difference between prophet and rabbi. The prophets demanded 'Keep the Sabbath'; the rabbis showed how this is done. The prophets demanded kindness towards one's fellow man; the rabbis showed how it is done. But in each *halachah,* including the *halachah* concerned with the rituals and with conformity to social laws, there remains one motive: to do the good deed, 'to walk wisely before God'. Never must a *halachah* be without that motive. A *halachah* can never be anything but a moral way. An immoral *halachah* must be eradicated from both biblical and post-biblical commandments. The *halachah* 'which Moses received on Mount Sinai' – to accept this solemn formula – concerns the moral law, the one moral law, obeyed on the numerous occasions when a man acts. A choice is before him: he can do right, or he can do wrong. He always lives under the rule of the moral law. In obeying this rule he obeys the *halachah* 'which Moses received on Mount Sinai'. The moral law speaks in each man's conscience. It is the categorical imperative demanding absolute obedience. 'The eternal stars above me and the moral law within me'– this Kantian formula expresses the text of Micah 6: 8, 'God has told you, O man, what is good . . .'

Why, then, does the word 'moralist' have a derogatory meaning? Are not Kant and Micah and the other prophets moralists? These men, who with so mighty a voice proclaimed the holiness of the moral law, should not be called moralists, because the moralist does not understand the sanctity which is in forgiveness, and because he does not know the miracle of atonement. The biblical prophet and all those who follow him, rabbis and ordinary Jews, and those who read the Gospels, are not moralists when they categorically demand: 'Do what is good, and avoid what is wrong'. Like the prophets the rabbis must demand a *halachah* in strict harmony with morality, and like the priest officiating on Yom Kippur in the Temple they must preach forgiveness and atonement. From the Book of Leviticus, in which the atonement service of primordial times is described, up to the huge neon letters on a New York skyscraper, shedding the word

Yom Kippur over the great city, Jews have combined their belief in atonement with rigorous ethics. Thus Jews did not become cheerless puritans, but remained merciful in their moral way of life.

It is not merely on liberal theological grounds that the term 'halachah of the prophet' has been introduced here. Obviously everyone using the term 'halachah' in the usual traditional way connects it with a decision handed down from the past to the present by a rabbi or by a rabbinical collegium. My reason for speaking of the *halachah* of the prophets has to do with something that has happened in Jewish history, indeed, in the history of mankind. This event is the new light in which our Holy Writ, the Bible, is seen in the post-medieval age. We see the Bible, the Torah, the Christian Gospels too, for that matter, as historical documents only and not as a kind of miraculous meteorite which has fallen from heaven. The Muslim sees the Koran in this unhistorical way: he sees it as a book, but as a book incomparable to any other book. Liberal Jews and liberal Christians see the Hebrew Bible and also the Gospels as we see any other book: a book written by writers who, whatever they were, were human beings. This is the effect which historical criticism has on our post-medieval generation. The authority of the Bible or of the Gospels is not impugned by this; it is the authority of men, but of men with a mission which is still meaningful for us today. This authority is that of the prophet. The prophet is a man, not a superman; the word he speaks is the word of God. To quote Franz Rosenzweig: 'The ways of God and the ways of man are different. But the word of God and the word of man are the same'. A man can speak, can write down what he says, and what he speaks and writes down is the words of God. So a man can be a prophet.

We need not be afraid or puzzled by the question: what is our *Tenach,* our Hebrew Bible? The question can be asked and answered. Our Torah is a book written by men. The men who wrote our Holy Scripture were lawyers, psalmists and chroniclers; above all they were prophets. What was possible in the past is possible in our contemporary history. Mohammed regarded himself as the 'last prophet': this separates him as a heretic from both Judaism and Christianity. The prophet speaks and makes his demands in any contemporary history.

The rabbinic *halachah* is justified through tradition. With the *halachah* of the prophet it is different. The prophet need not fall back on tradition for the justification of his message. His own personal conviction makes his message a prophetic one. The words in which he transmits it to those who do or do not want to listen to it start with the introduction 'Thus speaks the Lord'. Rashi and other medieval commentators did not understand what a prophet is. We listen to the 'thou shalt' speaking in man's conscience, and we walk, as the *halachah* of Micah 6: 8 demands, before God. We are able to revive, to reform and also to reject any *halachah*. In this way we arrive at a *halachah* rightly described as a *'halachah* of the prophet' and abolish the distinction between halachic and prophetic Judaism.

The battle for the rehabilitation of the rabbi was fought in the nineteenth-century theological seminaries and universities. There the rabbi of the past – the Pharisee of the New Testament – was at last shown to be an equal of the prophet. The historians dealing with the century in which the Gospels were written had to admit that Judaism is both prophetic and rabbinic. This victory has lost its relevance to the rabbinic Judaism of the present time. The Orthodox rabbis in Israel and in Diaspora Jewry today are not equals of the prophets: they are more like the *ulema* of Islam. Their *halachah* is based on antiquated tradition, not on prophetic conviction. A revival of Judaism will make it necessary to refer again to the controversy which once existed between the Pharisee as the Gospels saw him and the Pharisee of the tannaitic rabbinate. Today rabbis have to stop being what the *ulema* are: officials without the courage of a prophetic interpretation of a past tradition. Orthodox rabbis must be told that their *halachah* is an Islamic style *sunna*.

Jewish Orthodoxy as Islamised Judaism

The way in which we understand and translate the word Torah is of great significance. In Anglo-Jewry and, following Anglo-Jewry, in Israel and in other places of the Diaspora, Torah is often translated as (Jewish) law. In this translation, Torah is in principle made equal to, say, Roman law or English law, in short, to any law of a state. Yet any demanding word of a prophet is Torah. Torah can mean law, as it can mean guidance through doctrinal teaching. When Torah means law, it must not be reduced to a particular law, excluding the many applications to the situations of mankind. Torah understood as 'Jewish law' is reduced to a document, a book which lies conveniently on the table, to be used by a lawyer in his arguments. But the Torah is not a book, like the Koran.

Torah as law is universal law. Its universality makes it equal with love because it concerns the whole of mankind: law and love cease to be contradictions. A particular law, on the other hand, demands obedience in the way in which Allah has to be obeyed. The Muslim must obey Allah, but is not expected to love him. A sermon on the text 'God is love' does not fit into the atmosphere of a mosque. Allah is merciful, but except in Sufism he is not imagined as a loving God, who is more forgiving than punishing. This religious situation is mirrored in the everyday life of the Muslim. Marriage law and poetry reveal the Muslim as a responsible husband but not really as a lover.

To speak of the Torah as 'Jewish law' shows the deep penetration of Islam into Judaism. To struggle for a revival of classical, i.e. prophetic, Judaism, means to reject an Islamised Judaism which sees the Torah as 'Jewish law', as only relevant to the particular realm of Jewish life, and is blind to the universal relevance of the Torah to mankind. Islam is monotheism without prophecy. To understand the Torah as 'Jewish law', as is the way of Jewish Orthodoxy, means to reduce it to a Judaism without prophecy.

The Orthodox rabbis of today reveal themselves as clerics who are not rabbis but *ulema*. These '*ulema*-rabbis' teach that Torah means 'Jewish law', written and eternally unchangeable. A man can run away from it, but he cannot change it. This view of Jewish law is mistaken. With the prophetic element in Judaism alive, Jewish law can be changed. The term 'oral law' is only a legal fiction without a basis in history to sustain it, but it expresses the possibility that laws can be changed, and even new laws can be added to the bulk of previous ones, the so-called 'written laws'. With the prophetic character alive in a rabbi, he knows what can and what cannot be changed. He knows that with the progress from the Middle Ages into the modern western world a lot has to be changed. He also knows that the moral law remains unchangeable.

With the slogan the 'Torah is Jewish law' the Orthodox rabbi changes our Jewish monotheistic community into a monolithic organisation, and the Torah itself is changed into a political ideology. The Torah viewed as 'Jewish law' becomes what the flag of the state is to the citizen-soldier. He must not desert the flag; right or wrong, its command has to be obeyed. The Torah become 'Jewish law' robs the 'citizens of Yavneh' of their freedom, and makes them a mute part of a totalitarian system.

In Judaism two elements have to be alive: prophecy and piety. Living Judaism is sustained by both prophet and priest; both these religious types have to influence Jewish life. The prophet speaks the word of God. He speaks a demanding word, but he is not a lawgiver. The sad result of a study of contemporary Jewry shows it to be a pious community; pious, but without a sense of prophetic reaction to the events of its time. They are *froom* (pious), but solely *froom*. On the other hand, everybody who speaks up against an ossified Judaism and brings forward sound propositions leading to a revival not only displays piety but represents today those human qualities which made the prophet of biblical times a prophet. It goes without saying that with the prophet on the stage of history the false prophet too has to be reckoned with. But this is the price we have to pay for a history in which the prophetic controversy regains its creative power. Above all, the prophet must not be put on such a high pedestal that he is unthinkable in the human society of our day.

Franz Rosenzweig described the prophet walking among us and talking to us in our democratic era. Rosenzweig's description of prophecy is both monumental and simple. 'The ways of God are different from the ways of man, but the word of God and the word of man are the same. What man hears in his heart as his own human speech is the very word which comes out of God's mouth'. Commenting on Rosenzweig we can say: 'Listen to what man says to man, and you will hear the word of God'. Rosenzweig's description of prophecy – the word of God is a word spoken by man – is also expressed in Deuteronomy 30: 11–14: 'The commandment that I lay on you this day is not too difficult for you, it is not too remote. It is not in heaven, that you should say, "Who will go up to heaven for us to fetch it and tell it to us, so that we can keep it?" Nor is it beyond the sea, that you should say, "Who will cross the sea for us to fetch it and tell it to us, so that we can keep it?" It is a thing very near to you, upon your lips and in your heart, ready to be kept'.

The word of God become a written document, a book – this is Islam. The word of God become 'flesh', a church, a civilisation – this is Christianity. The word of God spoken by man to man – this is Judaism. When the word of God is no longer understood as addressed to man by man, but seen as enshrined in an unchangeable code, the Torah ceases to be the Torah of the prophets.

With the slogan 'The Torah is "Jewish law"', the theologically uneducated, yeshiva-trained rabbis drive away the intellectual and do not let his contribution, his 'oral law', become part of the dialogue in which the word of God is heard. The *ulema* and the *ulema*-rabbis both say: 'If you take a single stone out of the edifice of the Torah, of the *sunna,* the whole edifice will fall down'. Torah understood like the *sunna* of the Muslim – this is the teaching of the Orthodox rabbi of today. Jewish Orthodoxy is Judaism Islamised.

Judaism is not only in danger of becoming Islamised, it is also in danger of becoming Christianised. During the last two centuries continental Jewry was exposed to and in danger of assimilating to Pauline and Johannine Christianity. In the Anglo-Saxon world Petrine Christianity influenced Jews too weak to resist assimilation. Petrine Christianity, more than Pauline and Johannine Christianity, affirms law as part of Christianity. The result is a Christian shaped by devotion to law. Assimilation to British surroundings creates a Jewish type willing to obey the law. The strange situation arises in which Jews who in fact live outside Jewish life uncritically respect the

standards of Jewish Orthodoxy. They do not live the life of Orthodox Jews, but neither do they participate in a prophetic programme
of reform: it would be against 'the law'. These non-Jewish Jews
object to progress in Jewish religious life and display loyalty to
Orthodox established forms. The petrified details of the tradition
are, they say, 'the law'. 'Is that the law?', Shylock asks in humility
(The Merchant of Venice, Act 4, Scene 1). Shylock's belief in the validity of the law, even an absurd law, is tragic. But the situation can
change from tragedy to comedy when a non-Orthodox Jew in
Anglo-Jewry becomes a defender of Orthodoxy. He claims to be
Orthodox and joins the rank and file of Orthodox groups. A non-
practising Jew, assimilated to Anglo-Saxon surroundings, defends
the old petrified tradition more with upper-class snobbishness than
with Shylock's humility. 'Nothing can be done, nothing must be
done,' say the Jewish gentlemen confessing Jewish Orthodoxy. The
'law' makes any redeeming action impossible. In this case it is not
Islamised but Christianised Judaism which causes soulless stagnation.

Atrophy of Morality in Halachic Judaism

Today *halachah* can very well be defined as legality. There is a law of
some kind. Obedience to this law produces an action. The motive
for this action does not play any part in its performance. The main
thing on this level of activity is the result. I may give alms to a needy
person in order to get rid of the annoying picture of distress. On the
other hand I may act differently: I give my bit to the needy out of
charity. The result in both cases seems to be identical. But something
very important makes the actions very different: the motive.

Whether an action is in truth a moral action depends on its
motive. An action performed out of unreflecting obedience to a law,
military obedience for instance, is without the splendour of morality.
As an action on the level of mere legality something has been done
because it had to be done. It was done because others did it, or
because it had always been done. It was done because of legal obligation. The heart and soul of a moral motive is missing.

All this amounts to a weakness inherent in a Judaism reduced to
one-sided halachic order. *Halachah* demands obedience only in the
field of legal activity. The motive alone can make an action performed according to the *halachah,* indeed any action, a moral action.
In a Judaism which consists entirely of halachic precepts the absence
of consideration of a motive can lead to an atrophy of morality, of
moral thinking and of moral practice.

A limb of the human body may atrophy because it has not been used for a length of time. The same can happen to men's character. If action with negligence of its motive has lasted for a long time, in the end the sense of moral motive dies. If you teach a generation that mere legality suffices, moral cripples will grow up who will become convinced that the highest principle is not to be caught.

Numerous examples exist of rituals carried out mechanically. What kind of a man will a child grow up to be who is told that he is permitted to listen to the wireless on *shabbat,* provided somebody else, but not he himself, has switched it on?

Halachic precepts leave no choice: they have to be obeyed. In this the *halachah* is equal to a political order: it makes a Jew stand like a recruit before his sergeant-major. No room is left for argument. No freedom exists to choose the form of obedience. Obedience to the *halachah* is obedience without freedom, whereas moral actions presuppose freedom. Obedience to the *halachah* is legality in slavish submission. The Muslim calls himself a 'slave of God', and performs the deeds which he is obliged to do in an obedience which is identical with halachic legality. When Liberal and Reform Judaism teach that 'the *halachah* must not be dictated, it must be taught', the door to an end of halachic legality has been opened. The urgency of this emancipation from halachic Judaism in Israel and in the Diaspora cannot be stressed enough. A medieval rabbinate robs the population of the religious freedom which every citizen in the west possesses as a matter of course.

Halachic Judaism, as mechanical legality which neglects motive, is as medieval as was the sale of letters of indulgence by the Roman Catholic Church in the Middle Ages. Halachic legality and the trade in letters of indulgence expect religious and moral effects from mere mechanical means. 'When the coin is in the box, the soul is redeemed'. This magical materialism expects action without any participation of the moral motive to be pleasing to God.

The people which has given birth to Einstein, to Franz Rosenzweig, to a score of great inventors, scholars and Nobel prizewinners, is in danger of becoming primitive. Judaism a primitive religion? With the loss of our élite it can come to this. With the absence of the moral motive in a merely legalistic approach to actions a vacuum makes itself felt. The Jew may say his prayers according to the *halachah,* but if the motive for his prayer is not considered, phylacteries are supposed to fill the vacuum. The dull element in worship performed only in obedience to the *halachah* does not become less dull through wearing phylacteries. The phylacteries make Jewish prayer the worship of a primitive religion. The medieval Jew was not aware of this primitivity. After all, he was a medieval man. But for the post-medieval Jew phylacteries cannot but appear as a medieval device for the attainment of religious aims.

The great achievement of the historians of the *Wissenschaft des Judentums* school was the rehabilitation of the Pharisees. The rabbis were different from the prophets, but they were not in any way of lesser dignity. Judaism is the Judaism of the prophets and of the Pharisees. The words of abuse against the Pharisees in the New Testament are now recognised not as a rejection which condemns the very office of the rabbi but as a criticism of individual rabbis. The New Testament writer, in his invective against the rabbis, is like a pamphleteer, from whom historical objectivity is not to be expected. The Pharisee is not an impostor, but he can become one. No office is safe against the individual who misuses it. The rabbi can be a saintly scholar or a foolish holder of a clerical living.

The historian must beware of becoming an apologist. The historians of the *Wissenschaft des Judentums,* in rehabilitating the rabbis, performed an important task, which has changed our view of Jewish, and for that matter of Christian, history. The Pharisee, whether called rabbi or not, now stands before our eyes as different from and equal to the prophet. The New Testament, in referring to the Pharisees, records contemporary history. In this history the rabbis were like men throughout history: either rising to the height of their mission or abysmally failing in their holy duties. Above all, the *halachah* is not always the same. The *halachah* as Rabbi Yochanan ben Zakkai saw it in the year 70 is different from the *halachah of* the rabbis after the code of the *Shulchan Aruch* was written. It is therefore apposite to distinguish between the *halachah* of the classical rabbis and the *halachah* of a time which was without any creative element. The *halachah* has a history, in which there are some rabbis who successfully defend their intellectual freedom and others who belong to decadent periods in which scholarly activity is reduced to writing commentaries on commentaries.

Today the Orthodox rabbinate in Israel and in the Diaspora is without the prophetic element which should still be alive in their office. The rabbi without any spark of prophetic Judaism, who snatches power for himself from the state, is not a true servant of the Jewish people. There are, of course, righteous men who serve as rabbis and who are rightly revered by their flocks. But there is also the unfortunate fact of a rabbinate wielding power. This failure to separate state and religion deprives the Jewish people in Israel, and even in the Diaspora, of freedom.

Part II

Trialogue Between Jew, Christian and Muslim

Chapter 9

CHRISTIAN ANTISEMITISM

The two thousand years of Christianity have been two thousand years of hatred for the Jews. This is certainly no exaggeration. Rosenzweig even speaks of the eternal hatred for the Jew. If the Second Vatican Council really means a change in this respect, it would be an apocalyptic event bringing blessing not only to the Jews but to the whole of mankind, because both the murderer and his victim are afflicted with the curse which never gives peace to Cain.

Antisemitism, although the word was only coined in Bismarck's Germany, has always been present in the two thousand years of Christianity. We shall not understand antisemitism if we approach the evil only sociologically or psychologically. Only a theological approach will help.

'Before God, then, Jew and Christian both labour at the same task. He cannot dispense with either. He has set enmity between the two for all time, and withal has most intimately bound each to each'.[1] Rosenzweig does not speak here from the approach which the theologian must share with the scientist. He rather speaks with the sorrow which a mournful Psalmist expresses about an unalterable blemish which makes society, indeed the world, a valley of tears. One point we must accept from Rosenzweig: antisemitism means Christian antisemitism.

Western students of Islam have said that Christianity and Islam are irreconcilable opponents; had there been no strong anti-Muslimism in the Middle Ages, there would not have been the many outbursts of antisemitism by the Church. Paul and Mohammed are the

1. Rosenzweig, *Star of Redemption*, p. 415.

antipodes within monotheistic civilisation. The Catholic theologian Christopher Dawson called Islam the answer to Alexander the Great. The Semitic temperament opposed the *polis,* opposed Greek civilisation. In the same way, it can be said, Mohammed is the answer to Paul. Paul's belief, belief constituting Christianity, was replaced by the *sunna,* the *halachah* of the Muslim.

Mohammed against Paul, the crusader against the Muslim: this medieval hostility between Christian and Muslim is still alive. One has to understand the hostility between the intellectual and the bourgeois, the hostility between creative man and the man who repudiates creativity for the sake of resigning himself to the peace of God. That is what the Muslim does. Western man, this Christian Anonymous, has no love left either for the Muslim or for the bourgeois. Western Man, calling his civilisation Judaeo-Christian, is still in need of discovering the contribution of Islam. It is left to the enemy of Western civilisation, the Marxist, to see this contribution: he calls our Western civilisation 'bourgeois'.

The Jew, although not involved in the religious war between Muslim and Christian, was identified with the Muslim and was therefore persecuted. We must go back to Rosenzweig's 'God has set enmity between Jew and Christian'. How can the antisemite have a place in God's perfect creation? How can He who created the lamb have created the tiger? God is not responsible for antisemitism, Christians are.

Christian faith is constituted by the distinction between spiritual and secular. What is the spirit, the *pneuma*? The believing Christian believes in the reality of the spirit. The Jew, shaped by the biblical prophets, and therefore deeming possible a direct, unmediated encounter with God, does not need to contradict the Christian who aims at the inflowing of the spirit into his life and into his Church. The Muslim, on the other hand, does. He will not try to understand what the Christian means by belief, with its power of converting man to the spiritual existence achieved in his rebirth. (*Pistis* and *iman* never mean the same, although the Westerner translates both by 'belief'.) The Jew stands between the Christian and the Muslim, understanding both, identifying himself with neither. What the Jew will not accept is the exclusion of the distinction between holy and profane, between holy and human. The Jew objects to the assumption that only the distinction between spiritual and secular constitutes man's life with God. The direct unmediated encounter with God constitutes Jewish life, unquestioning obedience constitutes that of the Muslim, and 'the Damascus road' constitutes Christian life.

In his correspondence with his cousin Eugen Rosenstock, baptised into Christianity as a child by his parents, Rosenzweig argues about the reason for Christian antisemitism. Rosenzweig reminds his cousin of the Persian king Xerxes, whose servant, standing behind him at table, said: 'Master, remember the Athenians!' So far the story of Herodotus. But Rosenzweig changes the words of the servant. He writes to Rosenstock on 7 November 1916, that is seven years before he published *The Star of Redemption:* '*Despota, memneso to eschaton* (Master, remember what is absolute)'.[2] To comment on Rosenzweig's *eschaton:* Remember to whom we turn when we say 'Hear, O Israel, The Lord is our God, the Lord is One!'

No appeasing apologetics will eradicate the tension between Jew and Christian. The Christian reacts to the Jew with 'enmity'. The translator of the *Star* should have used the word 'hostility', as the word in the German original is *Feindschaft*. It is not enough to speak only of animosity. Here is that enmity which divides Cain and Abel.

The Jew bypasses the Christian doctrine of the Holy Spirit. He need not deny the existence of the spirit outright, but he will acknowledge it only as an aesthetic category: creative man is driven by the spirit. The prophetic attitude, never developing into an established religion, is critical of, but never aggressive towards, the existence of another established religion. Between Christianity and Islam, between Paul and Mohammed, enmity cannot but persist, but Christian and Jew are not irreconcilable. The Jew will only protest where the spirit becomes the enemy of reality. Reality is God-created. The Christian church is the monument of the spirit. The Jew will acknowledge the church as a place of prayer, just as he acknowledges the mosque; but he will not see the spirit as capable of creating a Christian institution with the right of denying that there is 'salvation outside the church'. The spirit, the Jew contends, is the spirit of man. To this the Christian responds with antisemitism.

The Jew must carry the kingdom of God and suffer antisemitism. He must say 'No' to all false absolutes. He must do so not only in the case of the church but also in the political field. The flag of the state is the most solemn symbol of Western man. Where the flag of the state is itself a kind of sacrament, the Jew says 'No'.

Medieval Islamic society tolerated Jews; Christian society was unable to do so. Christian doctrine according to Romans 11 saw Jews as part of the Christian commonwealth only when all the gentiles had become Christians: before this apocalyptic date 'they are treated as God's enemies' (Romans 11: 26, 28). In Islam, on the other hand, the Jews were *dhimmis,* free non-Muslim subjects of a Muslim government, who paid a poll-tax in return for which the Muslims were responsible for their security and freedom and toleration.

2. Rosenstock-Huessy, ed., *Judaism Despite Christianity*, p. 135.

However remote Islamic tolerance may have been in individual cases from what the liberal state calls tolerance, it was more than the Pauline world granted to Jews. Romans 10 and 11 may be read as a truly edifying sermon by Jews looking for an end of the 'enmity between Jew and Christian'. But Paul's admittedly sincere remark 'I am an Israelite myself, of the stock of Abraham, of the tribe of Benjamin' in practice means no more than the antisemite's assurance, 'Some of my best friends are Jews'. Much more thinking has to be done by the Christian antisemite to purify the world by fighting antisemitism.

Chapter 10

THE DOCTRINE OF THE TRINITY

The Hellenistic world, the West, responded to the biblical 'God is One' with the doctrine of the Trinity. To Jews this doctrine is, according to Samuel Sandmel, 'inherently incomprehensible'.[1] But the philosophy of Plato or of Kant may also be incomprehensible to many Jews. Like the philosophy of Plato and Kant, the doctrine of the Trinity has to be studied by Jewish scholars. The formula 'Father, Son and Holy Ghost', which for the devout medieval Christian denotes an inexplicable mystery, has an earlier history in which the Fathers of the early church were not merely devout believers, but proved to be thinkers engaged in a gigantic mental struggle. The philosophy within the doctrine of the Trinity is like a Gothic cathedral, an admirable monument of medieval piety.

The doctrine of the Trinity established that the God whom Christians address in the Lord's Prayer is the God of Genesis 1 and 2, the God who created the world. The doctrine of the Trinity established that the God who spoke (and is still speaking) through the prophets is the same God whom Christians hear speaking in the Gospels. In so doing, the doctrine of the Trinity rejected the heresy of the Gnostics, who contended that the 'old' God no longer reigned in the New Era. The Gnostic Marcion spoke of the 'unknown God' to whom a Greek arriving in an alien country would erect an altar as the true God. The Gnostics did not acknowledge the God of the Old Testament, who was God the creator. The doctrine of the Trinity, rejecting the various forms of Gnostic heresy, ensured that the Christians, like the Jews, glorified God as benevolent creator. The doctrine of the Trinity identified 'the Logos who was God' as the creator of the

---

1. Samuel Sandmel, *We Jews and Jesus* (London, 1965), p. 44.

world. But besides the God-created world there is history, which is the place of the creations of man. Hellenistic man could still marvel at the impressive achievements of the men of antiquity in literature, art and statecraft. They were acknowledged as the work of the Logos. The doctrine of the Trinity prevented **a** heresy which would have bypassed the creator-God of the Jews and worshipped the Logos instead. The Old Testament was not taken out of the canon of 'sacred books'; it was taught that the New Testament is not a substitute for, but an addition to, the Old Testament, which had become necessary through the impact of the surrounding Hellenistic civilisation. The doctrine of the Trinity emphasised that the New Testament did not bring a new revelation, but one that was implicit in the old revelation. The doctrine of the Trinity preserved monotheistic faith against heresies which relapsed into polytheism, seeing Christ in competition with, but on the same level as, the gods of Olympus. The doctrine of the Trinity preserved Jewish monotheism in the midst of Hellenistic civilisation.

Jews and Muslims decline to accept the Christian liturgical formula 'Father, Son and Holy Spirit'. Jews have known Christians for nearly two thousand years, and Muslims have known them for nearly fourteen hundred years. During all that time, up to the nineteenth century, to Hermann Cohen and Franz Rosenzweig, no attempt has been made, either by Jews or by Muslims, to elucidate the doctrine of the Trinity for non-Christians. A belief in the mystery of the Trinity dominates the Pauline centuries, usually called the Middle Ages. A mystery apprehended through faith alone is inaccessible to doctrinal comprehension. A philosophico-theological understanding of the Trinity, on the other hand, brings the Pauline centuries to an end and initiates a new era for Jew, Christian and Muslim. A trialogue between the three is possible when the doctrine of the Trinity, properly analysed, ceases to be the issue which disrupts the union of the three different but equally monotheistic faiths. When the Sphinx is made to yield her mystery and is addressed by her name, no longer veiled in secrecy, she sinks to the bottom of the sea, and time can flow forward to a new era.

The phrase 'through Jesus Christ our Lord' must not be seen as a spoken talisman. It has a similar function to the word 'name' (Hebrew *shem*) in biblical sentences like Psalm 115: 1, 'Not to us, O Lord, but to thy name ascribe the glory.' The Jew knows of 'the holy name' *(shem hakodesh),* which only the High Priest in the Temple was allowed to utter on the Day of Atonement. 'The holy name', which we do not pronounce, expresses God's whole nature. But there are 'a thousand names of God', to use a phrase of the Muslim, in which prophets, priests and laymen express His inexhaustible nature. God is our Father, our King, our Shepherd, he is the Husband of the bride Zion, and there are many other names which a prophetic imagination may discover. When we pray we want to turn to God, who is beyond our imagination. Jew, Christian and Muslim do not want their prayer to become a human monologue. All three turn to the One God. The Christian, weary of the misinterpretation of Greek monistic thinking, concludes his prayer with the words: 'In the name of the Father, the Son and the Holy Spirit'. This formula makes prayer a dialogue. The words of the human speaker have addressed God and have therefore ceased to be mere human speech and have become prayer.

With the formula 'In the name of the Father, the Son and the Holy Spirit' the fathers of the early church did not intend to contradict Jewish monotheism, but to oppose Hellenistic heresies. In a time of feverish messianic expectancy a new name of God came into existence. Any name of God is one of the 'thousand names' by which the One Name, the *shem hakodesh,* the holy name of God, can be expressed. The name 'Christ', the name 'Jesus Christ our Lord', the phrase 'In the name of the Father, the Son and the Holy Spirit' can direct the Christian to the One God and can distract him from the One God – as a Christian divine, the profound theologian Kenneth Cragg, clearly sees and admits: 'If some in the early church needed to bring their Christ-devotion more carefully "into God", are there not some in the contemporary church who need to reach out more readily from their Christology "into God"?'[2] The formula 'In the name of the Father, the Son and the Holy Spirit' is the Christian's Amen. The Muslim's Amen, relating human utterance to God, are the words 'as it is written'. What is the Jew's Amen? It is 'Amen'.

The early church pursued the religious aim of preserving monotheism. Eventually a political aim came to the fore which gave the dogma the function of establishing the One Church. By proclaiming that outside the One Church there was no salvation, the church separated the two monotheistic religions Judaism and Islam from Christian monotheism. The theologians were forced by the Christian emperor to submit to the *raison d'état.* The Pauline dualism – God and Caesar – created the political monotheism, or rather the political monism, of the Middle Ages: One God, one emperor, one pope.

All this needed to be said to those Jews, Muslims and also post-medieval men who say that the doctrine of the Trinity is 'incomprehensible'. But our effort to make this dogma comprehensible need not be understood as an apologetical attempt which still regards

2. Kenneth Cragg, *Alive to God: Muslim and Christian prayer* (London, 1970), p. 24.

scholastic metaphysics as a suitable medium for setting out the 'correlation' between God, man and world. The scholastic metaphysics which the church Fathers employed when they formulated the doctrine of the Trinity is out of date. The problems which the doctrine of the Trinity faced are still with us. Hermann Cohen elucidated the correlation between God, man and the world with the help of the triad of human reason: philosophy, ethics and aesthetics. This new method is no longer that of creating by means of abstract thought a system of ideas which by a kind of philosophical alchemy give information about God, man and the world. A post-medieval doctrine of the Trinity must express its content not with the help of scholastic metaphysics but with the help of anthropology. This anthropology must view man in his theomorphic reality, as the image of God. When thinkers leave the Middle Ages, a return to human reality is possible. 'What is man?' is the question that initiates the eternal enquiry. From this beginning we can hope to proceed to the second item of our enquiry: the world. Finally we hope to ascend to the summit and speak about God. This is the way of theological enquiry. But in actual human life it is different. When we start thinking in human life, not from playful curiosity but in unreserved commitment, our first thought is God.

Chapter 11

THE CROSS AND THE GALUT

We read in our portion of the Law about Rebecca's children. Before their birth, Rebecca knew that she was to have twins. The text reads: And the children struggled within her and she said: 'If it be so, wherefore do I live?' (Genesis 25:22). These words of despair spoken by their ancestress are a sombre introduction to the history of the Jewish people, destined to live in the midst of the gentiles. Why this foreboding? Are not Esau, the ancestor of the gentiles, and Jacob, the ancestor of the Jewish people, brothers, twin brothers? This brotherhood between the gentiles and the Jewish people must never be forgotten. But what does the mother of these twin brothers say? The children already fight each other as babes! If they struggle within their mother's womb, what can be the prospect for the future? Can their common origin overcome their inborn antagonism? Is Rebecca not right to be distressed about what is to come? But Rebecca received her consolation from a holy oracle which said: 'Two nations are in thy womb, and two peoples shall be separated from thy bowels; and the one people shall be stronger than the other people, and the elder shall serve the younger' (Genesis 25:23).

What is said here in the form of an oracle is not beyond rational exposition. We understand what is meant. The gentiles are stronger than the Jewish people. They have the vitality that comes of being rooted in the soil of their homeland; they are nations – that is the meaning of the word *goyim*. *Goyim,* nations, have the nobility and strength which surrounds nature and everything that grows from the earth. Mankind consists of gentiles. Dante, a devout medieval Christian, does not let the gentiles burn in hellfire, but in his poem of Heaven and Hell he gives them a place in Elysium, a kind of Greek paradise. The gentiles create the historic epochs, and they do this with the help of the state, not merely by right but by might. To be bound up with the state and thereby to wield power was and still is characteristic of the difference between the gentiles and the Jewish people, and the present little State of Israel will not change anything in this respect. The Jewish people, in remaining the people of the *galut,* the people of the Diaspora, is weaker than the gentiles. But Rebecca, our ancestress, received the promise for Jacob and his children that the weak will prevail over the strong. The spiritual forces that direct history do not possess the mighty vitality of natural forces. Justice, mercy, truth and holiness do not grow from the soil of the earth, but they win in history over those who have nothing but the strength of their natural status. The birthright derived from nature passes to him who in his weakness represents the power of the spirit: 'The elder shall serve the younger'.

The gentiles in whose midst we live are Christian gentiles. This fact does not change the picture of the antagonistic brothers which the prophetic narrator paints in our portion of the Law. As long as the Christian gentiles carry the Cross faithfully, they can, as children of Esau, become like the children of Jacob. But they always have the possibility of becoming the children of Esau again. We, in our own generation, have witnessed a gentile rebellion against the Cross. From about 1800, Germany introduced a philosophy of political idealism which had nothing to do with Christianity and which eventually led to Nazi barbarism. In the wake of this political idealism, that began as lofty utopian philosophy and ended as cruel barbarism, Zionist ideology grew and developed. The first language of the Zionists was German. When the Christian gentiles threw off the yoke of the Cross, Zionists thought they could throw off the yoke of the *galut,* the burden of an existence under the conditions of the Diaspora. The *galut* no longer seemed a necessary yoke for the Jews, as citizens of a western state and later as citizens of the State of Israel, to carry. But there is a difference. A Christian can either carry the yoke of the Cross or live without it; he can live his secular life together with Christian life or without it. A Jew has no such choice: the *galut* is his form of life. A Jew must be like Jacob; he cannot be anything else. It is not the soil of one individual country but the whole God-created world that forms his human existence, it is not nationhood but the fellowship of all men that provides the guarantee of his political and social existence; he exists not through might but through right. The Jew is always Jacob. The Christian gentiles have their secular life where they are like Esau and their spiritual sphere where they aspire to be like Jacob; but the Jew is always Jacob, in private life and in public life, in the family and in politics.

The *galut* has preserved Jacob. The *galut,* often but by no means always the place of martyrdom and persecution, of distress and tears, has preserved the Jew. Jacob's brother is Esau. We see the gentiles as children of Esau. We do not think little of our brother Esau. Our danger is rather that we admire the gentiles, the *goyim,* too much. They are admirable in their secular achievements, and when they are Christians they are often wonderfully capable of expressing the thoughts of Jacob in the language of the historic moment. But even as Christians the gentiles are always both Esau and Jacob. They can choose, and often they do choose, to throw off the Cross and be only Esau. We Jews have no choice. We cannot throw off the yoke of the *galut.* The *galut* is the unredeemed world, and the unredeemed world has to be faced. The Jew, faithfully carrying the yoke of the *galut,* faces this task: the unredeemed world must be redeemed through justice, mercy, truth and holiness. It is Jacob in the weakness of his *galut* life, not Esau with his strong might, who will prevail in the end. This is the message of our holy text: 'The elder shall serve the younger'.

Chapter 12

THE BINDING OF ISAAC

In the *Akedah* we have a story in which Abraham proves his complete devotion to God. Which commandment did they obey, the father and son, when they went, the father to sacrifice, the son to be sacrificed? It is the commandment of which we are reminded evening and morning in the words: 'Thou shalt love the Lord thy God with all thy heart, and with all thy soul, and with all thy might'. A man who loves gives everything, and retains nothing for himself. But does God's demand go to the extent to which Abraham was prepared to go? God does not want men to go beyond human power. This is the blissful experience of Abraham. He hears the voice speaking to him: 'Lay not thy hand upon the lad, neither do thou any thing unto him; for now I know that thou art a God-fearing man, seeing thou hast not withheld thy son, thine only son, from me' (Genesis 22: 12). God, who wants man to be God-fearing, does not want him to be a superman; he wants man to be human.

For three decades I have been preaching on the *Akedah*, sometimes twice a year, at New Year and on the Sabbath which has the *Akedah* as its portion. This Sabbath has other significant parts and I could have chosen them as the text of my sermon. I have never done so. I have always preached about the *Akedah*. Today, too, I shall not make it easy for myself and you, and I shall ask myself and you a pertinent question: when Ben-Gurion sent Jewish youths into battle, did the heavenly voice which could have prevented this sacrifice remain silent and not say to him: 'Lay not thine hand upon the lad, neither do thou anything unto him'? Ben-Gurion is a Jew, just like you and me. Why did he not hear these words which our father Abraham heard, rendering sacrifice unnecessary?

Ben-Gurion is a Jew like you and me, but, like you and me, he is a European, and as such he cherishes Greek tradition, the tradition of the noble soldiers who, at Thermopylae, defended freedom against slavery and sacrificed their lives so that others could live a life of freedom. Ben-Gurion became a keen student of Greek culture at a late age. He was fifty-two when he started to learn Greek in order to understand fully the splendid world of Greek idealism, which is also the idealism cherished by Western man. With Ben-Gurion the dilemma of the Maccabean chapter of Jewish history becomes the dilemma of our brethren in Israel. The Maccabees did not serve God in the way of Abraham, but by wielding the sword and by laying down their lives for their brethren. Without the Maccabees, mankind would not have the Bible and there would be no Judaism, no Christianity and no Islam: mankind would be without the monotheistic faith. But why go back to past ages, to the age of Thermopylae and the age of the Maccabees? We are contemporaries of the Battle of Britain. In those memorable days, when the fate of mankind was in the balance, the voice of the angel saying 'Lay not thy hand upon the lad' would have been out of place. We listened to the voice of Churchill, who told us that the lads fighting the invaders had to die so that we could live and be free.

Judaism, Christianity and Islam are fundamentally different, but compared with the numerous religions of this globe they are near to each other. This is no mere theory. You can say to a Jew, especially to a Western Jew: One false step and you are in the Christian camp! You can say to Jew and Christian: Are you what you think you are, or are you like the Mohammedan believers? The nationalist wars of our age have been fought as holy wars, and it is the Mohammedans who believe in a holy war. The word White Islam had to be introduced to characterise Europeans fighting their wars. I speak with respect of Islam and, I hope, with understanding. Islam demands unquestioned obedience to fate. Allah is God with his mercy hidden to man. In the two world wars Isaac, in the uniform of the various armies, marched into battle in unquestioned obedience, and Allah, not the God of Abraham, was his God. The voice saying 'Lay not thy hand upon the lad' was not heard. Isaac *was* sacrificed.

Our civilisation has three elements: the Jewish, the Christian and also the Greek. With this Greek element the soldier has his place of honour in our civilisation. Western man is a citizen soldier. Christianity's 'Love your enemies' does not stop wars and does not intend to do so. It spiritualises the combat and says to the soldier: 'Fight your enemy, but while you fight do not forget that he is spiritually your brother.' The noble expression 'fair play' is the result of this Christian spiritual approach to war.

And what is Christianity's message to Isaac himself, the son who fights wars for the ideals of his father? Is Isaac merely the helpless animal sacrificed on the altar without the intervention which could prevent his death? Christianity is different from Islam, which gives the soldier only the bitter consolation that his death in the holy war is itself a reward. Christianity attributes to the soldier not merely a passive but an active role. The dying soldier is seen as a mediator. Isaac, sacrificed on the altar, is a mediator between God and man. In the grave of the unknown soldier the nations of Christendom have revived the Cross: somebody died so that others can live.

The two world wars have led to the atomic age. The hope is growing that the atomic bomb will make wars impossible. Judaism is messianism; it is, above all, hope that there will be no more wars. Islam sanctifies war, Christianity spiritualises war, and Judaism sees a way to avoid war. Not by force but by persuasion, or – as the prophet says – 'with the rod of his mouth and with the breath of his lips' (Isaiah 11: 4), must the ruler settle conflicts. Where this is done, Isaac need not be sacrificed, the voice from heaven is heeded: 'Lay not thy hand upon the lad, neither do thou any thing unto him'.

The mountain where Abraham understood God is called *Adonai Yireh*, where the Lord is seen', where God reveals himself. Abraham went home a happy man. He had been prepared to give everything away and when his sacrifice was no longer necessary, he could himself say what he heard the heavenly voice saying: 'Now I know'. With his blissful experience Abraham could say of God: 'I have heard of thee by the hearing of the ear; but now mine eye seeth thee' (Job 42: 5). May God grant that, with the experience of two world wars, Western man may also say 'Now I know', realising the ransom which can be sacrificed in the place of Isaac. God wills that Isaac should grow up to manhood, marry and have a home.

Chapter 13

MORIAH, MASSADA, GOLGOTHA

We read in our portion of the Law the story which we Jews call *Akedat Yitzhak*, which means 'the binding of Isaac'. Christians refer to the same story as the sacrifice of Isaac. The difference is not only between a correct title, which makes it clear that Isaac was not sacrificed, and the other title which changes the content of the story by calling it the sacrifice of Isaac. The real difference which we face in these two titles of our story amounts to the difference between Judaism and Christianity. The great symbol of Christianity is the Cross which proclaims that somebody had to die that others might be happy. Abraham, on the other hand, stands before us as the happy father: he has emancipated himself from a tragic approach to life in which man is seen to be ennobled by accepting the destruction of human happiness. Abraham hears and obeys the heavenly message 'Lay not thine hand upon the lad' (Genesis 22: 12). In our story, as we Jews read it, he discovers the infinite mercy of God, who does not demand from man that he should be a superman or make a sacrifice which is beyond human ability. Isaac need not be sacrificed. If he were sacrificed, our story would point to the message of the Cross. As it is, our story of Abraham and Isaac is the story of a God-believing man; he is a happy father with a happy son. Our story tells us that the religious life leads to the good life, which can be exalted without tragedy. Our story, the story of Abraham on the mountain of Moriah, contradicts the message of the Cross erected by the Romans on Mount Golgotha.

I am not merely presenting theological subtleties to you. I explain the story of the Binding of Isaac as a contemporary witness of the noble idealism which has been displayed and is still being displayed by all those who demand and make sacrifices for our State of Israel. Two million Jews live in this state. My prayers for them are the prayers for our fellow Jews. May they prosper as citizens and may they be privileged to make the contribution which 'maketh the Torah great and glorious'. But there is one particular prayer which I pray for my brethren, the citizens of the State of Israel: may the political leaders in their noble idealism never regard the citizens of the State of Israel as material which can be sacrificed for the sake of the state. The State of Israel is for the Israeli Jews and not the other way round. The happiness of the Jewish population in Israel must never be sacrificed for the noble idea which some may see embodied in the modern state. May the tragic sacrifice of human happiness on the altar of the state, with fathers sacrificing their sons for a deified state, never happen in the land of Israel of our time.

It happened once. We have only to mention the word Massada to recall a tragic past. Massada was the name of a small fortress in which the zealots after the fall of Jerusalem offered useless and senseless resistance to the Romans and eventually committed suicide. It is disquieting to watch how often this word is mentioned in present Zionist political discussions. A few years ago it had not yet been reintroduced into modern use; the word Massada was not even mentioned in Valentine's Jewish Encyclopaedia of 1938.[1] Today the name is well known even to people whose knowledge of past Jewish history is very small. Massada has become a slogan signifying the mood of our modern Jewish zealots. Our State of Israel can only exist in an atmosphere of international goodwill towards this small state. Owing to the present Cold War, the final settling of frontiers and the solution of many other problems are postponed for the day when the great world powers will unite to make their decisions. When this day comes, we shall plead our cause and represent its justice with all the moral force at our disposal. But the decision will be made by the world powers. On our side prudence must prevail, excluding violence and armed conflict. But this is not the view of our modern zealots, who scorn the advice of reason and patience and call those of us who give it 'trembling Israelites'. These modern zealots have their slogan, Massada, as their answer. They are prepared to sacrifice an idealistic Israeli youth for the state. They are prepared to sacrifice Isaac. This shows that the faith of Abraham is beyond their understanding. They are willing to submit to tragedy and to suffer the inevitably heavy cost in blood and tears. With Massada as the image of their political programme they move away from

1. [Albert M. Hyamson and A.M. Silbermann, eds, *Vallentine's Jewish Encyclopaedia* (London, 1938).]

the faith of Abraham who when he left Moriah was a happy father; they proceed to Golgotha where the Cross comforts the prisoners of tragedy.

At present, Christian missionaries work with some insignificant success in Israel. Should the Levantine proletariat in the countryside and in the cities of the State of Israel become numerous, the success of the Christian missionaries might increase. Schools are too few, and good education is therefore expensive. The missionaries are richly endowed and can offer free and good education. We can only despise this kind of soul-snatching. Taking into account the circumstances and the results issuing from them, the Christian mission to the Jews presents no danger to us, and it never did. The danger comes from our own midst. If Jewish zealots succeed in converting our youth to a political idealism which glories in tragedy and sacrifice, a movement will start which will lead from Moriah to Massada, and from Massada the signpost points to Golgotha, where the Cross of Christianity pronounces a message so different from that of Judaism. We are always tolerant; we say, today more often than in the past, that Christianity is the daughter religion of Judaism. But we must never lose sight of the difference between Judaism and Christianity. The zealot, as a political idealist, is prepared to sacrifice Isaac. He does not hear, or is not willing to hear, the message which made Abraham the father of our Jewish faith. The message, the wonderful message, is, was and will always be: 'Lay not thine hand upon the lad'. May this message from heaven be heard when the citizens of Israel have to make their decision against the patriotic zealots in their midst.

Chapter 14

THE YEAR ONE

History is the history of states. Hegel, Bismarck, Nietzsche, Spengler and Hitler hammered this doctrine into German minds. History is seen as progressing from battlefield to battlefield. It is not true that this doctrine, dominating the fascist era, revived the spirit of the Greek *polis*. To the Greek citizen-soldier the *polis* was both state and church. In war he defended both hearth and altar. In the Christian era state and church, at one in the *polis* of antiquity, proceed along different roads through history. *Arete*, the religio-political virtue of the citizen-soldier, was split into two different functions in the Christian era: one was that of the hero, the other that of the saint. The man who lives in the private sphere, the father of the family, being neither hero nor saint, has no place of honour in the feudal, hierarchical Christian system of the Middle Ages. Crusaders and celibates make history progress; this was the view prevailing in the Christian Middle Ages, in which there was no acknowledged place for Jews, as there was none for women. The Exodus from Egypt ends slavery, or to put it in the affirmative, it establishes the private sphere as man's greatest privilege. After recording the Exodus, the prophetic writers of the Hebrew Bible recorded the stories of the patriarchs, showing men living the good life, outside a history reduced to a political sphere. The Book of Genesis contradicts the doctrine that history is nothing but the history of states. In fact both Judaism and Christianity contradict this doctrine, but each does it in a different way.

Both Judaism and Christianity distinguish between the temporal kingdoms and the Kingdom of God. But where the Jew looks forward to the goal of all history, to 'the end' (Daniel 12: 13), to the complete arrival of the Kingdom of God which in history is still in the process of coming, the Christian looks back to the beginning of the Kingdom of God. According to the Jew this beginning is already praised as 'very good' within the act of creation; according to the Christian it has taken place in the midst of recorded history. The Christian is at his most Christian when celebrating Christmas, the Jew most Jewish when celebrating the Day of Atonement.

In the midst of the worship of the Day of Atonement there is a vision of a mankind with all its families liberated from 'Egypt' and united in the worship of the One God: 'When the world will be per-fected under the Kingdom of God and all the children of flesh will call upon thy name ... Before thee, O Lord, will they prostrate themselves and worship.' In the Gospels this vision of the great pros-tration of mankind takes place before a child: the church celebrates the epoch-making event when the word going forth from Jerusalem reached the gentiles. With this event a new era began.

Jesus the child, the newborn babe – not Jesus the teacher, whose teachings were no different from rabbinical teaching, nor Jesus the crucified Messiah, who suffered the same fate as was meted out to many other Jews who were followers of the Zealots, the idealistic opponents of Rome – was already the Saviour, the *kyrios* (Lord) of the gentiles. Jeremiah's 'Before I formed thee in the belly, I knew thee, And before thou camest forth out of the womb I sanctified thee' (Jeremiah 1:5) was made understandable to the gentiles, who did not understand the status and role of the biblical prophet, but clung to the age-old myth of a merciful God coming down from heaven as a human person in order to help suffering mankind.

The arrival of the kingdom still to come, the whole of mankind united in its peace, so longingly expressed by the Jew in each *Aleinu-*prayer, in each *Kaddish,* is to the Christian only a *theologoumenon,* a secular proposition or a problem of church diplomacy. In the heart of the Christian there is no place for this hope. He does not look for-ward towards 'the end', he looks back to the birth of the Messiah, to the beginning which changed history. On *Kol Nidrei*[1] the Jew antici-pates the future arrival of the Kingdom of God; on Christmas Eve the Christian, rejoicing with the sound of the bells, proclaims the new era. These two faiths, so near to each other, can never become one.

The Christian knows of one single point in history where history was not history. It occurred in the Year One of the Christian era. Since then history has changed and through the mediatory agency of this changed history the Christian regards time after the Year One as different from time before the Year One. A myth recorded in the

1. [The eve of the Day of Atonement.]

Book of Joshua also speaks of an event within history when time ceased to be time, stopped flowing and stood still. It was not a prophet but a soldier who prayed: 'Sun, stand thou still upon Gibeon; and thou, moon in the valley of Ajalon. And the sun stood still and the moon stayed, until the nation had avenged themselves of their enemies' (Joshua 10: 12–13). In so far as history is the history of states, 'the miracle' at the conquest of Gibeon repeats itself.

The history of states is the continuous, never-ending flow from episode to episode. The politician strives to create stability, and tries to do so with the help of the state. State means status, standing time; time should stand still. With the aid of power and violence, with the aid of the sword, the politician – both as soldier and as law-giver – forces time to persevere, makes the state a barrier against time. Behind the barriers of his state there should rule an unchanging law, first established by force and afterwards dispensing justice and peace, the justice of the victor and the peace made possible by the conqueror.

The state is the attempt to bring eternity to the gentiles, to plant eternity in the midst of temporal order. It is also only an attempt, and it has always to be renewed. The Jewish people, as a priestly people, not formed by the *polis* although able to live in it, praises God in the benediction: 'Blessed art thou, O Lord . . . who hast planted eternal life in our midst'. The eternity of God is not merely time standing still. But the author of the Book of Joshua speaks of the miracle in which time stands still. 'And there was no day before it and after it, that the Lord hearkened unto the voice of a man; for the Lord fought for Israel' (Joshua 10: 14). The victory of Joshua is acknowledged as an extraordinary date of history, but of his prayer it says that it was a prayer 'of a man': it was not a priestly prayer, a prayer for the coming of the Kingdom of God. Still the 'miracle' of Gibeon, the political miracle of making time stand still for a while, helped men. People rejoice in the peace created by the politician.

When a state is newly established, it is always a Year One in the eyes of those who rejoice in the success. A Year One is always celebrated when war or revolution create a new era. The French and Russian revolutionaries, trying to introduce a new calendar beginning with the year of their victory as the Year One, were unknowingly imitating the first Christians, who put the beginning of the new era between themselves and the Caesars.

The Roman background of the Gospel story must not be ignored. After the Roman soldiers had crushed what was left of Maccabean Judaea, rabbinic Judaism on the one hand and the New Testament on the other began their way into history. The Roman soldiers had their share in the creation of the new era; the Year One is a date in the time when the Roman Empire was at the height of its power. The participation of the Roman soldiers in the rise of Christianity, growing out of Judaism, is even emphasised in the medieval passion play which, for all its anti-Jewish display, does not forget to bring the cruelty of the Romans to the stage when the crucifixion story is performed.

The role of the Roman soldier is played on the true stage, that of history, by the crusader. Like his predecessor the Roman soldier, the crusader is celebrated as a heroic figure. In spite of all the controversies between crusader and pope, the church always acknowledged the crusader as serving the Christian cause. Heroes and saints co-operate in the two thousand years of Christian history, and both hero and saint can become inhuman for the simple reason that they aim at becoming super-human. Where man is not permitted to be human unhappiness reigns. The path of the crusaders and Templars into the countries of Eastern Europe and the eastern Mediterranean was a trail of blood and misery. A crusader castle, from which the pious warriors sallied forth to attack and plunder, still looks out today with the grimness which in the past made it an Auschwitz for the local population. The Templars in Poland and Russia behaved like the SS in Hitler's war.

No one needs to identify the Christian and the crusader: it was not the church but the crusaders who murdered the Jews. But the church is responsible for the deeds of the crusaders. In the years 1933–1945, when the world was harassed by the Germans, the churches, among them the Roman Catholic Church which had still retained its great power with its medieval framework, forsook this responsibility. This new era heralds the end of the Middle Ages. With Auschwitz as an indictment against the Middle Ages, the medieval chapter of Europe closed and the democratic age was established. In this new age a social sphere which is neither a political sphere nor a sphere constituted by the Christian church has its rightful place: the civic society. With its bourgeois features Western society gives the Jew the place which he was denied by the church triumphant of the Middle Ages.

The post-medieval Jewish–Christian fellowship has to be based on an understanding of the difference between Jew and Christian. It is necessary to see the difference clearly: to minimise it out of the friendliest of motives helps no one. It must be understood that the role of the Christian in history cannot be played by the Jew, and the role of the Jew cannot be played by the Christian. The Christian needs the Jew at his side. Where the Christian rejoices in the salvation brought by the Year One, where he rejoices in the Messiah who has changed history, the Jew, without becoming anti-Christian, without contradicting Christian dogma with any dogma of his own, says by his mere existence: not yet, the world is still waiting for redemption. Creation is complete; it is 'very good'. Redemption is still incomplete. In a world celebrating Christmas, in this great part of the globe which is now the realm of Western civilisation, the Jew stands in prophetic loneliness and says to the celebrating millions: not yet; the Messiah has not yet arrived, there is still war, strife, lack of justice and not enough love. The Jew is the messianic watchman of Isaiah 21: 11. People ask when the hope of mankind will be fulfilled. The watchman, with his 'not yet', urges them never to allow their hope to stop asking 'when?' The Jew's 'not yet' is his faithful co-operation with Western civilisation. He also gives important help to the Christian directly: he reminds him that besides approaching God through a mediator – typical of any form of pietism, Jewish, Christian or Mohammedan – there is the possibility of prophetic directness and independence. The Jew trusts God as a son trusts his father. Every man is a child of God, and every man enjoying the privilege of a son can enter his father's house; a son need not become converted in order to love his father.

The Jew represents man such as he is since creation. The family is outside history: father, mother, child represent the family as holy order, because it springs from creation which is 'very good'. The gentiles represent man as the product of history. The Christian church directs the gentiles into a new history, makes them citizens of the 'new era', converts them. The mission of the church is to convert the gentiles.

For converted man a new era begins. Conversion is an act of mind which must be repeated as a constant beginning. Conversion, as it changes the individual, changes political situations. Rome was the first gentile power to be converted by the church. Other gentile powers followed. With its Christian element within it, Western civilisation today is bringing youth, new life, a 'new era', to the old stagnant civilisations of Asia. To establish civic society does not belong to the sphere of Christian activity. The Old Testament was always the guide of the Christian gentiles for the establishment of human order, as distinct from the political life of the state and the religious organisation of the church. The Jew is better equipped than the Christian to establish civic society, the private realm of life, where neither the hero nor the saint provides the model. The Christian is better at converting the gentiles, in persuading the gentiles to abandon their own history and to make a new beginning. The Christian co-operates best with the politician, the Jew co-operates best with the man who is a private individual. The private sphere of man always remains the source from which everything originates, including politics and art: every saint celebrated in the Christian calendar had a father and a mother.

When Hegel called the Year One 'the axis of world history' he was speaking as a provincial. Europe at his time was a small province; the global world did not really enter into minds of European provincials in 1800. Today the whole world is integrated into history, which is for the first time a history of the whole of mankind. In the democracy of the West we have for the first time an order outside the Christian church heralding hope for all the nations of the world. The dogma *extra ecclesiam nulla salus* (outside the church there is no salvation) is contradicted by the mere existence of Western civilisation. To regard the present era as an era of accomplished redemption because of the Year One of two thousand years ago would rob the present generation of the opportunities which are now offered to mankind. The two thousand years of the Christian era were two thousand years of war; all the wars of Christendom were fought as holy wars. Today for the first time it is possible for man to destroy the globe. Only by turning in awe to God the creator of the world can man survive the atomic age. God the creator is worshipped by the Jew, while Christian adoration is more of the 'Son' than of the 'Father'; but history now includes the globe, the whole created world. For the church, this is another reason for considering its relationship with the Jews and for closing its medieval chapter.

For the Jew, too, a chapter is closing. With the Emancipation, the Western Jew became a citizen of the state, and with the establishment of the State of Israel we are ourselves in charge of a state. A situation has arisen which did not exist in the two thousand years of rabbinic Judaism. We ourselves are now responsible for history. When Franz Rosenzweig spoke of the Jew wandering *seitenblicklos* (without a sideward glance) through history, he wanted to emphasise a Jewish messianism consistently and always directed towards the redemption of the whole of mankind, as in the vision of the *Aleinu* prayer and the intercession of the *Kaddish*; his intention was not to plead for a devaluation of history, as in the decadent phase of Hasidism and in any escapist pietism. We Jews must go through history. Our task is to be, whether in a Jewish state or in the Diaspora, that people which began its way with the Hebrew Bible, continued it under the conditions of the medieval hierarchical structure of life, and will now pursue it in the democratic era, both as Jewish citizens of the various states of the Jewish world Diaspora and as citizens of the State of Israel.

In a demythologising exegesis, the Year One is the moment when Judaism was planted in the history of the gentiles so that they became Christians. Both Yehudah Hallevi and Maimonides acknowledge the importance of this date in the Hellenistic period of history. The philosopher Karl Jaspers sees another date as the most

important: criticising the statement of Hegel cited above he places
the 'axial era' at that point of history when prophecy arose in Palestine, philosophy in Greece and Buddhism in India. We can well
agree that with the biblical prophets mankind received everything it
needed to have revelation from God.

The modern historian who has learned his lesson from the
prophets has demythologised the ideas and institutions of the Middle
Ages. The air, without incense, is clear like the morning of the new
day. The meeting with God can take place. 'Prepare, to meet thy
God, Israel' (Amos 4: 12).

Chapter 15

THE MEDIEVAL PASSION PLAY

The medieval passion play is performed in Oberammergau and other places on the Continent. Recently it could be seen in England. If we were to give a title to the tragedy represented and enacted here, it would surely be 'deicide', the 'killing of God'. The notion of 'deicide' has traditionally been associated in Christendom with the Jewish people, with the idea that in the crucifixion the Jews were responsible for the 'death of God'. Deicide has been much under discussion, especially during and since the second Vatican Council. Accusations levelled at the Jews have been softened, or modified, or even retracted. But the issues at stake, from a Jewish as well as a Christian standpoint, have still not been thoroughly clarified.

The formulation 'the Jews killed Christ' does not dominate the New Testament. It is not a dogma. Yet it is a doctrine for which the Church is fully responsible. The Church is responsible for the fact that the Jews were branded with the stigma of deicide. Yet Paul's words about the Jews in Romans 11 are inseparable from the New Testament: 'God has not rejected the people which he acknowledged of old as his own'.

Christian theology is now duty bound to emancipate the concept of deicide from a pre-Christian myth, and from serving as an antisemitic doctrine. That is why those of us who are committed to the Jewish–Christian dialogue must include the passion play in the agenda of our discussions.

How does the medieval passion play in fact envisage the event of the crucifixion? The question 'Who killed Christ?' makes anyone who watches the play look automatically to Pilate and his soldiers. They represent imperial power, which holds sway over the life and death of all. The Jews were the unfree subjects of this power. They obeyed, either with the resentment of the opponent or with the bad conscience of the collaborator. To those who staged the passion play in the Middle Ages, the role of the Romans was clear. They were the central figures.

The passion play shows Christ on his way to the crucifixion accompanied by the Roman soldiers. Christ carries the cross, the instrument which the Romans used for capital punishment. The Roman soldiers carry their weapons. The crown of thorns on the head of Christ is a torture invented by the brutal soldiers. The onlooker sees all this: Christ in the hands of cruel heathens. He also sees the Jews walking with the soldiers. But the Jews are merely there in order to offer themselves to the gaze of the crowd. They are nothing but extras. They are ridiculed as fat and bearded bourgeois; the fattest and most bourgeois looking of the Jews is represented as the High Priest. The action of the play, in spite of its crudeness, is in harmony with the truth that the Romans, not the Jews, are charged with cruelty towards Christ. The play ends, of course, with the cry: 'Crucify him, crucify him!' But even here the visual side is correct in its portrayal of history. The shouting is addressed to Pilate, who alone has the power to crucify anyone, so that the lesson of the play, 'The Jews killed Christ', is not borne out by what the onlooking mob really sees. As long as the play remains in its visual frame, it gives the real content of the Gospel story which states – as historical exegesis now emphasises – that the Jewish court, the Sanhedrin, had no power of capital jurisdiction. Jesus of Nazareth was crucified by the Romans, who alone had the power to do it. Christ and the Jews were both the sufferers. The man executed by the Romans on the cross and the Jews were one in the misery which a triumphant Rome heaped on their shoulders.

Recently the passion play as performed in Franco's Spain was shown on television. It was grand theatre. The armour and weapons of the Roman soldiers were authentic, and the costumed Jews were just as medieval men imagined them. It was a first-class production. Hollywood could not have done better. Franco was on view, too, in a large saloon car; and Christ was there with his crown of thorns, bent under the burden of the heavy cross. The visual effect of the play was inevitably that of a triumphal procession. The man who triumphed was Franco. The man bearing his cross represented all those whom the triumphant man had sent to their death, all those who languished in the Spanish prisons, all those who had to leave Spain and become homeless. Any passion play is a triumphal procession; and the watching audience must recognise who plays which role. In Auschwitz Hitler was the triumphant Caesar; and at Golgotha it was the Roman Eagle that triumphed.

What a display of barbaric pomp is in the triumphal procession of the Roman Caesar! His face is painted red with minium like the statue of Jupiter on the Capitol. In his hand is the eagle sceptre. Over his head are held the insignia of glory, the triumphal wreath of gold and diamonds. His quadriga is drawn by snow-white horses, and around it the soldiers prance in three-step as worshippers of the Caesar-God. Triumph in origin means 'three-step': in the triumphal procession men do not walk the ordinary way, they walk one step and then stamp with both feet in the orgy of their victory. Hitler danced his jig in front of the film cameras after the fall of France, and Franco rode in his saloon car in the passion play to celebrate the anniversary of his victory in the Civil War. The Roman triumphal procession had its many horrors. The prisoners were tortured, female prisoners had to lift up their skirts while walking in the procession, everything indecent was permitted to the soldiers with impunity. Victory meant that the Caesar was God, creating his own law.

If the passion play makes the Jews a defeated and guilty group – as the medieval play does – then it becomes a pagan triumphal procession. It makes the Cross a sign of victory over the Jews. The Cross ceases to tell of the God of Abraham, Isaac and Jacob in the clash with Rome, but tells instead of the victory of Rome over the Jews, as the Arch of Titus glorifies it. *Judaea capta*: behold, Judaea is defeated – an event no longer celebrated by Roman heathens, but staged in Oberammergau, in Tegelen in Holland, in Mexico and in South America.

It is important to establish what the Christian doctrine enshrined in the passion play has in common, first, with the theme of the suffering servant in the 'Servant of God' texts of the Old Testament, and then with the Promethean myth of the Greeks. It is also important, however, to discern the differences between them. Christian exegesis, searching for Christian teaching within the Old Testament, has, traditionally at any rate, pointed to the 'Servant of God' texts in the Book of Isaiah. The Servant of God, this prophet whose name we do not know, is brought to his doom by a power outside the Jewish people, probably by the last Babylonian king. So far it is exactly like the narrative of the Gospels.

But there is a striking difference. The Babylonian wielder of power does not enter the stage on which we see the suffering prophet. There is no stage. There is no Babylonian Pilate in the 'Servant of God' texts, nor is there a Herod. According to the Synoptic Gospels, on the other hand, Pilate and the Roman soldiers are manifestly involved in the crucifixion of Christ. No parallel exists in the 'Servant of God' texts to the variety of roles and scenarios in the New Testament.

The 'Servant of God' texts, on the one hand, and the synoptic Gospels recording the Passion of Christ, on the other, are, as literary types, as different from each other as for example a prose epic from a tragic play. The authors of the Gospels followed the Greek prototype of classical tragedy and dramatised into a clash between individual and authority what is in the Hebrew text the story of a Jew, the story of a man chosen by God and, in the words of Isaiah, 'despised and forsaken by man'. The Gospels bring on the stage Jews and Romans, Christ and the High Priest, the disciples and Pilate. When the authors of the Gospels make the Jews shout 'crucify him, crucify him!' it is clear that the Jews have been given the role of the chorus of Greek tragedy. The chorus makes articulate the will of one individual or of several individuals which decides the way in which the tragedy inevitably develops. The chorus is the voice of fate. Has the High Priest or Pilate, have the Jews or the Romans, become articulate in the voice of the chorus shouting 'crucify him, crucify him!'? The tragic playwright does not give an answer to such a question. He lets his audience watch the play. They have eyes to see and can judge for themselves. The medieval passion play starts in the Gospels.

In the Greek story of Prometheus we find points of both identity with and difference from the Gospels' narratives of the 'deicide'. According to Greek mythology, Prometheus, who represents creative man, is chained to a rock. Vultures eat the liver from his living body. The rebel who wants to be what God is, a creator, is punished for his *hubris*, for his sin of attempting to be God-like. The story expresses the deep pessimism of the Greek who, above all, wanted to be a *poietes*, a maker of things, whether these things were marble wonders of sculpture, works of literature, states or empires. In this, his deepest desire, he was stricken with the knowledge of the futility of his desire. He knew he would not reach final success. The absolute solution would evade him.

Five hundred years after the myth of Prometheus was expressed as the philosophy of pessimism, a cross was erected on Golgotha. It became a symbol which brought hope to the languishing Hellenistic world of the Mediterranean basin. In the symbol of the Cross the old symbol, that of Prometheus on the rock, was still recognisable. But the new symbol changed the gentile world. The philosophy of despair was silenced. The Cross had a message of good tidings for man who suffered in his Promethean enterprise as artist, politician, planner, in short, as a *poietes*, a maker of things. The message was: death on the cross is not an end; it is a beginning. It is the death of a son who ceases to be a son and becomes in his own right what his father is – a creator. The man on the cross is not a Prometheus, a rebel. On the cross he is at one with the father.

Christians and Jews must both surely object to the one-sided way in which Freud deals with deicide as the outcome of the father–son conflict in the subconscious mind. Freud only sees a cruel father and a rebellious son. In Auschwitz rebellious sons have killed fathers. Freud saw it coming. But this depth psychology, developed in anti-semitic Vienna, did not enable him to see the sacrificial love of the sons uniting them with the fathers. Yet the sacrifice of the sons in their attempt to improve the world of the fathers, the sacrifice of the sons on the battlefields of history, is enormous.

In view of what has been said, it is a travesty of the Gospels from Christian premises themselves to ask 'Who killed Christ?', as if his death could have been avoided like a mishap or a judicial murder. From the point of view of the synoptic Gospels, the deicide could not have been avoided in this way. The Gospels used the image of dei-cide to contradict the Greek tragic playwrights, who speak of fate inevitably leading man to his doom. In the deicide the Gospels describe a tragedy, but one which in a most un-Greek manner leads to a happy ending. The peace-lacking gentile at last receives the mes-sage of peace.

Those who have killed Jews, from the time of Constantine's union of church and state up to Auschwitz, are themselves involved in the sacrilege of deicide. They have shouted their antisemitic 'crucify him! crucify him!' and with this same cry demanded the death of the Jews. The antisemitic 'crucify him, crucify him!' became the Nazi slo-gan 'Perish Judah!' The first crusade was also a pogrom.

The present discussion about deicide will not change Christian faith, and is not intended to do so. Jewish semantics have the figure of a king and father, or of a prophet who, as Messiah, leads towards the goal of history. The Jewish people faithfully waits for what is not yet but what will come: the kingdom of justice, mercy and truth. 'Jews as Jews walk through history without a sideward glance', said Franz Rosenzweig.

The Christian cries out in jubilation: the tragedies of history have a happy ending, the Cross contradicts tragedy, the sacrifices on the battlefields of history are not meaningless. All those who stand astride the path of history have a guarantee of victory and bliss in the crucified and resurrected God-man. History is not 'a tale told by an idiot', it is Golgotha and Calvary, crucifixion and resurrection. The deicide in which the servants of God suffer and die makes history progress ever nearer towards redemption.

The Jewish jubilation about the God-created world sees the world of the fathers as the blissful habitation of man; as for history – the miracle at the Red Sea guarantees God's victory outside the world of the fathers. In the world of the fathers men are born, grow up, woo, marry and beget children and live under eternal laws in the happiness of the creatures of God.

The study of the difference between Judaism and Christianity is the heart and soul of any Jewish–Christian dialogue worthy of the name. With regard to the concept of deicide the difference between Jew and Christian is clear, and must not be blurred. A Jewish theology, faithful to the content of the Hebrew Bible, can see no reference to deicide either in the 'Servant of God' texts of the Book of Isaiah or in Genesis 22 which tells mankind that Isaac was not sacrificed, and proclaims the message of love uniting father and son. Jew and Christian are both witnesses of God: for the Jews there is rejoicing that Isaac is not sacrificed, while Christianity is the triumphant faith that a sacrificed Isaac bestows the glory of redemption on mankind.

Chapter 16

ISLAMIC SUBMISSION TO THE LAW

At the centre of Gotthold Ephraim Lessing's play *Nathan the Wise* stands the parable of the three rings. By means of this parable Lessing explains his attitude towards the three monotheistic religions, Judaism, Christianity and Islam. A father has three sons. In his possession is a precious ring. To which son is he to bequeath it? He loves his three sons equally. He finds a way out of the dilemma by asking a goldsmith to make two more rings in such a way that no human eye can discern any difference between the three rings. When the father dies each of the sons inherits a ring, and each can claim that his is the genuine one. The moral of the parable is that the question 'who possesses the genuine ring?' cannot be answered. But Lessing adds a postscript. It is only at the end of days that it will be known just what the whole truth is; in the interim each man, be he Jew, Christian or Muslim, must live according to what he believes is the truth, and must try, by his good deeds, to prove that he is on the right road. This means that he has no theoretical proof for the truth of his religion, but that he does have the practical solution of making it apparent that his life is guided throughout by the truth of God.

Lessing's parable of the three rings advocates an open society. The Middle Ages had periods in which an open society existed. The reign of the Emperor Frederick II was one of those periods. At his famous court in Sicily Jewish, Christian and Islamic scholars discussed their philosophical, political and theological problems. With the death of Frederick II in 1250 everything changed. Historians have compared the year 1250 with the year 1914: 'the lights went out all over Europe'. The creative forces of the High Middle Ages came to a halt. Christendom and Islam no longer penetrated each other beneficially. From the thirteenth to the nineteenth century Islam was in a state of stagnation: for the Sharia innovation meant heresy – deadly sin. In the Christian West it was not much different: *reformatio* and *renovatio* did not mean progress but return to the sacred old order. Everything had to remain according to the old principles. The decadence of the Middle Ages speaks out in the encyclical *Quanta cura* of Pope Pius IX, issued on 8 December 1864, which refers to the revolution of 1848 with utter condemnation: 'Revolution is the inspiration of the devil; it aims to destroy Christianity and build paganism on its ruins.'

The impact of Islamic civilisation on Christianity was considerable; it was made possible by the great mobility of Mediterranean men. Pilgrims, scholars, crusaders and Jews travelled on the roads connecting north and south, east and west. The Jewish ghetto was not yet a prison; it was still a home. The Mediterranean Jew, as physician, as translator from Arabic into Latin, and as trader, connected provincials with the intellectual climate of the world. *Ubique sunt Hebraei* (everywhere there are Jews), reports a chronicler of the early thirteenth century.

The twelfth century was the age of the religious disputations. Heinrich Heine, in his charming poem *Disputation*, is sarcastic about the religious value of such meetings and he mocks them as tournaments of clerics. Above all, 'rabbi and monk' are both not to his taste. Heine has, in this case at least, the approach of a liberal to whom the Middle Ages means nothing but a dark age. Lessing's parable recaptures the seriousness of the medieval discussion between Jew, Christian and Muslim. Europe was open to Islam, Islam to Christianity, and the Jew lived in both the Christian and the Islamic world. This co-existence of Jew, Christian and Muslim did not necessarily create the cynicism of which the story of the 'three great deceivers', Moses, Jesus and Mohammed, is proof. Mohammed has been accused of being, partly at least, responsible for this story. He calls the Old Testament, the New Testament and the Koran the three successive forms of revelation. This robs each of them of its unique truth and makes Moses, Jesus and Mohammed, as human vehicles of revelation, equally lacking in undisputed authority. From here it is only one step to the cynical story of the 'three great deceivers'. Lessing's parable recalls the seriousness and the creative possibilities of the dialogue between the three monotheistic religions. Islam preserves the spirit of antiquity. Our present civilisation is not only a Judaeo-Christian civilisation but has a third element: the Graeco-Roman element. Islam points to this element.

A religious dialogue is not an exercise in comparative religion. Where the Jewish–Christian dialogue sinks to the level of an intellectual duel without commitment, cynicism will creep in, as it does in the transformation of the parable of the three rings into the story of the 'three great deceivers'. Lessing's parable points to a possibility for our own future. In the dialogue between Jew, Christian and Muslim a new search for God can come to life. If this dialogue is not a search for God but has the hidden aim of conversion by intellectual means, the scepticism of Heine's poem is justified. The dialogue of the members of the monotheistic family is an undertaking comparable to worship, from which it is different. (A Jew, Christian and Muslim can attend each other's services respectfully and even devoutly, but they cannot give up the differences between Jewish, Christian and Islamic divine service.)

For Franz Rosenzweig there are not three but only two ways of testifying to the one truth – the way of Judaism and the way of Christianity. Rosenzweig does not acknowledge Islam as a monotheistic religion. To him, Islam is a religion of reason and duty, and it is without revelation. Rosenzweig was unfair to Islam, precisely like many Christian theologians who have seen it as Semitic Hellenism or as a Christian heresy. Mohammed has been called the greatest plagiarist of world history. More to the point is the German Islamist Karl Becker, who has called Islam a 'carrier of religions'. Indeed, the Jewish and Christian elements in Islam cannot be overlooked. An attack on Islam is therefore often a boomerang which rebounds on Judaism or Christianity.

Rosenzweig's misconception of Islam has consequences for his understanding of Judaism. The Jewish people has lived for centuries, indeed up to the present day, under the influence of Islamic civilisation. In the Middle Ages, the Jewish people had, in its own cultural setting, an Islamic way of life. Rosenzweig defends such forms of communal life as Jewish, although they have their origin in Islam. When he writes 'you can run away from the Law, but you cannot change it', he is not aware that what he is saying could well be a quotation from the Sharia. Since Mohammed is regarded as the last of the prophets, prophecy as the continuous force of criticism and free enquiry is excluded from religious life, which is only accorded recognition in its character of unchanged tradition. Rosenzweig's dictum about Jewish law obliterates the difference between the Jewish and the Islamic doctrine of law. He wished to be thought of as a liberal Jew, but becomes rather an advocate of a Jewish *status quo* and a defender of the Jewish Middle Ages – a thinker who, it is now even alleged, stands on the side of Orthodox Jewish obscurantism.

The second consequence of this error regarding Islam is of wider relevance. The Christian theologian who does not understand Islam is not able to make sense of the European class founded on reason and law. That class, standing in the midst of Christendom but never acknowledged by Christian doctrine, was the bourgeoisie. A Christian rehabilitation of bourgeois life has never been forthcoming. The very word 'bourgeois' has a derogatory meaning. Whereas in France the *citoyen* has the halo of citizen-soldier and patriot, the French *bourgeois* is without such glory; he represents nothing more than good living. In Germany the word *Bürger,* although imbued with respectability, carries the stigma of inferiority engendered through not belonging to the aristocracy. Above all, if a Christian becomes a bourgeois he ceases to be a Christian. Why? The world of today is divided into two halves, one of which is called the bourgeois West. Is the West, then, in so far as it is bourgeois, not Christian?

Lessing's parable sees the three monotheistic religions as equals, but it does not draw any distinctions between them. But their equality need not be understood as identity; as between themselves they are different. Their difference becomes clear when we look at the Jewish, Christian and Mohammedan exegeses of Genesis 22. The great message of this chapter, according to the Jewish understanding of it, consists in exactly what the text says. God does not want Isaac to be sacrificed. God's love and mercy are available to man without having to be earned by sacrifice. Isaac returns home, marries, and himself becomes a father. That is the story of Abraham – a story dubbed by Kierkegaard a 'bourgeois idyll'. But is it possible for God to be revealed in greater glory than as giving us life although we have done nothing to deserve it? The Christian exegesis of Genesis 22 changes the story. Isaac is sacrificed. Some one has to suffer and die, in order that man may live and be happy. Love is sacrificial love. The Koran has but a short extract of the story. Abraham is bidden, 'Sacrifice your son', and he obeys. That is all. The faith of the Muslim is the submission of his will to the will of God. He turns to God with a radical 'Thy will be done', and his obedience is his faith.

It is not possible, on the face of it, to determine whether any one of these three interpretations is more profound than the other two. We come back to Lessing's parable, with its emphasis on the indistinguishable equality of the three religions. Even though it is not possible to call any one of the three 'higher' or 'lower' than the others, their differences are apparent and must be carefully investigated.

It was a Christian mystic, Angelus Silesius (1624–77), who transplanted the threefold form of the foregoing exegesis into the heart of Christianity itself. Just as we distinguish between Judaism, Christianity and Islam, so he saw three different forms within Christianity itself, explaining the doctrine of the Trinity not as three static ideas, but as referring to a process within the history of mankind.

> *First was the Father, now is the Son:*
> *The Spirit will be here on earth on the day of glory.*

Accordingly Schelling – and after him Rosenzweig – distinguished between the Petrine Church in the era of the Catholic Middle Ages and the Pauline Church which begins with the Protestant Reformation and lasts until the French Revolution. The church which then enters history is the Johannine Church which is nowadays superseding the Constantinian Church. The Petrine Church, that is to say the Constantinian Church, uses law combined with power to sanctify human order, it is a denominational imperialism: the church militant aspires to make all infidels into believers. The Pauline Church, on the other hand, christens the human soul; it converts the poet within man, transforming the ever-changing imagination into an ever-identical faith, into 'faith alone'. But with its 'naught but faith' this church lets the world slip away, and the Johannine Church has to take over. The Johannine Church likewise christens man, but the whole of man and not only his soul; man, endowed with body and soul and living his life in society, is summoned to become a Christian on a non-political, spiritual pattern.

How can Judaism fit into this philosophy of history? Here we have to set another parable at the side of Lessing's parable of the three rings and Angelus Silesius' vision of the three Churches. It is the parable of Judah Hallevi about the seed and the tree. He saw Christianity and Islam not as new religions but as monotheistic civilisations, as one tree with two mighty branches growing from a common seed. That seed is Judaism.

Judah Hallevi's parable of the seed and the tree with its two branches puts Christianity and Islam, those two differing forms of monotheism, on an equal level. That equality consists in a fact which, although overlooked up till now, is nevertheless clearly visible in the two thousand years of Christian and fourteen hundred of Islamic history. Both Christianity and Islam created their own respective cultures and civilisations. The history of the West represents, for all to see, two civilisations – one Christian and one Islamic. The dialectic between love and law cannot be resolved either within a single institution or within a single civilisation. The civilisation of the West is based upon the two monotheistic civilisations, Christianity and Islam. To speak of 'Jewish culture', or (what amounts to the same thing) a 'Jewish civilisation', is a misconception. In so far as Judaism holds fast to its prophetic element it is debarred from the possibility of fulfilling itself in the sort of creativity that establishes states, cultures and civilisations. What is Jewish about the so-called 'Jewish intellectual'? With his uprootedness from reality, he has his habitat in the spiritual and intellectual sphere created by the

Christian division between spirit and flesh, soul and body. What is Jewish about the so-called 'Jewish bourgeois'? With his trust in reason, and his submission to the moral law, he has his habitat in a sphere which is a colony of Islam planted in the midst of the Western world.

Everyone agrees that the bourgeois era began with the French Revolution. When Shelley wrote a poem about it he gave it the title *The Revolt of Islam*. He castigates the zealotry of the demagogues, but does not disapprove of the aim of the Revolution itself; he can write 'the sympathies connected with that event extended to every bosom'. (The words are quoted from the preface to his poem.) Like others of his contemporaries, he found Islam more natural and more human than Christianity. Islam rejected a dualism that would exalt the soul above the body. Islam keeps faith with man, who is permitted to remain a whole man. At the same time as Shelley was calling the French Revolution the revolt of Islam, Goethe was writing his *West-östlicher Divan*. With the French Revolution, according to Schelling and Rosenzweig, the Johannine era begins – a Christianity without dogma and, unlike Petrine Christianity, without a Christian law. In the present Johannine epoch the intellectual and the bourgeois become visible, and at long last justify themselves in the sense of finding their rightful place within a monotheistic civilisation. To move on from this point of our religio-sociological analysis and to speak of a *Jewish* intellectual or of a *Jewish* bourgeois involves us in an enquiry of some importance. In what way, we must ask, has Judaism been the leaven that has changed in the one case a Christian and in the other an Islamic character to such a degree that the attribute *Jewish* can be at all apposite?

That which appears, in institution and civilisation, as love and law in counterpoised opposition, as the contrast of mercy and justice, can live side by side within the man who is not shaped by civilisation but retains his human wholeness. No institution, no civilisation, no achievement of creative man can have the attribute 'Jewish'. There is, of course, the Hebrew word *avodah,* which has a double meaning. It comprises two actions which are elsewhere generally thought of as contradictory to each other. *Avodah* means both *work* and *worship,* worship of God and ordinary work, the work which man must needs perform in order to maintain himself. Promethean man – every creative man, that is – knows of a third activity: self-fulfilment in art and in politics, in culture and in civilisation. Christianity aligned art with worship and built the church alongside the state. Christian civilisation is a superstructure built by Promethean man who has been christened. Marx condemned the Christian superstructure as a betrayal of the material world. So did Islam. Islam turned aside from spiritual holiness, and worshipped instead terrestrial holiness: the world itself is the creation of God. Man can of himself, without any change effected by an inner conversion, turn to God. Islam never came into contact with a polity in which man is free. Islamic Hellenism never encountered Athenian democracy, but only the tyranny of disappearing antiquity. It was not the state, but private society and the family that were sanctified by the Sharia, the holy law of Islam. Religion and law became identical. Nothing whatsoever of the social and material world was to be excluded from sanctification through the legal supervision of the Sharia. But nor was the material world itself intended to be raised to a spiritual level. Why should it be? 'The substance of the matter is obedience', said Simone Weil. That is, indeed, a statement begotten of piety, albeit not of Christian piety. Christianity and Islam, so close to each other because of their common origin in Judaism, are, as civilisations, divided by an unbridgeable gulf. The Jewish people had its history within Christian and Islamic civilisations and yet remained different from both of them. Seen from the standpoint of the Hebrew word *avodah,* the work-and-worship enjoined upon the Jew, Christian civilisation is but spiritual superstructure. What did the Jew contribute, then, to these two civilisations? He gave himself, and in so doing gave humanity. The Jew, as the word *avodah* implies, has no mission other than to work and pray. He must be a *Mensch* – he must be human. It is man's humanity which can combine love and law, mercy and justice. But in Christianity love supreme and in Islam law supreme constitute two different civilisations.

In our nuclear age, which has put all established civilisations into a state of crisis, it is a consoling thought that man need not be identified with his own civilisation. Standing aloof from that civilisation, he is at once in the situation in which the biblical prophets found themselves. The prophet was taken apart from the multitude, and had the task of telling others that in the destruction of the Temple it was not God but man who had suffered defeat. The work of man's hand, a civilisation, was being thrown into the melting pot. The very word 'religion' has become discredited for many people, because it represents a civilisation in which a monotheistic religion appeared on the stage of past history. Bonhoeffer demanded a 'religionless Christianity'. Rosenzweig stated, with satisfaction, that in the whole of his substantial work *The Star of Redemption* the word 'religion' does not occur once. Both Bonhoeffer and Rosenzweig are expressing what Schelling, with reference to Angelus Silesius, called the 'Johannine age'. Of these three witnesses of the coming age, which has already begun, two are Protestants and one is a Jew. They are joined by Friedrich Heer, a Catholic historian. Heer demands that conversion should not be the first thought in the mind of a Christian when he meets a non-Christian. Rather, it should be his task to give himself to his fellow man as a Christian personality.[1] Jew, Christian and Muslim can enter into a true dialogue because they have to express what they stand for in their personal existence, and because they are no longer represented by a Jewish, Christian or Islamic civilisation styled the Jewish, Christian or Islamic 'religion'. The Jew has always been a human type. This now applies equally to the Christian and the Muslim, because the two monotheistic civilisations which they represented so mightily in the Middle Ages no longer have any impact upon the world. The world today is divided into the democratic West and the communist East, and neither of the two can be fittingly identified with either Christianity or Islam. Both Christian and Muslim have entered a new era since the French Revolution. Progress has taken place: to put it in the words of Bonhoeffer, 'the world has come of age', or, to use the terminology of Angelus Silesius, 'the Johannine age is here'. Neither the church nor the Sharia makes our new age. It is neither a Christian civilisation in the West, nor an Islamic one in the East, that dominates our modern world. The world is one. East and West have met, and the world will be shaped anew through three types, the Christian, the Muslim and the Jew. In Christianity the sacrificial love of sons offering themselves for others, in Islam obedient submission to the authority of the fathers, and in Judaism the happiness in which fathers and sons are united – here is a trinity in which Christian, Muslim and Jew can co-operate.

There is no disintegration here, amounting to an end, but rather a regrouping. Medieval Christianity and medieval Islam break up, and a Jewish, a Christian, and a Muslim form of personal existence are set free. The 'Johannine age', the Christianity without law and dogma which Schelling and Rosenzweig saw as entering our life after the French Revolution, does not involve the abolition of what Petrine and Pauline civilisation, the Christianities of law and dogma, have contributed. What is truly new does not destroy the old, but revives it. Freemasonry misinterprets the Johannine age as being severed from the past. The well-known nineteenth-century Viennese Jewish preacher Adolf Jellinek was influenced by this misinterpretation when he said, 'Judaism is now called upon to build on the ruins of religions its Third Temple, of the true religion.' The Austrian rabbi, in the days of the virulent antisemitism which preceded Hitlerism, could place no hope in the church which he observed participating in that antisemitism. Probably unknowingly, he was preaching Freemasonry, not Judaism. Lessing was interested in the

---

1. F. Heer, *Offener Humanismus*, p. 359.

Freemasons but never joined them. It seems that in the days of classical Enlightenment Freemasonry was not yet what it is today, a travesty of monotheistic religion. The Johannine age of which Schelling and Rosenzweig hopefully spoke does not rest upon the 'ruins' of the two preceding ages. In the regrouping that takes place intellectual and bourgeois come forward anew, as far as their manifest presence on the scene is concerned; but they were in fact born and bred in the preceding Christian–Islamic civilisation.

Beside the intellectual and the bourgeois there stands the soldier. War as a crusade, as the 'holy war' of the Muslim, did not end with the Christian and Islamic Middle Ages; it merely transformed national wars into 'zoological' wars. Among the types of human character to which our civilisation has given birth the soldier must not be forgotten. Citizen soldiers of the two world wars suffered as did those who died in Auschwitz. We may observe these soldiers in their obedience to authority – the great virtue of the Muslim. We must also view them in the setting of the sacrifice in which they died so that others might live. The tomb of the Unknown Warrior revives the symbol of the Cross: no one can pass a war memorial without being reminded of the Golgotha of our own time. The inhumanity of Auschwitz began with the inhumanity of the trench warfare of 1914–18. The youth that died in Flanders died in their own Auschwitz. The genocide of Auschwitz began in Verdun, which a German general called his blood-pump; and the French commander who opposed him was no less limited mentally in allowing himself to accept a method of fighting which made genocide an instrument of war.[2]

The two thousand years of Christianity have been two thousand years of war. The 'Holy War' which Mohammed taught the Muslims to fight was a Christian conception. In Christendom the principle of 'Render unto Caesar the things which are Caesar's' is no less important than the second half of the saying. It is a principle which makes of the soldier who sheds his own blood for his country a Christian figure; and it makes the state, though it be different from the church, its equal. The state is a secular institution, but a secular institution that exists because the church exists.

Rosenzweig was aware of the Christian element in the secular civilisation of the West. In his youth, when he first encountered Zionism, he was afraid that a Jewish state might transform Jews into Jewish Christians. The Christian mission to Jewry has never had the slightest effect on the Jews. But a situation can arise – as it did in the

2. The last sentences of this paragraph must not be taken out of the context of this book. What the Germans did to the Jews was a unique criminal act without parallel in the history of mankind.

early church – in which Christianity grows out of Judaism. Christianity always grows out of Judaism: that is the glory of the Jew. The Hebrew Bible in the hands of Christians, the *opiniones Judaicae* adopted by Gentiles, create Christianity. Whether Jews are present in the flesh or not, Judaism is an element in Western civilisation. A further probability arises when the Jew, deeming himself to be a faithful Jew, becomes in thought and action a Christian. Rosenzweig, realising that the state as a secular institution is still under the influence of the church, pondered about a Jewish future in a Jewish state. Just as the church is a state transformed by Judaism, so might not a Jewish state transform Judaism into elements of which one – the necessary spiritual opposition to power – is a Christian element?

In the Hebrew Bible the message for the servant of the Lord is a message for priest, teacher, preacher or prophet. It is the call to be ready for martyrdom. The soldier has the message of the Cross. In both instances the message is that someone must die in order that others may live. In the soldier's case the martyr's death is offered to a hero who no longer, like the Greek hero, dies for his own glory, but for the glory of God. The message of the Cross makes of the soldier a Christian figure. The Jew of the Diaspora fought in two world wars and yet remained a Jew. A dilemma now begins to face the Jew who, with his own State of Israel, has now entered the realm of the *polis*, and faces something of which he is morally bound to take cognisance: the rise of a tension between teaching and governing, between persuasion and the application of power, between spiritual and temporal power. In Jewish existence – in the private existence of any person – no such dualism comes to the fore. As citizens of the Jewish state Jews will therefore be able, step by step only, and in continuous watchfulness, to preserve their own Jewish existence.

The Christian controversy between state and church is today[3] reappearing in Israeli affairs. In her unavoidable *Kulturkampf* Israel will have to learn from church history how, in the European Middle Ages, the struggle between church and state made Western civilisation a fortress of the freedom of man. Christianity also has to be duly appraised for its faculty of paving the way for technological civilisation. The Jewish doctrine of creation, taken over into Islamic teaching, sees the world as 'very good' (Genesis 1: 31) and leaves man, as the creature of God, with his human status unchanged. Christian doctrine sees the world as not yet redeemed on its first day, and remaining unredeemed until the coming of Christ. The Christian division between creation and redemption – redemption being the

---

3. [The book in which this extract appeared, *Creation and Guilt*, was published in 1969.]

cosmic correction of creation – between flesh and spirit, can tell of a world which is material, neutral or even wicked, and at the silent disposal of man. The Christian view of man's status made it possible for him to become the subtle workman – a technological man who applies to his work only one side of his human existence, his mental faculties. Adam works on the land with his physical strength; but technological man is no longer Adam. He is the 'second Adam'. He is man shaped by the division between spirit and flesh. The progress of technological civilisation has been bought at a price. Man has lost his wholeness – a unity undivided into spirit and flesh – and the world has lost its glory which the Psalmist praises and has become instead mere neutral matter. The priestly father of his family – negatively assessed by Christianity as a 'bourgeois' but sedulously safeguarded by the law of the Torah and by the Sharia – is threatened with being edged out of the realm of technological civilisation altogether.

The Islamic countries realise perfectly well that they have to pay for their westernisation. The West has freedom, Islam has equality, a brotherhood not compromised by any Christian division between the highly specialised scientist or technician on the one hand and, on the other, the masses who are to become cogs in a vast machine-civilisation. Islam was once capable of affording a dignity to the man of the Hellenistic mass age, and it has retained this capacity of making any impoverished beggar as much a Muslim as the man who is independent, fearless, and a gentleman; it summons the pauper to worship at the mosque on equal terms at the side of prince and scholar. In the Middle Ages Islam and Christendom confronted each other as two civilisations: Islam, like Russian communism later, offering equality without freedom, and Christianity, like American capitalism, torn asunder into rich and poor, offering freedom without social equality.

Whenever an Islamic state was established the ambition of the Islamic divines was to have a Western state as well as an Islamic way of life regulated by the laws of the Sharia. Israeli Orthodoxy likewise wants it both ways: a Western state and Jewish law as interpreted in the Middle Ages. But an informed Western observer of Islam has this to say: 'As the state formed on a Western model comes increasingly to be the norm in Muslim countries, so the experience of the Muslim believer comes more closely to resemble that of the practising Christian in Western states.'[4] 'Talking of an Islamic system and thinking in terms of the Western system (wrote a Pakistani in 1951) is an incongruity which is visible all around us. The spirit soars to the lofty

4. *The Times Literary Supplement*, 4th March, 1965.

heights reached in Omar's time, but the eyes are fastened on the spires of Westminster.' What Rosenzweig said about a 'Jewish' state Islamic theologians are now saying of an 'Islamic' state. Egypt adopted a Western constitution in 1954, thereby making the United Arab Republic a democratic socialist state, and in consequence of that decision abolished the Sharia courts. In Algeria Islam became the 'state religion' in 1963; Iraq is a 'democratic socialist state in the spirit of Islam'. How can all this be possible? In fact, of course, it is not possible. The Western state is of Christian origin and it remains a Christian institution. An 'Islamic' Western state is embroiled in the same difficulties which must beset a 'Jewish' Western state. Jews are happy to have achieved the State of Israel; but amid their enthusiastic joy the question has to be asked: 'where does the road lead for the Jew who knows himself to be shaped by the prophets and classical rabbis?'

In Israel, the rabbis of the Sephardic community are totally unaware that their own Sephardic way of life is influenced by Islamic civilisation. No intelligent statement of their difference from either the Ashkenazic community of Israel or from the Israeli political leaders has been forthcoming from the Sephardic rabbis; they merely defend their own vested interest as religious professionals. Something quite different has to be said of the rank and file of the Sephardic community. They form a valuable part of the Israeli people rooted in the life of their family and, untouched by westernisation, dignified in their practical style of life. This will not, of course, remain so for long. The Israeli army is the great educational instrument of westernisation. Soon the difference between the Sephardic community of Israel that comes straight from the Islamic Middle Ages and the Ashkenazim who come straight from the civilisation of Eastern and Central Europe will have disappeared.

The Islamic situation of the State of Israel was not introduced by the Sephardic Jews, but arises with an inner logic out of a peculiar political predicament. Owing to the electoral system, a socialist party group has to make some concessions to religious Orthodoxy. It is for this most disreputable of reasons that religious law has been made obligatory for the citizen of Israel. Identification of political law with religious law is Islam; it is this which now governs the life of the Israeli citizen. A Jewish Orthodoxy, established as 'state religion', is Islam, and something of which Jews cannot, with consistency, approve. A religious state is a caliphate. The fact that in Israel religious law is applied with the support of the state is a step back into the dark ages, into the Islamic Middle Ages. A Jew robbed of his freedom cannot live a Jewish life. We must opt for the West. In the century and a half since Mendelssohn, Jews have proved that they can be both Westerners and Jews.

We see today that Christianity, Islam, and Judaism are disappearing as watertight groups, each separated from the others by their hitherto individual cultures and civilisations. Christian, Muslim, and Jew are all forced into a situation in which they have to assert themselves as three different types. To the Jew, there is nothing new in this situation. The Middle Ages had two complementary civilisations, the Christian and the Mohammedan. Judaism, with its prophetic roots preserved, never represented a civilisation. If an architect were to reconstruct a model of the Herodian Temple, we would see the kind of building that stood everywhere around the Mediterranean world. The earlier Temple of Solomon was a work of Phoenician architecture. The Hebrew Bible itself has Canaanite, Egyptian, and Babylonian elements. The Jew, as we have said, is a Jew by virtue of being engaged in *avodah,* worship of God and work for his livelihood. He is not called upon to erect a 'Jewish' culture. It is only the apocalypticist who will condemn the superstructure over Adam's field as an illusion, and as a quickly fading, sinful Babylon. The so-called superstructure, condemned by the apocalypticist and by the Marxist, is a home for man to live in. It lasts just so long as man can keep out the decay. This he can endeavour to do by his moral actions, by doing justly and by loving mercy. The Jew co-operates with the creators of culture and civilisation. But to speak of a 'Jewish culture' is to be misled by an ideological fallacy. We shall either establish Western civilisation in Israel, or, if we fail to do so, we shall become involved in Levantine disorder and corruption. We cannot preserve our Jewish identity by pursuing the phantom of a Jewish culture. We must either stand in the midst of Western civilisation as God-worshipping Jews, or we must disappear.

As Western civilisation becomes global civilisation, Christianity and Islam cease to stand apart behind the cordon once provided by their geographical separateness: they now permeate each other. The Christianity of the bourgeois West gains in non-spiritual humaneness; and Islam, adopting the Western state, leaves terrestrial holiness behind and rises to a spiritual status that enables man to become the architect of the superstructure of art and of technical miracles. The Jewish people, divided in the Middle Ages into two groups, one Ashkenazi and the other Sephardi, according to their respective habitation in either Christian or Islamic countries, is today losing the complexional differentiation conferred on it by these two different civilisations of the medieval past. After Auschwitz, and after the exodus from the Arab countries, the Jewish people has one cultural prospect only. What is to be mankind's prospect in this new world, in which Christians and Muslims will no longer exist as closed groups separated from each other, and in which the Jew can no longer maintain his distinctive medieval form of life? What is the human situation in an age described by Angelus Silesius, Schelling and Rosenzweig as the Johannine age? It is not the Christian of the Petrine, Constantinian Church, with its militant programme of converting non-Western civilisation, who will survive, but rather the Johannine Christian, offering himself, as a Christian person, to the family of man. It is not the Muslim dreaming behind the legalistic walls of his Sharia of an eternity that stands still in human life who will survive but rather the Muslim as a God-believing humanist, united in equality with his fellow believer. It is not the Jew integrated into a life of separation by his ritual codes which reduce Judaism to a Jewish pietism who will survive, but the Jew who meets God under the same conditions as those under which the Biblical prophet met him. It is the Jew, the Christian, the Muslim, without the support of their past Jewish, Christian and Islamic cultures but as three different types of man meeting God in three different ways, who will constitute the future.

Chapter 17

THE ISLAMIC GOWN OF JEWISH ORTHODOXY

The German Islamic scholar Karl Becker states that 'the gown which Christianity wore in the Middle Ages was woven in the orient'. The supremacy of Islamic culture over Christian culture in the Middle Ages is an established fact. Viewed from the high civilisation of the Muslim cities of North Africa and Spain, Christian Europe could be called a Balkan country. But this Islamic cultural frame of medieval Christianity and Jewry must not allow us to forget the differences between Christianity, Islam and Judaism. In a moving letter written in his old age to a Muslim pupil, the great Jewish Islamic scholar Ignaz Goldziher writes: 'We are brothers. We have the same God'. This is true. But as theologians we must be clear about the differences which a Jewish–Christian–Islamic trialogue must articulate for the benefit of the three monotheistic religions.

Hasidism shows the impact of Christian culture on Judaism. Hasidism is part of European Christian pietism. Before the Hasidic chapter of Jewish history, in the geonic period and in the period of the codifying rabbis, Islamic cultural influence prevails. In fact during the whole of the Middle Ages there was no difference between Jews and Muslims in Christian eyes. A historian who is an expert in these matters says: 'had there been no great outburst of anti-Muslemism there would have been little if any antisemitism in the High Middle Ages.'[1] Right from the beginning Christianity refused

1. A. Cutler, 'The origins of modern anti-Semitism: a new hypothesis', *Judaism* 17 (1968), p. 472.

to acknowledge Islam as a monotheistic religion in its own right. For the Christian, Islam is a Christian heresy. This hostility between Christian and Muslim is significant for the Middle Ages; it is out of date in our post-medieval age. This does not mean that we should play down the difference between love and law, between book religion and prophetic religion. This difference makes the Christian and the Muslim, the twins coming from Rebecca's womb, brothers in doctrinal disagreement. The parable referring to the Jewish mother, to the womb of Rebecca containing the still united brothers, is significant. It is even more satisfactory than Yehudah Hallevi's parable of the seed bringing forth the tree with two branches, Christianity and Islam. Doctrinal differences between Christian and Muslim will remain unresolved on the dogmatic level. Yet what Christianity and Islam as organisations, as denominations, cannot unite can be united in the human existence of the Jew.

The controversy between Progressive and Orthodox Jews remains unresolved so long as it is not seen that Jewish Orthodoxy defends a position which is Islamic, not Jewish. The Orthodox rabbis in Israel and in other parts of our Diaspora are *ulema,* Islamic divines, rather than rabbis. Both in the rabbinic assemblies of 1844–8 and in the dialogue between Rosenzweig and Buber of 1923 the case of Progressive Judaism would have been much stronger had it been understood that Jewish Orthodoxy was still influenced by Islamic thinking. In the rabbinical assemblies of 1844–8 Zacharias Frankel opposed the Progressive rabbi Abraham Geiger with the statement: 'What is accepted by the community as custom no authority can abrogate.' Frankel's statement is the exact formulation of what the Muslim calls *ijma*: Orthodox Judaism is defended with the help of an Islamic tenet. Other instances of the same approach will be seen when we turn to Franz Rosenzweig's dialogue with Buber, as recorded in his pamphlet *The Builders* (1924), and to his other references to the controversy between the Orthodox and Progressive interpretation of Judaism.

Franz Rosenzweig writes about 'the law which cannot be abrogated by a revolution; one can run away from it but one cannot change it'.[2] It is surprising that Rosenzweig describes Jewish law in these words. What he says here and – as we shall see – soon retracts, is the very description of the law as the Muslim understands it. The Muslim is convinced that he is in possession of a historic written law which is a 'revealed law'. Sharia, which includes the Koran, is indeed, in the opinion of the Muslim, the law from which one is able to run away, but which no man can change. In the clashes with rulers

---

2. Rosenzweig, *Star of Redemption,* p. 304.

and intellectuals the *ulema* could always point to the holy law which they had no power to change. Chief Rabbi Dr Jakobovits[3] says to this day in London what the *ulema* said. The tradition, the *ulema* say, is established, innovation is neither desirable nor possible. Every traditionalist, be he Jew or Christian, will argue in the way of the Muslim who turns to the *hadith,* the pious search into transmitted traditions. He is persuaded that only there will he find the truth for which he searches. With its faithfulness to the existing tradition Islam could mix with various cultures, could soon absorb them, and yet remain unchanged.

It has been said that Pauline Christianity can become 'faith in faith'. A faith in faith can cease to be faith in God. In adjustment to the new era created by Paul, the word Torah was translated for Greek-speakers by the word *nomos,* which means law. But the protest against Paul's faith on a world historic scale did not come from the Jews, it came from Islam. The Torah is both law and doctrine; it has both nomistic and anti-nomistic features. While the Christian tries again and again to unfold the content of faith as doctrine, it is the Muslim, not the Jew, who has rejected this spiritual enterprise. Let God be God: not doctrinal search but obedience is due to Him. Here, where he should totally agree with the Muslim, Rosenzweig joins the Christian and says that the formula 'there is no god but God' (*la ilaha illa'Llah*) is a tautology. Christian theologians have said this throughout the centuries since the rise of Islam. Rosenzweig should have acknowledged the very nearness of this statement to, if not its identity with, our 'The Lord is One'. This is not an arithmetical statement. It tells all mankind in solemn triumph that no doctrinal subtlety or prophetic metaphor can express what God is. 'Who is God?' a child asks when he hears of him for the first time in a story narrated in the Bible or the Koran. The teacher, as a resolute pedagogue, answers: 'Don't be silly: God is God.' We too must be satisfied with the answer 'God is God'. Rosenzweig, one could argue, is guilty of the same 'tautology' of which he accuses the Muslim. He writes: 'The content of revelation is revelation'. Very well; but is this not also a 'tautology'? Muslim law and Christian revelation are never wholly transferable to the situation of the Jew. The Christian knows the time and place of the one Revelation; the Jew, upholding prophetic Judaism, can only speak of revelations, in the plural. Every Jew must 'stand at Sinai' in his own lifetime. There is no biblical Hebrew word for revelation. The Hellenistic Jew who translated the Hebrew Bible into Aramaic found 'He came down' (Exodus 19:20) too anthropomorphic and

---

3. [Immanuel Jakobovits (later Lord Jakobovits of Regents Park), British Orthodox Chief Rabbi, 1967–91.]

translated 'He revealed himself', creating a new word, revelation, for the vocabulary of mankind.

The holy law of the Muslim and the faith of the Pauline pattern, faith in the one revelation, became the two irreconcilable forms of monotheism. Judaism recognises the two opposing partners, Islam and Christianity, as blood from its own blood and flesh from its own flesh. But Judaism remains different from both of them. To understand Judaism as a 'religion of law' is to misunderstand it. It is to identify Judaism with Islam. This has been done by Christian theologians in the past and is still done today.

Rosenzweig acknowledges only Judaism and Christianity as monotheistic religions; he does not acknowledge Islam as monotheism. This is a mistake, but when a man of the stature of Rosenzweig makes a mistake, there is still a lot left to learn from him. Rosenzweig sees Islam as a 'religion of reason and duty' and with this mistaken premise he is successful in grasping the true essence of the humanism of his time. This humanism was indeed a 'religion' of reason and moral duty. Protestant ethics and German philosophical idealism made this humanism a force of German bourgeois civilisation. It cared for the welfare of men and believed in the regulative idea of a united mankind. It was belief in man, not belief in God: it was not monotheism. Islam, as a religion of reason and moral duty, stemming from a belief in God, *is* monotheism.

The dispute between Jewish Orthodoxy and Progressive Judaism has so far – to say the least – always led to a stalemate. But those who argue with the help of Christian or Islamic doctrines are unaware that they are not defending Judaism but Christian or Islamic thoughts and behaviour which have penetrated Jewish life. Emancipation from the Middle Ages means emancipation from medieval Christian and Islamic culture. Reform Judaism today is the refusal to go on wearing 'the gown woven in the orient'. In rejecting the rabbi who teaches what the *ulema* teach, the Jew is not merely a Western Jew, but a Jew emancipated from a past which has become meaningless. But we cannot oppose Islamic law and Christian doctrine with a Jewish doctrine pronouncing the Jewish point of view *ex cathedra* against Christianity and Islam. No such Jewish doctrine exists. Instead we must put forward our Jewish approval or disapproval step by step. Above all we must always see ourselves involved as Jews when Christianity and Islam are under critical investigation. Judaism must regard the two other monotheistic religions as its descendants and as fellow fighters. All three monotheistic religions must unite to combat the dark age which threatens our civilisation.

In Islam the formula 'as it is written' has a sacrosanct character. Rosenzweig's hostility to Islam makes him differentiate it from a

Judaism in which the prophetic elements are alive. A prophetic understanding of Judaism prevents it from becoming a book-religion. Our faithful, unending study of the Holy Scriptures, to be pursued by young and old, does not let us lapse into book-idolatry. Rosenzweig writes: 'Should God residing in His high heaven have to give man – a book?'.[4]

The Muslims have a 'holy book'; the Jews do not. The term in Jewish tradition is not 'holy book' but 'holy books'. The Sadducees upheld the Torah as a closed book and guarded it against any contamination from additional interpretation, but our Judaism is Pharisaic Judaism. The Pharisaic doctrine of the 'oral tradition' is a mere fiction, but it became a blessing: it opened the door through which new ideas, new interpretations, new customs and new laws could enter, and become Torah. The Pharisees succeeded in preventing the Torah from shrinking into mere books. The Torah is not a book in the sense of the Koran. Nor must revelation be understood by Jews in the Christian sense as an event which took place at one time (in the Year One) and at one place (in Palestine). 'God came down', as recorded in Exodus 19:20, is the content of revelation; the words which follow, 'upon Mount Sinai' and 'The Lord said to Moses', are already *midrash,* pious narrative, interpretation of the revelation, not the revelation itself, 'God came down': man does not need more than these three words. In these three words he has revelation.

The tradition recorded in the Talmud must not be identified with *sunna* (the unchangeable path to be trodden by the Muslim). The Talmud can be called a 'Hansard': free men discuss their problems, and the Talmudic Hansard reports them. In the Talmud we still breathe the air of the *polis,* of the city with its free citizens. The Muslim never experienced freedom. He knew the difference between master and slave. But the fight for freedom, in which the Popes rose against the emperors, has no equivalent in the history of Islam. In Western civilisation's passionate concern for freedom Islam does not participate. Whether happy and content in the benevolent tribal democracy, or suffering under the cruel authoritarianism of sultans and feudal lords, the Muslim must do without freedom. In their submission to God Muslims do not see themselves as 'children of God' but as slaves of God. Where Jewish Orthodoxy succeeds in establishing community life, the members of the flock are denied freedom of thought, and the authority of the rabbi has to be acknowledged like that of the *ulema.*

The sermon plays a great role in synagogue, church and mosque. The sermon interprets texts and doctrines, demands commitments of various forms and presents moral admonition. Where laws are

4. Rosenzweig, *Star of Redemption,* p. 166.

proclaimed as holy laws, the man who speaks to a congregation becomes a legal scholar rather than a preacher. Nevertheless, the mosque had its pulpit, and sermons were preached there. This was most of all the case with the Sufis, who were more under Christian influence than Islam as a whole. It was in the Jewish communities of Eastern Europe, in the time between the expulsion from Spain and the rise of Hasidism, that the sermon was neglected and that the rabbis became similar to the *ulema*. When Progressive Jews in Berlin introduced the sermon into their divine services, Orthodox rabbis complained to the government about Jewish heresy. Their point was that the sermon is right for the church, but not for the synagogue. At that time the elders of the Berlin Jewish community commissioned Leopold Zunz (1794–1886) to write a learned essay about the sermon. He proved that the sermon had always flourished in the classical periods of Jewish history. It was a sign of decadence that the Eastern European rabbi refused to preach, regarding it as beneath his dignity as a legal scholar to do so, and left the preaching to the *maggid*, who was popular but seen as possessing a lower status than the rabbi.

Leopold Zunz was a kind of family saint for the Rosenzweig family. But Rosenzweig did not agree with Zunz when he wrote: 'As long as the Talmud is not dethroned, nothing can be done'. This was the view of the Jewish Enlightenment movement. Rosenzweig already lived in the light which the great historians of the nineteenth century bestowed on a new generation. Guided by these historians they moved away from the Middle Ages. The *Wissenschaft des Judentums,* that vigorous and creative offspring of German historiography, dissolved the Talmudic block into its many parts. The historic, linguistic, doctrinal and legal parts became separated from each other and modern Talmudic study lost the dreariness and abstruseness which had made Zunz despair, taught as he had been in his youth by the old, unpedagogic method of his masters. Today the Talmud is a valuable source book. It has been demythologised by the historians. The Progressive Jew, who has shed the medieval gown woven in the orient, sees the Talmud without any numinous quality, which it could never claim. The Progressive rabbis have emancipated us from the Islamic concept of the 'holy book'.

Montgomery Watt, an authority on Islam, points to the danger of the 'fixational' attitude of Islam. 'The conservative attitude loses its justification and becomes fixational if it goes so far that an adjustment to changed circumstances becomes too difficult. Most religions were in some periods of their history too conservative'. The post-Talmudic literature becomes a literature of commentaries on commentaries. A lack of creative new formulation becomes characteristic of Islam after the canonisation of the Koran. The Jewish literature of the geonic period and of the period of the codifying rabbis is also devoid of any creative clement. Tradition becomes fixation on the past, making any adaptation to a new situation impossible. A fixational attitude leads to the fundamentalism from which the Jewish people, deprived since the holocaust of numerous scholars, suffers today. The civilised Orthodoxy of what was once German Jewry has become primitive, narrow-minded fundamentalism. Rosenzweig's pamphlet *The Builders,* written ten years before the outbreak of the catastrophe of 1933, gives for the last time an intelligent exposition of the controversy between Orthodoxy and Progressive Judaism. But we have to enquire whether the dialogue between Buber and Rosenzweig, in which German Jewry participated, still has some meaning for us.

Rosenzweig, at the time of writing the *Star,* is a convert. He turns away from German philosophical idealism, and becomes a Jew. Entering his newly-acquired commitment to the world of Judaism, he is prepared to accept everything; he is unwilling to be critical about the difference between medieval and post-medieval Judaism. The difference is ignored. He encounters the term Jewish law and is prepared to accept it. But even in the youthful fervour of his new discovery, in which he writes *the Star,* he distinguishes between commandment *(mitzvah)* and law. The *mitzvah* is action, performing a ritual. It is significant that the terminology is 'one performs a *mitzvah*', not 'one obeys a *mitzvah*'. The Jew who performs a *mitzvah* obeys a commandment which in some instances is of minor importance or of no importance at all and which is never legally binding. Rosenzweig is not criticising Jewish law but the law of the Muslim, and the reader who studies the *Star* has to find out for himself where he is speaking of Jewish and where of Muslim law. It must be pointed out that a distinction between commandment *(mitzvah)* and law is not applicable to Islam. In Islam everything is law, the highest ethical commandment as well as some minor religious practice. On the other hand, Rosenzweig understands rituals as gestures of love. This concept contradicts the Christian theologian who – identifying Judaism with Islam – calls Judaism a religion of law, Christianity a religion of love. Unfortunately, Rosenzweig gave his pamphlet *The Builders* the subtitle 'About the Law'. The beautiful description of rituals as gestures of love is not considered. Rosenzweig suggested that Buber should enter the world of Jewish rituals. Buber – rightly – refused to accept rituals which were described to him as laws.

In the third part of his *Star* Rosenzweig deals with the calendar of the Jew. Describing life in the synagogue and in the family, he seems to be dealing with the same material as the *Shulchan Aruch,* the code

which is still regarded as authoritative by Orthodox Jews. Yet there
is a decisive difference. Rosenzweig writes what has become his personal conviction. He demands nothing. He describes a way of life.
He writes his confessions, the confessions of a modern Jew who has
discovered Judaism of old. The *Shulchan Aruch*, on the other hand, is
a book of law, just like any other law-code; the Orthodox Jew has to
obey it without asking questions, like a Muslim. He does not obey as
an autonomous man, but by way of heteronomous allegiance. It is
the law, the Law of God.

Rosenzweig deals with questions like these. No doubt his view is
his personal opinion, but it has a quality which no dry jurist can
achieve. Those who accept Rosenzweig's description of Jewish life
are invited to do so voluntarily, not with the unquestioning obedience of the Orthodox Jew, who does, in the field of rituals, what the
din, what the *halachah,* stipulates. Rosenzweig does not say in any
one case 'You have to do it', He only says 'You are able to do it', He
appeals to the autonomous man in the Jew. *Din* and *halachah* address
the man of the Middle Ages, who has not achieved the emancipation
which could have made him autonomous. In our post-medieval age
din and *halachah* foster Islamic rather than Jewish piety. *Halachah* has
become identical with the Muslim's *sunna,* the way everybody is supposed to walk. With such an Islamic interpretation of *din* and
halachah an individual selection of fewer rituals is out of the question.
Orthodox Judaism, influenced by Islam, accepts the dogma of the
ulema: the doors of *ijtihad* (prophetic interpretation of tradition) are
closed. For Rosenzweig they were not closed. Nor are they closed for
any Jew of the Progressive sector who has thrown away 'the gown
woven by Islam'.

Two years after finishing the *Star* Rosenzweig emancipated himself from the Islamic interpretation of Jewish law. No longer did he
see the Jewish law as 'the law which no revolution can change and
from which one can run away, but which one cannot chang'. Post-
medieval Jewry had not run away from the laws and rituals which
under the conditions of the Middle Ages had united the Jewish people, dispersed among many nations, into one closely-knit community. Most of these laws and rituals had fallen away from the Western
Jews like leaves falling from the trees in autumn. Rosenzweig
acknowledged the new situation. He no longer spoke of Jewish law
without qualification, he spoke of the 'law of western Orthodoxy of
the nineteenth century'.

Eventually Rosenzweig arrives at this formulation: 'Judaism is *not*
[his italics] law, Judaism creates law. But Judaism *is not* identical with
law. Judaism "is" to be a Jew.' This is Rosenzweig's Copernican turn
from medieval metaphysics concerning the Jewish law to the Jew

himself. The Jew as a 'peculiar' type of man is in the centre; 'Mount Sinai' and 'the *Torah* [Law] *from Heaven'* are demythologised. The two-thousand-year-old covenant with God depends on the fragile, embattled, persecuted, earthly figure of the Jew. No longer is the Torah understood as eternal law, the guarantee. The Jew is the guarantor of the eternal Torah. The modern, post-medieval understanding of Jewish existence is already formulated in Isaiah's "'My witnesses", says the Lord, "are you"' (Isaiah 43: 10).

The new situation is clearly apparent in our use of the word 'ritual'. Pre-modern man did not speak of rituals. A medieval Christian would have regarded it as blasphemous to call the performances of a Roman Catholic priest at the altar 'rituals'. To the Muslim, too, the minutiae of his pious behaviour, from his movements while praying to the rules for his pilgrimage to Mecca, were more than mere rituals. The pre-modern Jew performing the rituals demanded from him by the *Shulchan Aruch* thought himself obedient to a law; he did not use nor did he even know the semantic formula of the word 'ritual'.

Rosenzweig describes the time in which we live today when he writes: 'The Jewish law distinguishes today more between Jew and Jew than between Jew and gentile'. In this situation modern Jews ponder which rituals, how many or how few of them, they are obliged to perform. Rosenzweig's advice is: 'Try them out, do what you are able to do, but what you are able to do, do!' He also says that our inability to accept the obligation to perform some of the rituals may be a true and genuine contribution to pious Jewish behaviour. Modern Jewry, however, began to reduce the number of rituals and to select from them those which were able to bring holiness into their lives.

Rosenzweig did not succeed in weaning Buber from a Judaism reduced to Jewish nationalism. Buber was acquainted with the piety of Poland, where Jewish rituals were alive as ethnic forms and as popular religion without individual reflection. Buber also rejected 'the law of western Orthodoxy of the nineteenth century'. It was, he argued, not a national expression of the Jewish people; it represented only a congregation, the small band of men and women who followed Rabbi S. R. Hirsch as their pastor. Rosenzweig, on the other hand, was attracted by the pietistic warmth of the German Orthodox Jewish communities. He criticised, however, S. R. Hirsch's primitive theology. When Rosenzweig was acclaimed by Orthodox speakers as a Conservative or even as an Orthodox theologian, he protested and said: 'I am a Liberal Jew'. He was a Liberal: he subscribed to the method of biblical criticism.

Like Rosenzweig in his youth, Hermann Cohen turned away in his old age from philosophical humanism and became a Jew in the true sense. He revealed to an Orthodox rabbi his feelings about the few rituals which he performed. 'When I make *kiddush,* when I say *motsi,*[5] when I say grace, I am so moved that tears come into my eyes'. The Orthodox rabbi, when telling me about Cohen's confession, commented: 'Why is he moved? When I make *kiddush* or say *motsi* or say grace, I do it to be *yotse* (to fulfil my duty)'. A man shaped by autonomy and a man of the heteronomic pattern are absolutely different, even when they seem to do the same thing. The heteronomic man is still standing in the Middle Ages; the autonomous man has left the Middle Ages behind. At the start of his theological pilgrimage Rosenzweig thought he could embrace the whole of Judaism by ignoring the difference between medieval and post-medieval Judaism and the difference between law and ritual. He therefore spoke of the law which no revolution can abrogate and from which one can run away but which one cannot change. He later realised that with these words he had defined Islamic, not Jewish, law; he had not defined the Torah. Soon he found the one, unalterable, eternal Judaism, not to be changed in its essence in the course of history. In the end he therefore attached a different meaning to the unalterable law. He saw Jewish existence as eternal existence, and the law constituting this existence as eternal and holy law.

5. [The blessing over bread.]

Chapter 18

VICARIOUS SUFFERING

Within monotheistic civilisation Jews move between Christianity and Islam, always scrutinising them critically, assimilating themselves to them, always seeing them as partners in a world-historic dialogue, always seeing them as flesh from their flesh, but never identifying themselves with them.

The role of standing between Christianity and Islam and deciding whether to agree with one or the other has fallen on the Jew. Shall he learn from the Christian creed to emulate the leap into the realm of the spirit, or shall he, like the Muslim, reject it? Shall he follow the method of the Muslim and accept the medium of the law to create a social life which is human and has a character of holiness? A Jewish groping between the Christian and Islamic approach will become evident in the Jewish decision concerning vicarious suffering.

Chapter 53 and other texts from the book of the so-called Second Isaiah preach the message of vicarious suffering. In Western Jewish religious thought from Geiger to Baeck the text 'to be a light to the nations' (Isaiah 49:6) was explained as the Jewish contribution to mankind. Yet today, after the Holocaust, the third *churban,* during which six million Jews were tortured and murdered, there are second thoughts. We are not so sure now about the doctrine of vicarious suffering. Muslim theologians call vicarious suffering immoral. 'Why should anybody else suffer for me?' they ask, rejecting the idea propagated in Christian lands through the symbol of the Cross. Many Christians who were sincerely shocked by the suffering of the Jews during the Nazi persecution appeased their troubled consciences in the end with the pious sigh that Jews had always had to pay the price of vicarious suffering for being the chosen people. This is the point where the Muslim's indictment is right. To make the doctrine of vicarious suffering the excuse for inflicting or ignoring suffering is indeed immoral.

Islam still remembers and reveres the wandering preacher Husayn ibn Mansur al-Hallaj (858–922), who died a martyr. In his biography are all the elements which could have made him the Jesus of the Muslims. In him vicarious suffering could have been extolled as necessary for the salvation of man. Islam avoided the temptation. Eventually the execution of al-Hallaj was said never to have taken place, just as the execution of Jesus is denied by Islam. Allah does not need the sacrificial death of men for the sake of their salvation. But the stories of the miracles performed by this Persian martyr who announced 'I am the Truth' (*ana al-Haqq*) are still reverently told today.

For the Muslims Jesus is a prophet, and it would be blasphemy for them to believe that God would let his prophet suffer ignominy, torture and death through execution. Sura 4: 157 therefore announces concerning Jesus: 'They did not kill him, they did not crucify him, it was made to appear so to them'. In the Cross, in the doctrine of vicarious suffering, Christian and Muslim convictions oppose each other irreconcilably. The Cross reminds man that there is an inevitable tragedy and that he owes it to God to remain involved in it. Like the outcome of a Greek tragedy, the tragedy on the Cross is inevitable. Islam rejects the belief of the crusaders, of any creative man, that the way to the crucifixion has to be trodden. Invited by the muezzin the Muslim sets out for *falah,* for the good life. In the spirituality of the Christian and in the humaneness of the Muslim, civilisation has two denominations, two established religions, which contradict each other. Writers, thinkers, artists, soldiers, all those who give their lives on the altar of history, are the eternal crusaders, looking to the Cross as their archetypal symbol. In obedient resignation to the will of God the Muslim sees the whole world as a mosque and as in no need of redemption. He gathers all the forces of his heart and his mind for prayer. Crusader or worshipper, Christian or Muslim – which is more favourable in the eyes of God? A prophet is needed to answer this question. Jewry, with its prophetic Judaism still alive, is forced to answer, and it is to be hoped that it will answer in the right way. For a thousand years – from the geonic period up to the rise of Zionism – we lived in such a symbiosis with Islam that medieval Christians identified Jews with Muslims. It is owing to the apocalyptic character of our time that we joined the crusaders of our day and fought Muslims on the battlefield. Our beloved youth who shed their blood in the Six Day War died the death of vicarious suffering. Their vicarious death saved the Israeli

Yishuv[1] from extinction. We say: 'Glory to the Jewish soldiers of the Six Day War, glory to all those who gave their lives for the State of Israel'. In so saying we contradict the Muslim's negative evaluation of vicarious suffering. But does Auschwitz not make us unhesitatingly agree with the Muslim?

Is it not 'immoral' to 'explain' Auschwitz with the doctrine of vicarious suffering? For two thousand years this doctrine has been preached by the Cross. Does Auschwitz not make an end to the sermon of the Cross? It does, says Emil Fackenheim in his deeply moving theological reactions to Auschwitz. He also draws a consequence for Jews themselves. Jews have always seen it as their duty to sacrifice their lives for the sanctification of the Holy Name *(kiddush hashem)*. After Auschwitz another duty remains uppermost: our continued existence. We have to endure as Jews. If we were to disappear from the stage of history, Hitler would have won.

No less a man than Goethe finds the Cross to be a terrifying symbol, ghastly in its very appearance. In his pedagogical programme for a reformed school he demands that the cross be veiled in order to prevent it from being seen by the young; they should be protected from the trauma which the man cruelly hung on the cross must inflict on their minds. But is not the martyr to be acknowledged in his holy mission for his fellow man?

Muslim theology makes an important contribution to the dilemma posed by the doctrine of vicarious suffering. The Cross is a sign of victory. It is not that this victory is not credible – the Jew will not doubt the credibility of the idea that the merciful God has the last word. But the Cross stands in the glory of publicity, and in this it does not represent a man who suffers in the anonymity of his own fate. Men suffer far away from their fellow men, not recorded by any gospel writer, historian or any justifying authority. Job represents the anonymous sufferer. The Cross is a victory sign glorifying vicarious suffering in history. Muslim theology has nothing else to say of the saint than that he was a good man. The Church acknowledges saints only when the *gesta sanctorum,* the deeds of the saints, prove their graduation to sainthood. The Cross is the promise that creative man is lifted up and brought home to his Creator. The Servant of God in Isaiah 53 does not merely stand for creative man, he stands for mankind. The Jew is anonymous man. Behold the Jew: that is how mankind suffers.

For the pious Christian the Cross is the symbol of martyrdom. But we must ask whether the killing through burning, torture and sophisticated executions practised in the Middle Ages had its brutalising

1. [Jewish inhabitants of the Land.]

cause in the image of the Cross. People came to watch an execution armed with supplies of food and drink. The men with their wives and children watched someone executed on the wheel – a very long-drawn-out process. What steeled the nerves of these people? Was it perhaps the sadistic contemplation which any cross could arouse throughout the years in a primitive mind? In the churches paintings drew attention to the saints with realistic illustrations of the forms of their martyrdom, their execution, showing their mutilation in stages, the ground strewn with severed limbs. An eyewitness tells us how long the strongly-built Jan Hus battled with the flames and how hideously he screamed. The screams were ignored by the recorder of the *gesta sanctorum*. Thus arose a generation which tortured, burned, killed millions of Jews and non-Jews in the Nazi period.

They did so in countries where the Cross was exhibited everywhere. In Poland one could not walk down a country lane without encountering again and again the stern spectacle of the man dying in agony from his cruelly inflicted wounds. In the countryside, where the Nazis built Auschwitz and Treblinka, the Cross was the distinctive characteristic. Vicarious suffering is holy. Cruelty is demonic. The Cross preaches about both. So does the text of Isaiah 53. But the sermon of the Cross turns to the onlooking eye. Chapter 53 in the Book of Isaiah preaches the same sermon, but the cruelty is not visible. The eye is not chaste, it is lustful. The word spoken or read addresses the thinking man, feeling with and responsible for his fellow man. The lustful eyes of the gentiles gaze at the Cross and reveal what no evangelist had any intention of revealing: the lust of perverted men, inflicting pain on a human being and enjoying it. The image of the Cross and the Christian imagery of heaven and hell are creations of an imagination which needs purification through analysis. Jews have a vested interest, in fact mankind has a vested interest, in a revived Christianity. 'Strike the Jew, and you strike man' (Kafka).

The Zionists took a leaf out of the book of the Muslim theologians and cried out: *'Genug gelitten!'*, 'We have suffered enough!' The Zionist agrees with the Muslim theologian who says that vicarious suffering is immoral. The Zionist rejects the Christian interpretation of Isaiah 53. But Kafka's religious poetry might teach us that vicarious suffering is there in mankind's history. This Jew, sensing the years of the Holocaust to come, describes the lot of such a one 'who bore our sufferings' (Isaiah 53: 4) in his novel *Die Verwandlung* (*Metamorphosis*). There is nothing of the trappings of the Hellenistic history of the Gospels, there is no Roman cross in Kafka's 'crucifixion' story: Prague at midnight; a dehumanised commercial traveller breathes for the last time, after his thoughts have turned in love to his family.

It is the view of Kafka that somebody must suffer unhappiness, even die, so that others may live and be happy. Of the death of him who represents Isaiah's Servant Kafka writes: 'He died like a dog'. We can accept Kafka's interpretation of Isaiah 53 even with the experience of the Holocaust and ask: Who are the Christ-killers? The answer is clear: The gentiles are the killers.

Besides the acceptance or rejection of the doctrine of vicarious suffering the clash between personal morality and social legality divides the Christian from the Muslim. Obedience to the law can be simply 'the done thing'. Actions performed in obedience to personal morality rank higher than actions performed in obedience to social legality. This is self-evident to the Christian. But unlike the Christian the Muslim sees with satisfaction the good end result achieved through social legality. The Muslim is human, the Christian strives rigorously for perfection. Christian scrutiny discovers that man guided by social legality lags behind his real moral obligation. Somebody who seems to be 'a good man doing good things' may in fact be deceiving himself and others by his public image. He stands there 'among the righteous' and may be nothing of the kind. Living in harmony with social legality the bourgeois can say, 'I have a clean record.' He and people like him make the city and the suburb a place of law and order even if not a place of saints. This counts for much. Respectability and moral perfection are different from each other, but society owes a lot to men who stick to the rules of respectability. 'No cries of distress in our public places' says the Psalmist with satisfaction.

The words of Psalm 144: 12–15 are a prayer of thanksgiving coming from the heart of the bourgeois. But they also express *al-falah,* the 'Good' to which the muezzin invites all men in his call from the minaret. Messianic dreams no longer move the heart with restless desire. The world is at peace when families dwell in their homes. In these homes a human, not a spiritual, happiness prevails. Who does not wish to achieve this happiness? The call of the muezzin announces that this happiness exists and is available to all humankind. Nobody needs to be ashamed of longing for this happiness. The words of the Psalm express what any man who is honest with himself desires:

> Happy are we whose sons in their early prime stand like tall towers,
> our daughters like sculptured pillars at the corners of a palace.
> Our barns are full and furnish plentiful provision; our sheep bear lambs
>   in thousands upon thousands; the oxen in our fields are fat and sleek;
>   there is no miscarriage or untimely birth, no cries of distress in our public
>   places.
> Happy are the people in such case as ours;
> happy the people who have the Lord for their God.

To the Islamic rehabilitation of social legality one has to add the fact that Islam is a religion aiming at the good life. Islamic society purports to be a welfare society. The call of the muezzin from the minaret invites the worshippers to an alert response to *al-falah:* 'Come ye unto the Good'. *Falah* is the state of welfare and prosperity of the people of God, fulfilled in communal existence and realised in social life. The call of the muezzin invites to prayer *(salat)* and to the good life. The Muslim, satisfied with social legality, and the Christian, discovering sin and selfish motives in man even while he obeys the laws, are radically different from each other. The Muslim will be seen by the Christian as a bourgeois. The Christian is not a bourgeois. The Cross shatters the peace to which the muezzin invites the worshippers. The Cross makes the longing for the good life a treasonable enterprise. Christianity has never come to the defence of the bourgeois. The man who lives his life according to social legality, and the man with a restless conscience about his involvement in the immoral are two different human types of man. In the realm of monotheistic civilisation the Muslim can be praised for being human, the Christian for being spiritual. But only the man who is neither a Muslim nor a Christian can combine Muslim humaneness with Christian spirituality. The Jew is this man. He is a Jew not through the spiritual faith of Paul nor through law of Mohammed. Neither creed nor law constitutes prophetic Judaism. A Jew need not be expected to be what those giants, the prophets of the Bible, were. A simple Jew speaking of God and seeing his life bound up with God, without a 'leap into faith' and without slavery to social legality, is the man guided by prophetic Judaism. There are many doctrines and many laws recorded in the Jewish Scriptures which Jews cannot afford to ignore but which they have to re-interpret again and again. But no doctrine, no theory, no creed nor any law makes a Jew what he is as a Jew. He is a Jew by listening and responding to the call of the One God. From state and culture many and various calls come and make their demands. They cannot make a Jew a Jew. There is no 'Jewish' state. There is a state of which Jews are sovereign citizens. There is no 'Jewish' culture, although Jews can be passionately and successfully engaged in culture. What is Jewish is the Jew who hears and understands the message that God is One.

Chapter 19

SECULAR AND HOLY

Judah Hallevi and Maimonides see Judaism as the seed which brings forth the tree with two branches, Christianity and Islam. They dare to see Judaism, Christianity and Islam, in spite of their differences, as identical in so far as they are forms of monotheism. But it is an entirely new interpretation, not envisaged either by Judah Hallevi or by Maimonides, when we say that there is Christianity and Islam within Judaism, that Christianity and Islam are already there within the 'seed' itself and not merely later in the tree with the two branches. Anybody who accepts the metaphor of the seed and the tree in this new way has left the Middle Ages.

The metaphor of the seed and the tree can, indeed must, be understood by the post-medieval Jew as meaning that Christianity and Islam are within Judaism. To call Elijah the Mohammed of the Old Testament is only one example; we can add many others showing an Islamic or Christian doctrine or form of behaviour within Judaism, even within the Jewish Scriptures. It is not enough to talk of a dialogue between Jews, Christians and Muslims. Such a dialogue is valuable and takes place now wherever peace and reconciliation between Jews, Christians and Muslims are pursued. A dialogue can take place between people who are different from each other. In pointing to Christianity and Islam within Judaism we recognise that they are often not different from each other. With this understanding the dialogue ceases to be an intellectual enterprise and becomes a meeting of kinsmen. Brothers meet brothers.

This absolutely novel perspective makes our age as revolutionary as the age which followed the year 70 CE, the year of the destruction of the Temple. 'How shall we remain Jews without the Temple?'

asked the Jews of that cataclysmic era. 'How shall we remain Jews?' asks the present generation, 'without the shelter of that separate identity which makes us different from Christians and Muslims? Are we not deprived of that shelter when it is said that there is Christianity and Islam within Judaism?'

Far from being weakened, the knowledge of our difference from the other two monotheistic religions has been strengthened by three things. Firstly, the recognition of Christianity and Islam within Judaism shows the Jewish people as giving birth to Christianity and Islam. Secondly, historical criticism and demythologisation have made Jewish history and Jewish principles truly visible, and put an end to the falsifying approach of medieval apologists. Thirdly, there is the State of Israel as the preserver of the separate role of Judaism at the side of Christianity and Islam. With the establishment of the State of Israel the 'fence around the Torah' is no longer needed for the protection of individual Jewish identity.

Jew, Christian and Muslim must necessarily remain different from each other. The world of the Christian is formed by the categories spiritual and secular. The world of the Jew is formed by the categories holy and profane. The Jew does not need to step towards a spiritual sphere in order to meet God. He has been told: 'Ye shall be holy, because I, the Lord, am holy'. The Jew has been told that nobody is holy but God. Whereas the Christian enters the realm of the spiritual by entering a church, the Jew does not need the atmosphere of the spiritual when praying to God. Yet modern Jews know and cherish the spiritual art of Western culture. The Jew, like any Christian, is uplifted by listening to great music, by reading poems, in short, by meeting the artist and admiring his work. Here, Jew and Christian will not agree with each other; it is already much that they understand each other's different approach. The Christian most emphatically rejects the Jew's view that spirit is always the spirit of man. It is already a step forward, a step away from the Middle Ages, that the Jew understands the Christian's objection to identifying spirit with the spirit of man. It is already a step forward that the Christian understands the refusal of the Jew to transform his Judaism into a spiritual Judaism. A spiritual Judaism exists: the Christian church is spiritual Judaism. A Judaism without participation in history becomes spiritual Judaism. Thus it will remain: Jew and Christian, so near to each other, so much dependent on each other for a mission common to both of them are, and indeed must remain, different from each other.

The Jew does not, like the Muslim, reject spirituality in the realm of culture. The Muslim is afraid to be led into apostasy by spirituality, in fact, he dislikes spirituality: the sweet sound of the church bells disgusts him, still reminds him of the pigs which the crusaders herded in mosques. The Jew is without the Muslim's antipathy. He likes, loves, approves of the spirituality which he finds in Western culture, to which he makes his own valuable contribution. Of course, the Western 'Jewish culture' is an offshoot of Christian culture. It is the 'Christianity' within their Judaism which enabled Jewish intellectuals to render an important contribution to Western culture. But all avenues of culture have been trodden and the *fin de siècle* spirit begins to make itself felt. Is the end of culture ennui? Some say so. But a way out is possible, and is given to our generation through the example of Franz Rosenzweig. At the height of the culture of his time he turned away from the belief in a solution through culture, through art, philosophy and literature. He turned to the biblical world. He learned Hebrew and read the Bible as he had previously read Goethe.

Jewish novelists in America delve deep into the important content of twentieth-century culture. If they emulate the conversion of Franz Rosenzweig – not a 'Damascus', but a conversion just the same – these gifted writers like Isaac Bashevis Singer, Bernard Malamud and Saul Bellow, have much to give to our embattled age. But what these Jews have to undergo, like Rosenzweig, is the conversion from literature to theology.

Secularisation has made all three monotheistic religions leave their ghettos. The Christian church – that splendid Christian ghetto of the Middle Ages – is today like Judaism and Islam a denomination furthering its religious aims. This does not mean that secularisation has made the three monotheistic religions disappear from civilisation. They are present in a new form. Western man of the secular age, whether or not he confesses his loyalty to one of the three religions, remains a Jew, a Christian, a Muslim. The walls of the ghettos have disappeared, and this makes monotheism even stronger than it was in the Middle Ages. Shakespeare is a typical man of the Renaissance, but in his sonnets or in *The Tempest* he is a most articulate Christian. Secularisation does not obliterate any of the three monotheistic religions. The danger which secularisation carries in itself is in the political field. Secularisation, particularly that of the Christian church, brings the naked state, the dreaded Leviathan, to the fore. A secular state, a state not restrained by any form of monotheism, leads to fascism.

The bourgeois, also a product of secularisation, is an important carrier of monotheism. In our secular age a church-going Christian, a practising Jew, a pious Muslim need not in truth be adherents of that form of monotheism which they affirm. The three monotheistic religions are now like sparks which are around us and influence, say, a Christian with Jewish ideas or a Jew or a Muslim with Christian ideas. This seeming disorder has its reason in the strength of monotheism in the secular age. It is not at all a sign of weakness. It is not monotheism but theology that is weak in our secular age. We have to acquire a theological training to see the numerous instances in which the three monotheistic religions penetrate each other.

The bourgeois may seem to be far away from Islam, but his devotion to law and his exclusion of love at the side of law make up a man who is essentially a Muslim. It is the philosopher Ortega y Gasset who in two books, *On Love* and *The Revolt of the Masses,* has taught us to see that the bourgeois and the Muslim have something to do with each other. 'It is difficult for the bourgeois and the Muslim... to fall in love in an authentic manner. For them life consists in an insistence on what is known and habitual, an unshakeable satisfaction with the same daily routine.'[1] Ortega, like Franz Rosenzweig a pupil of the Marburg philosopher Hermann Cohen, recognised the bourgeois as the conservative element in Western civilisation. Instead of using the word bourgeois as a word of abuse – as our left-wing youth does – we must see the bourgeois as a religious figure, as he is according to the Islamic, though not the Christian, values of our secular age. Whatever the economic foundation of a society may be, it is a society enjoying the good life if the bourgeoisie can prosper in it. The working population of the West has opted to be a bourgeoisie. Our Western civilisation is often (especially in America) called Jewish-Christian civilisation. The bourgeois reminds us that it is a Jewish-Christian-Islamic civilisation.

There is a poetic image of the wolf and the lamb lying together in peace. A bourgeois society has this fulfilled peace as its goal. Without engagement in war and without the political manipulation of power the bourgeois is different from creative man; he is, on the contrary, the product of the creator of the world and of all men. The bourgeois is more of a creature than the intellectual, the politician, or the artist. In the bourgeois we therefore meet man as God created him. The family is economically a bourgeois social group. In this Karl Marx and Friedrich Engels are right. But when Engels ironically speaks of 'the holy family' the pietism of his upbringing is still there in his philosophy of materialism. Priest, prophet, intellectual and artist, the genius and the simple eternal man, whom we see in Adam, each of these varieties of human beings is the offspring of a bourgeois family. Civilisations do not 'decline and fall' with the bourgeois in their midst.

Man grows to full humanity by experiencing the guidance, security and love which only a father and a mother can provide. Everything is said about the bourgeois family and every praise of the bourgeois family is expressed when we can say about it that a father is there, a mother is there. This makes the bourgeois family the holy family of the secular age. Secularisation destroys the myth but makes truly visible what is holy.

1. José Ortega y Gasset, *On love ... aspects of a single theme*, translated by T. Talbot (London, 1967), p. 150.

Chapter 20

THE HOLY SEED

The steadily rising number of intermarriages begins to worry even the most tolerant defenders of Jewish universalism. The Jewish liturgy reminds the worshipper again and again that the election of the Jewish people cannot and must not be explained away by universalism which, to be sure, both prophets and rabbis preach as the content of Judaism. The rabbis, although excluding proselytisation, teach Jews to welcome proselytes with kindness. On the other hand the election of the Jewish people is upheld as valid in all history, past, present and future. 'He has chosen us from all nations'. No conversion can transform a gentile into a Jew, no anathema can exclude a Jew from his Jewishness. Jewishness has no door through which Jews can get away from their Jewish existence and none which could let gentiles enter into the intimacy of the common Jewish bond. A Jew is born a Jew. He is part of the Jewish people through his physical existence. And a Jew cannot stop being a Jew. During the Holocaust many a Jew may, like Jeremiah and Job, have cursed the day that he was born a Jew, but there was no way for him to get out. Considered in this way – and it is in this way that it must be considered – intermarriage does not bestow the Jewish particularity on the non-Jewish partner. Our praise of the universalism of Jewish teaching is sincere, but our insistence on the particularity which the election of the Jewish people implies cannot be given up. The objection to intermarriage is not primitive clannishness or tribalism left over from the past, it is not racialism. Particularism is as justifiable as universalism. As universalism is the hallmark of our service to mankind so is our Jewish particularism. God has chosen the Jewish people, has set it apart from all the nations and has done so for the benefit of mankind. Jews are withdrawn from mankind in order to serve it.

The praise of Judaism as a universalistic faith abounds in modern Jewry. The defender of Jewish particularism is a lonely figure in our modern world. On the Jewish side there is only Franz Rosenzweig who defends it as a theologian. On the side of the Christians I know only Kenneth Cragg, who as a Christian theologian has profound things to say in defence of Jewish particularism. Here is a Christian who is not scandalised by Jewish particularism, but sees it as the fertile ground from which his own Christian universalism grew.

The confrontation between particular and universal is formulated by Franz Rosenzweig in the confrontation of 'spiritual' and 'a community of common blood'. 'We' – note the proud 'we' – 'have no need to hire the services of the spirit: the natural propagation of the body guarantees its eternity'.[1] Ezekiel's 'In thy blood live!' (16: 6) demands loyalty to the election of the people. This election is not divine favouritism. It is the God-created way through which the particular can serve the universal, the Jewish people can serve mankind. The promise of God to Abraham, 'So shall thy seed be' (Genesis 15:5), is the promise to every father who is truly human in his hope that he will be the progenitor of descendants who will not quickly disappear but will last 'from generation to generation'. Intermarriage cannot but be a sad interruption or even an ending of this flow of blood, sanctified for perpetuity, for eternity.

The loyalty of Jewry to its common blood community is not racialism. Blood is not holy, what is holy is God's promise of eternity which the blood is destined to carry through the ages. Blood is the human vehicle. All men are human creatures in whose veins flows the same blood.

Any vocation is open to abuse. Yet community of birth, common ancestry, the awe in which we speak of the 'holy seed', the precious intimacy which cannot be decried as clannishness – all this served as a mighty constituent of Jewish loyalty. All this gets lost – or at least can get lost – when intermarriage takes place. That Jews throughout the centuries willingly listened to those who preached against 'marrying out' explains the miracle of the continuity of the Jewish people. In the self-understanding of the Jewish people as 'the chosen people' the outcry 'our fathers' is not a reference to a genealogy but a confession of the abiding trust which preserved the Jewish people for its vocation throughout history. The proud 'we' – the Jewish cry 'but *we* are eternal' – is in the key of a passionate, humble and blissful psalm.

Of course every people is a chosen people. Nature, territory, climate, history create a unique identity in every nation. The gentiles become nations by claiming the possession of a unique identity. But

---

1. Rosenzweig, *Star of Redemption*, p. 299.

the unique, mysterious identity in the ethnic existence of the Jewish people is not the work of nature, territory or climate. It is not enough to say, as Bishop Kenneth Cragg does, that Jewish election exists in the belief of those who believe themselves to be chosen. This statement is true but not sufficient; above all, it misses the crux of the matter. The Jew is chosen, whether or not he accepts or knows this fact. The election of the Jewish people is not a mere belief, a mere doctrine or – least of all – a mere idea. It exists in brute actuality. We can see the actuality of Jewish election at work, as we see the dark skin of a negro or the colour of a person's eyes. In order to make Jewish election visible like any matter which can be seen and touched, like any event which can be witnessed as occurring in history, we must keep in mind the situation of Jew, Christian and Muslim in their relationship to the state.

The Jewish people living under the conditions of the Diaspora, as a people of exiles, has an attitude to force, to political power, which is different from that of Islam. Christianity is sometimes 'Jewish' in its attitude to the state, sometimes, especially as a Constantinian church, its attitude to the state is identical with that of Islam. Islam is a political religion; the caliphate is a state religiously conceived and revered. Islam finds this natural and even stipulates that the prophet becomes ruler. This contradicts everything that we know of the biblical prophet. Islam understands piety as obedience; it looks for piety not in conviction but in a legal attitude. Victory on the battlefield is the victory of God. Success in political affairs is proof of God's intervention. God is identified with success. The community of the faithful is 'the party of God' (Sura 5:56). The state is called to assist religion, violence is necessary. The Muslim sees his political enemy as an enemy of God. But all this having been said, it must also be remembered that Islam is a monotheistic faith and one which can penetrate into Judaism and into Christianity. Jew and Christian have to be aware of this ever possible penetration.

The Jewish people, dispersed among the nations, has no access to power. To exist in history without power – is this possible? From the year 70 CE to 1948 the Jewish people could not shape its fate by using power. The establishment of the State of Israel has changed this predicament. Geography, however, makes any state established on Israel's soil a buffer state dependent on superpowers. It rules out a reliance on power alone. There is now a difference between Diaspora and Israeli Jewry: the latter has access to force. But this difference is not such as to allow Israel the reckless use of power. The refusal to employ force to destroy evil can be seen after Auschwitz as belonging to the realm of eschatology, which must not guide men destined to live in history. The blessing and the curse of existing without power is at the root of the election of the Jewish people. The Jewish people calls itself 'the merciful people, children of merciful people'. This is not sermonic hyperbole. It means what it says. The social and political circumstances shaping the Jewish people as the people of the Diaspora made it a 'merciful people'. Christians hail mercy as a Christian virtue, Muslims call mercy the foremost attribute of God – *Allah rahman* – but mercy as a Christian and Islamic dogma is one thing and mercy as a Jewish ethnic characteristic, another. Mercy – *rahmanut* – is the characteristic feature of the 'chosen people'. The Jew, by always reacting with *rahmanut*, displays his psychological nature.

This characteristic feature of the Jewish people is threatened when Judaism becomes a political religion. The urgent aim is to be a devoted Israeli patriot and to remain a Jew. The Jew of this post-Holocaust age will be able to be a loyal Jew in Israel and everywhere in the Diaspora and yet refuse to have the Torah politicised. Every national war tends to be a holy war, a *jihad* as the Muslim calls it. We shall have to avoid this temptation. A 'promised land' is not a national territory but the land which 'God will show' us, in Israel and in the Diaspora. 'Service', *avodah*, does not merely concern citizenship. For the Jew service is the worship of God.

The Christian church is a spiritual institution. Islam as a post-Christian religion regards such an institution as not viable in history and supplements it with its concept of a religious state. Neither church nor caliphate should be a blueprint for a Jewish state. The Jewish people living under the conditions of Diaspora is called by the biblical prophet a 'remnant'. The prophet says of the 'remnant' that he will 'remain': the man without power will not be devoured by those who have power. If this is true – and the history of the Jewish people shows it to be true – it is a miracle manifest as truth. This miracle surrounding the Jewish people as the 'remnant' makes it the 'chosen people'. In his *Star of Redemption* Franz Rosenzweig gives us a portrait of the remnant:

> Judaism, and it alone in all the world, maintains itself by subtraction, by contraction, by the formation of ever new remnants. This happens quite extensively in the face of the constant external secession. But it is equally true also within Judaism itself. It constantly divests itself of un-Jewish elements in order to produce out of itself ever new remnants of archetypal Jewish elements. Outwardly it constantly assimilates only to be able again and again to set itself apart on the inside. In Judaism there is no group, no tendency, nay barely an individual who does not regard his manner of sacrificing incidentals in order to hold on to the remnant as the only true way, and himself therefore as the true 'remnant of Israel'. And so he is. In Judaism, man is always somehow a remnant. *He is always somehow a survivor* [my italics], an inner something, whose exterior was

seized by the current of the world and carried off while he himself, what is left of him, remains standing on the shore.[2]

Rosenzweig was not inclined to write a pamphlet against intermarriage. Nor did he in his time see any need for it. He was and remained a Germanophile and lived in his small closed Jewish–Christian circle which listened to his interpretation of Judaism. Standing out in this interpretation is the statement quoted earlier: 'we [Jews] have no need to hire the services of the spirit: the natural propagation of the body guarantees its eternity.' Actually this was not written against intermarriage, of which it implies a condemnation; it was written to exclude a spiritual, i.e. a Christian, interpretation of Judaism. The 'remnant' exists in history, real and visible. He walks on the roads of the world, and people who meet him find him different from others who pass by and call him Jew.

The Jewish people is the 'chosen people'. This privilege, which we hold in trust for the benefit of mankind is – as was pointed out earlier – threatened by two facts: by the rising number of intermarriages and by the politicisation of the Torah. Will there now be two forms of Jewish existence, one for the Diaspora Jew and one for the Jewish citizen of the State of Israel? Only the former will be the Jew with his unique characteristic of being chosen. Europe has lost its aristocracy in the various wars and revolutions. Shall we – in this political ice age – lose our Jewishness of being 'merciful children of merciful fathers'? We feel we shall overcome the great crisis.

Those who 'join the House of Israel' are called 'proselytes of righteousness'. They may very well enrich the Jewish people. We should not call them 'converts' to Judaism. Conversion is a Christian, not a Jewish, experience. Race is not an obstacle to joining the House of Israel. There is the promise of the biblical prophet that 'a remnant will remain'. The Jewish people with its proud 'we' will continue to sing: 'We are thy people, and thou art our God'.

We live in a time when Judaism, Christianity and Islam penetrate each other doctrinally. But neither Jew nor Christian nor Muslim wants this doctrinal penetration to lead to a loss of religious identity. There is a difference between believing and belonging. What the *beth din* (the rabbinical Court) has to find out concerns the second more than the first. When the proselyte says 'we Jews', he should be accepted into the Jewish fold, even if his doctrinal knowledge of Judaism is not yet satisfactory. Are Jews born as Jews always more erudite in this respect?

Here we can learn from Islam. The Muslim stresses belonging, the Christian believing. Sura 49, which has the title *The Private*

2. Rosenzweig, *Star of Redemption*, pp. 404–5.

Apartments, refers in verse 14 to some Bedouin people who came to Mohammed after he had become the ruler in Medina. These Arabs from the desert, who were not yet familiar with the details of the new faith of Islam, avowed their allegiance to it. Mohammed was fully aware that their determination to belong to Islam could not be a belief in Islam. The difference between believing and belonging must not be ignored. It was true kindness on the part of Mohammed that he was satisfied with the wish of these newcomers to belong to Islam without being capable of satisfactorily believing in Islam. Only the future can show whether their belonging to Islam will make them true believers. When a father gives his daughter away at the wedding, it is in God's hand whether the marriage will turn out to be successful. Rabbis, accepting a proselyte, cannot, even after their scrutinising interrogation, know if the newcomer will adapt himself to the Jewish community, and they will have to leave it to God who, if he wills it, will enrich the House of Israel by the entry of a new member.

Chapter 21

SHYLOCK, THE TRAGIC CHAMPION OF THE LAW

The Merchant of Venice belongs to Shakespeare's 'problem comedies'. The problem in this play is the clash between justice and mercy, between law and love. In its attitude to love and mercy Judaism does not contradict Christianity as Islam does. Shakespeare, the Renaissance playwright, is also highly praised for his thorough understanding of the Middle Ages. As I have pointed out previously, in the Middle Ages Christians identified the Jew with the Muslim. Shylock's belief in the ultimate validity of a written law is characteristic of the Muslim. The Jewish attitude to law is different. But Shakespeare's Shylock is introduced as a Jew who has an absolute belief in the concept of law. 'I crave the law', 'I stand here for law', says Shylock. Driven into a corner by Portia, Shylock asks: 'Is that the law?' He asks this question in humble submission: the letter of the law must be obeyed; there is no way out. This is Islamic belief. Judaism, on the other hand, since the Pharisaic interpretation of the concept of law, has a different approach to legal arguments. One has only to turn to the traditional texts and one will find a way out of every dilemma; the wisdom of the law, of the Torah that is, is inexhaustible. 'Turn it [the Torah] and turn it again, because everything is in it' *(Abot* 5:25).

In Jonathan Miller's production (The National Theatre, London, 1970), with Laurence Olivier as Shylock, Jessica stands in the last scene on the darkened stage, silent and motionless, holding a sheet of paper – the law. As she looks at it she faces the merciless legal inevitability. The law, however hurtful to man, cannot be changed.

The Muslim accepts this situation in submission. The Jewish understanding of the law makes no such inhuman demand. Jewish casuistry becomes an instrument of mercy; interpretation becomes
liberation from the rigours of a written law. In Shakespeare's portrayal of Shylock, the difference between Jew and Muslim does not
always come to light. Under the conditions of the Middle Ages this
difference often disappeared, and Jew and Muslim stood undifferen-
tiated in the Christian world. Shakespeare is therefore not wrong in
ascribing Muslim features to the Jew Shylock.

The Marx Brothers, philosophical clowns of great human insight,
reveal the Jewish attitude to the law. In one of their films one brother
holds a huge piece of paper with all the clauses of a contract in his
hands. As they negotiate, they tear strip after strip of paper off the
long roll of the document until they reduce it to nothing. This clown-
ing is profound, and it is symbolic that it is brought onto the screen
by Jews. Jews feel that written laws can and must be interpreted for
use in daily life until they cease to be harmful. Modern Orthodox
Jews do not have such a liberal approach; in ossified tradition they
uphold the medieval situation in which Jews were influenced by
Islamic civilisation. The Jewish law, the Talmudic rabbis said, is a
'law of mercy'. The clownery of the Marx Brothers made these rabbis visible on the screen; Shakespeare makes the Islamic obedience
to the law visible on the stage.

Shylock's insistence on the law – 'my bond, my bond' – is manly
morality. He must not be played as a monster. Shylock has greatness,
the greatness of moral conviction. 'What judgement shall I dread
doing no wrong?' 'I stand for judgement, – answer, shall I have it?'
No respectable puritan could address judge and jury with a more
impressive display of moral integrity. Shylock does not beg for
mercy. He can rely on the law. He stands for the law like a Muslim:
a written law has been brought from heaven and given by God to the
Muslim believers. The law is holy.

The popular concept of the Jew, which is represented to the full in
Marlowe's play *The Jew of Malta*, was overcome by Shakespeare.
Marlowe's Jew was comical, cruel, satanic. Shakespeare had to
reckon with the fact that an Elizabethan audience, though they
hardly met real Jews, would see Shylock in this way. But Shakespeare, being Shakespeare, changes the monster of the fairy tale into
a human being before our very eyes. The laughter freezes on the
faces of the watching audience, and behold! – they become passionate witnesses. They see a suffering man, a Jew in the hands of cruel
Christians. Portia pleads that if law is adduced as an argument
against mercy, it is cruel. Her plea for mercy has the glowing fervour
and the sweet persuasiveness of 1 Corinthians 13: 1: 'I may speak in

tongues of men or of angels, but if I am without love, I am a sounding gong or a clanging cymbal'. Here Paul attempts to translate the word *rachmanut* (mercy) for a Greek-speaking audience. He succeeds, as far as success is possible here. So does Shakespeare in Portia's speech 'The quality of mercy . . .' But their success lies in the words which Paul and Shakespeare find to enhance the importance of a Christian doctrine. *Rachmanut* is not a doctrine, it is more a bodily response than a mere cerebral expression. One can mentally approve of mercy and at the same time fail to live up to the human response which mercy demands. Portia proves this. After reciting her wonderful hymn to mercy she is most cruel towards Shylock. To show mercy is the demand of Christian dogma. The Muslim obeys laws, not dogmas. Mercy is also an Islamic law. God, Allah, is *al-Rahim*, the compassionate one.

It is debatable whether mankind benefits more from the dogma of mercy or from the law of mercy. Where the treatment of Jews is concerned, Islam was merciful to those outside its denominational walls. To the Muslim, Jews were infidels, as were Christians. But Jews and Christians were both respected as 'people of the Book' and given a place in humanity by Islam. Christianity with its *nulla salus extra ecclesiam* did not grant a Muslim or a Jew a place in humanity before the Second Vatican Council. They were seen as the Elizabethan mob saw Shylock, as wicked people, as monsters.

Rachmanut, the Hebrew word for mercy, denotes neither a dogma nor a law. It means a human reaction of both a bodily and a spiritual nature. True man reacts with *rachmanut.* Man created in the image of God and preserving this image in himself is always fraught with waves of *rachmanut,* that mercy which is an attribute of both God and man. *Rachmanut* is neither a dogma nor a law, but is that truly human experience which the dogma of mercy and the law of mercy try to make articulate.

Shylock is the warm-hearted Jew, who, we feel, knows both the call of *rachmanut* and the majesty which the law wields. He appears as the father of a daughter. True, Marlowe in his *Jew of Malta* also tells a story of father and daughter. But the story is not credible. Fairy-tale villains may make the audience's flesh creep in terror, but at no moment is the fairy-tale taken as reality. Shakespeare makes us look into reality. A Muslim wants sons. Daughters are not greeted at birth with particular joy. But Shylock loves Jessica. He remembers Leah, his deceased wife. He remembers the years of his courtship. He worries about Jessica's future, distrusting Christian husbands. When Bassanio admits that he would be able to sacrifice his love for Portia for the sake of another love, that for Antonio, Shylock is disgusted. Marriage, initiated and preserved by love, is always safeguarded by law.

Shylock stands for law. He mistrusts a 'love affair' as a basis for marriage. Poor Jessica, the Jewish girl among Christians!

These be the Christian husbands! I have a daughter –
Would any of the stock of Barabbas
had been her husband, rather than a Christian. (Act 4, Scene 1)

Love exalts the children of men. 'Love is strong as death' (Song of Songs 8: 6). Law provides stability both in marriage and in all the various transactions of a great city such as Venice. Jew and Muslim respect the majesty of the law. Love is not bound by law: it is lawless. Youth needs the protection of the law against love. Poor Jessica – a Jewish girl alone, unprotected in the world of Christians.

The Muslim rejects the spiritual concept of love. As for the Jew, who knows that even the non-spiritual can be holy, he acknowledges love as being not spiritual but holy. The words 'My sister, my bride' in Song of Songs 4: 9 have been understood by Jews both as a dialogue between God and Israel and as a dialogue between a man and woman in love. These words are not spoken in the realm of Christian love which does not, indeed must not, be fulfilled in the cohabitation of the two sexes. Christian love is not consummated love. This cruel spirituality hurts the female partner more than the male. Shylock sees Jessica in the cruel world of Christian love. He weeps over Jessica, who has not listened to the warning in the Song of Songs against permissiveness: 'I adjure you, O daughters of Jerusalem . . . that ye awake not nor stir up love until it please' (2: 7). Now Jessica is with a Christian man who, not uniting love and law, will not be able to soothe his girl with the words 'My sister, my bride!' Love and law, which cannot be united doctrinally, can be united where both heart and mind are alive and guide human behaviour.

Shylock is a Jewish father, mourning the loss of a daughter. In the noble Belgravia of Venice, in Belmont, Shylock's rejection of lawless love is repeated in another key, in the language of poetry and music:

Tell me where is Fancy bred:
Or in the heart, or in the head?
How begot, how nourished? (Act 3, Scene 2)

In Shakespearean English, fancy means love. In the Belgravia of Venice, in Belmont, the answer to the question about love is the same as the answer which would be given by the law-abiding Puritans of the merchant city of Venice themselves. We can safely put the words of Proverbs 31: 30 into their tight-lipped mouths: 'Charm is a delusion and beauty fleeting: it is the God-fearing woman who is honoured.' We are even allowed the suspicion that Portia is directing Bassanio with the song 'Tell me where is Fancy bred . . .' to bypass gold and silver in the lottery of the caskets and to choose lead. The little song distinguishes between illusion and reality in the Christian Manichean distrust of reality and of love of the flesh. In this, Shylock and Portia come to the same view concerning love. 'Head and heart', law and ecstasy, fight a battle where love takes hold of man. Love

> is engendered in the eyes,
> With gazing fed.

The Christian is no longer in the Hebrew tradition, but is a captive of Greece where the eye provides the momentary revelation. Love sees heaven open; it is faith, nourished by faith, and is certainly not based on law. But the Hebrew view is expressed in the line which is a dirge about the death of love.

> Fancy dies
> In the cradle where it lies:. . .
> Let us all ring Fancy's knell.

Human life without the direction of law ends in destruction. Human life without love is unthinkable. As a father and husband Shylock testifies to the holiness of love. The bridegroom in the Song of Songs testifies to the holiness of love when, in the midst of his passion, he says 'My sister, my bride!'

The love/law issue dominates merry Belgravia–Belmont itself. In the humorous ring scene an assumed infidelity is taken lightly. Permissive tolerance, not the strict rule of the law, seems to be the code of Belmont's youth. The inscription on one of the two rings reads 'Love me but leave me not'. In the dialogue between the two principal lovers of the play, Portia and Bassanio, the often-repeated word 'ring', 'ring', 'ring' does not sound like a severe reproach, but like a warning uttered in friendly understanding. Nothing has happened, and nothing, it is understood, will happen. It is all a joke. What is missing in Belgravia–Belmont is the seriousness which the word 'law' denotes to Jew and Muslim. Surely, the repetition of the word 'ring' is a reminder of what the law stands for. But Belgravia–Belmont seems smilingly to forgive, where Jew and Muslim adopt a puritanical outlook in respect of marriage. A Muslim girl says to a male who is eyeing her: 'Fear God, I am a virgin'. Would the merry youth of Belgravia–Belmont not giggle and snigger at the puritanical Muslim girl? The Old Testament values virginity; ascetic discipline in the pre-marital state is recommended to the youth of both sexes. There are instances in which Jewish and Muslim law provide important protection to daughters and wives. The spiritual sublimity in the picture of the Madonna can impart a status of inferiority to ordinary women who are more connected with earthly nature than men. To the medieval Christian women were mere chattels; they had no place in a Christian society governed by

celibate priests. What will happen to Jessica in a Christian world?
Shylock is sorely aggrieved.

Antonio is both a Jew-hater and a Christian, cherishing spiritual
love. A Freudian might see suppressed homosexuality in Antonio's
love of Bassanio, thus inviting the contemptuous, antisemitic taunt of
'Jew'. Antonio need not be seen as a homosexual. His love is spiritual love, not consummated in the sexual act. The love between Tris-
tan and Isolde is not, indeed, must not become, love consummated
in marriage. 'Wagner: background music for a pogrom', writes Saul
Bellow in *Mr Sammler's Planet.* Saul Bellow's sharp criticism need not
be understood as a denigration of Wagner's great art. He is a truly
Christian artist, as Kierkegaard is a truly Christian theologian. Both
interpret love as Christian Manicheans. Jew and Muslim may not
understand such an attitude. Their lack of understanding will be irk-
some to Christians of the ilk of Kierkegaard. Christians will even
hate those who refuse to acknowledge, let alone approve of, the spiritual quality of love. The Christian, distinguishing between spiritual
and secular, does not regard Jew and Muslim, who distinguish
between holy and profane, merely as belonging to a different school
of thought. Uplifted to his spiritual realm, he reacts with hatred to
those who differ from him and deny what he regards as the truth, as
the basis of his existence. Here the Christian cannot simply agree to
differ. Here antisemitism is built into Christian faith. True, the Christian who, in upholding his belief, turns to a spiritual existence is
more a Manichean Christian than a Christian as the dogma of the
church understands him. The dogma of the church, accepting the
Old Testament, was forced to turn a somersault and to come to terms
with the antisemitic hatred built into Christianity. Thus there is hope
for a Jewish–Christian understanding. But those who work for this
understanding have courageously to face the Jew-hatred of the
Christian. Antonio also teaches us that 'sadness', as Shakespeare calls
it, is built into the Christian way of life. He confesses:

> I hold the world . . .
> A stage, where every man must play a part,
> And mine a sad one. (Act 1, Scene 1)

Spiritual uplift says farewell to life as ordinary humans live it.
Christian saints and ordinary Christian believers derive happiness
from their spiritual way of life, but it is a sad happiness. It is a happiness plucked from a sad withdrawal from the world. The happiness
of the Psalmist, on the other hand, is happiness in the midst of
unchanged reality: in marriage, in fatherhood and motherhood, in
the family, in short, in an ordinary way of life. Christians of the type
of Kierkegaard, Schopenhauer and Wagner regarded the patriarchs

in the Book of Genesis, who led this way of life, as bourgeois. How annoying that these 'Jewish materialists' refused to see reality as illusion. Schopenhauer expressed his Christian Jew-hatred when he spoke of 'cursed Jewish optimism'.

Sociology and psychology cannot succeed in explaining anti-semitism. Theology has to be consulted in order to explain Christian Jew-hatred. Jewish and Islamic unbelief in the face of the miracle of the transfiguration through love – Wagner's *Liebestod* and the Cross, symbolising not death but resurrection – remains the scandal which every Jew represents by his very existence. No true Christian can feel at ease facing what is a *skandalon*, a stumbling-block, in Christian eyes. Here the Jew has nothing with which to appease the Christian antisemite. But he can say to him: Mind your stumbling block.

In Shakespeare's play the medieval form of *disputatio* is discarded. Instead, Jew and Christian face each other, the one not really representing only the teachings of his church, the other not really representing only the Torah, the teachings of the Synagogue. Jew and Christian are two types of man: the clash is not merely between representatives of two different doctrinal systems. The Christian is a man whose humanity is Christian, just as the Jew is a man whose humanity is Jewish. This means that Jew and Christian meet in Shakespeare's play on the same level. In all walks of life, in business, in war, in his private life, in love and in marriage, the Christian acts as a Christian, the Jew as a Jew.

Can a leopard change his spots? Can a Christian leave the Jew, who refuses to give up being different from the Christian, alone? Is this refusal of the Jew to become a Christian merely the rejection of Christian doctrine? What does Shylock know about the details of Jewish law? He is not a rabbi. A rabbi would teach Shylock that the 'righteous of the gentiles' are justified in the eyes of God. A rabbi would demand that Shylock stop hating and pursuing revenge. Shylock is a Jew hated by Christians, and he responds to the hatred of his persecutors with the hatred of the persecuted. 'I hate him for he is a Christian', says Shylock of Antonio (Act 1, Scene 3). No redeeming distinction is made between gentile and Christian. The cruel gentile and the Christian are seen inseparably as one character, and the persecuted Jew ends up as a hater. The Christian made him that. But Shylock hates the gentiles, not, as he says, the Christians. The Christian Jew-hatred, on the other hand, is directed against the Jew, with his Jewish faith. Peace between Jew and Christian can only be achieved by the Christian on one condition: the Jew must be forced to become a Christian. The unbaptised Jew is an offence to the Christian; the Jew denies what the Christian believes. Christian Jew-hatred cannot be resolved. Shylock leaves it at that. His noble speech

'Hath not a Jew eyes? . . .' is humanism. It is spoken to the gallery, to people who are shaped more by the Renaissance than by the Christian church. But with his 'I will not . . . pray with you' Shylock makes it clear that he is not a humanist, he is a Jew. He prays to God. This is something the humanist does not and is not able to do.

I was reminded of Shakespeare's penetrating new insight into the Jewish–Christian relationship when I spoke on a platform for Jewish–Christian fellowship. Whenever I used the expression 'the Christians' I saw a shadow of annoyance come over the face of my Christian chairman. Had I said something disagreeable? So it seemed. My Christian friend, a staunch Methodist, would not have minded hearing critical references to the historical church. He himself indulged in them. But he had nothing to do with these sins of the church. He felt himself, as a Christian, to be an exponent of an unassailable doctrine. But then he heard my 'the Christians'. This dragged him from his doctrinal ivory tower on to the stage where Christians are exposed to the world like the Jews in their hatred and love, and recognised in the open marketplace by their human behaviour without the fig-leaf of doctrinal justification. Hatred is not theoretical or doctrinal disagreement. Hatred is the most murderous weapon of the persecutor. The number of martyrs in our time has grown to millions. Hatred has risen from the dark recesses of Christian souls.

I have no desire to indulge in apologetics which seek to white-wash what is black. The history of religion has its numerous black chapters. But is Shylock speaking as a Jew when he says: 'I hate him for he is a Christian'? Here he is the stage Jew, the Jew as the mob imagines him, not the Jew whose humanity Shakespeare has discovered with the eyes of a genius, and with his heart, which sees the image of God in every human creature. The Christian Jew-hatred, on the other hand, is a fact proved by two thousand years of Christianity. Hatred of the Christians is not a historical characteristic of the Jewish people. The novel *Der Weg ohne Ende* ('The Way without End'), by the German Jew Gerson Stern, impressively testifies to the absence of hatred of Christians in Jews. In this novel a Christian lad says to a Jew who has just suffered antisemitic abuse from a Christian, 'you must really hate us.' The Jewish answer is: 'If we were to hate, we could not live.'

Shakespeare's *Merchant of Venice* speaks of Jews and Christians. In fact, the play shows persecutors and persecuted. It shows the Christian as persecutor. Yet Christian doctrine must not be denounced as a superstructure simply overlaying material interests. The doctrine of Christian love becomes the mighty motive for superhuman action. Following the doctrine of Christian love the Christian nurse overcomes the heavy burden she carries day and night, the Christian missionary dares to go forward into the jungle and into barbarian surroundings, and the Christian soldier sacrifices his life in order to defend the freedom and wellbeing of his kith and kin.

Shylock is a Jew; Antonio is a Christian. Bassanio, Portia and the others are not merely citizens of Venice: they are Christians. Shylock has his Jewish gabardine, the Italian noble citizens have their Jew-hatred. Jew-hatred is 'the mark of *their* tribe'. In Jonathan Miller's production the Jewish gabardine was replaced by the respectable coat of the Victorian banker. But the Jew-hatred undergoes no change. It has been the same throughout all the centuries of Christianity.

The Christian is the noble member of the establishment. The Christian in the lowest station of life feels superior to the Jew, who is and remains a foreigner. Shakespeare marked Shylock as a foreigner through the name he invented for him. These are the names of the gentlemen of Belmont: Antonio, Bassanio, Lorenzo, Gobbo, all of them ending with the letter o; the names of the women have an a as their last letter: Portia, Nerissa and Jessica – already assimilated through her name to the noble crowd which will later receive her as an equal. The name 'Shylock' does not fit into the society of Belmont. It is an embarrassment. When in the court scene the duke commands 'Antonio and old Shylock, both stand forth', Portia knows very well who is Antonio and who Shylock. But icily she asks: 'Is your name Shylock?', and Shylock has to reply, as if to admit a wrong: 'My name is Shylock'. He is singled out through his very name. What is his crime? He is a foreigner.

'God loves the foreigner.' This is what Jewish Holy Scripture tells us (Deuteronomy 10: 18). The laws of Venice protect the foreigner. But in the whole of Shakespeare's play not a single word of love is said, not a single act of love is shown to Shylock by anybody. They only hate him, mock him, despise him. Shylock responds in the same way. His rebellion against his tormentors is just as articulate as his conviction that he is seen, protected, and indeed revenged by God. Summing up the various passages about the Servant of God in the Book of Isaiah, we feel prompted to say: the Servant may very well have had experiences not so different from those of Shylock. The Servant of God faces hatred, scorn and contempt. Shylock carries his burden with normal human reactions. When the play ends, Shylock is still alive. We are allowed to ponder about his fate after the fifth act. The great Shakespeare stops with the fifth act; the Bible's narratives lead the reader beyond the fifth act. Where Shakespeare has no hope to offer, the Bible offers hope. Shylock's, the Jew's, survival offers hope to all men. Shakespeare's Shylock is nothing but a man. A Jew is nothing but a man, loving his kin, suffering pain and reacting to love and hatred as any man does. A man of this kind, an ordinary man, Everyman, can – after the fifth act – achieve the holy status in which the Book of Isaiah introduces the Servant of God to us. The Jewish survivor of a pogrom can and will often be a broken man, a Shylock in the fifth act. But, as he has not been killed but still lives, he can leave the fifth act behind and proceed to the holiness which the Christian worships in the symbol of the Cross and which in Jewish everyday life is holiness become reality.

The actor Paul Rogers played Shylock in a mask whose features reminded me and others of the conventional Christ-face. Shylock, a victim delivered into the hands of cruel torturers: the modern audience of Shakespeare has become mature. Shylock with his red wig, Shylock as an objectionable character, has disappeared from the stage. Laurence Olivier plays a Shylock who is impressive in his conformity with pious Jewish ritual. He wears a skullcap, he has a prayer shawl at hand and, in the sad moment when the loss of Jessica has to be accepted as final, the audience hears the sombre tune of the *Kaddish* prayer. Jonathan Miller's production brings Shylock on the stage as a pious Jew. He is pious like Job, thundering words to heaven about his misfortune, a Lear deserted, a dethroned king. He is always greater than the businessmen of Venice and the idle crowd drawn to Belmont.

The 'usurer' Shylock angered a Victorian Jewish audience and still annoys American Jews. Today we understand the 'financier' Shylock. The acquisitive man can be reproached with religious arguments, but is today also recognised as a guardian of the competitive, that is, the free society. The communist world may have checked the acquisitiveness of man, but at too costly a price: communist society is without freedom. 'Usury' is taken by a modern audience as the old-fashioned term for interest on capital. What is wrong with Shylock's usury? The Bank of England announces the interest rate at intervals and makes it known how much 'usury' is granted to those who give loans. This is the capitalist era which was just being ushered in in Shylock's days in place of the feudal economy. Money replaced land as the measure of value. The medieval Christian was a Manichean: the world was evil, money and sex were the very elements of an evil world. But the new age of bourgeois values put an end to the aristocratic style of life. The gaiety, ease and colourful scenery of Belmont rests on money. Money breeds money. This still shocked Elizabethan society, which itself only slowly and painfully awoke to the rise of capitalism. Shylock represents the new age.

A modern audience of *The Merchant of Venice* is no longer inclined to despise a representative of the acquisitive society, which is what Shylock is. R. H. Tawney[1] pioneered a fair understanding of Shylock. 'Which is the Merchant here? and which the Jew?' asks Portia, disguised as a young doctor of law (Act 4, Scene 1). The distinction between the royal merchant Antonio and the Jew, the moneylender, is difficult to make. Antonio in his distaste for usury lends money without interest. But where does his money come from that permits such generosity, such 'Christian courtesy'? From his argosies, his ships, in short, from his trade. Antonio, the merchant, is also dedicated to making money, to profit. And profit, when analysed, is often 'usury' in a more respectable form. Antonio, in despising Shylock, is acting in self-hatred. 'Wilt thou whip thine own fault in other men?' cries Timon of Athens. But there remains the outcry: 'My daughter! O my ducats! O my daughter!' (Act 2, Scene 8). Do these words not make Shylock a monster? It is often forgotten that we do not hear Shylock say these words. They are brought to our knowledge in a report by Solanio, who tells us that Shylock, driven in his pain to the frenzy of madness, runs about, muttering and crying 'Justice, the law, my ducats, and my daughter!'. He addresses nobody, he is oblivious of 'all the boys of Venice', who follow him and witness the old man's breakdown with cruel curiosity. A breakdown, a madness which robs the old man of his senses, makes him curse: 'I would my daughter were dead at my foot, and the jewels in her ear: would she were hears'd at my foot, and the ducats in her coffin' (Act 3, Scene 1). It has to be remembered that Shylock does not speak here as a rational being. True, these words come out of his mouth, but a raging passion drives him to utter this curse. The cursing old man reveals himself as a man of deep emotion. He loves his daughter. He is the father betrayed by his child, whom he never stops loving. In the moment of unbearable grief he curses his beloved child. In his powerless state man has only one way out. Blessing and cursing, like love and hate, lie near to each other in man's heart. The cursing Shylock of the third act is Shylock in the moment of greatest tragic pain. But in spite of the curse, Shylock will not cease to be the loving father. When in Jonathan Miller's production Shylock leaves the stage after the court scene (Act 4, Scene 1), he cries out in pain like an animal, mourning the loss of his daughter. He is no longer seen but his cry of anguish is heard. This inarticulate cry repeats Jeremiah's lament: 'Rachel weeping for her children. She refuses to be comforted, they are no more' (Jeremiah 31: 15).

The actor Schildkraut, as a Jew committed to vindicating the

1. Introduction to Thomas Wilson, *A Discourse Upon Usury* (London, 1925).

humanity of Shylock, played a father who remained unforgettable to those who saw him on the stage. Although the old man babbles and mutters, unceasingly lamenting the stolen treasures, only his daughter, who has left him, is in his mind. Schildkraut's way of acting this role is justified. But Shakespeare requires us to live up to his genius. To Shylock, the persecuted, offended, despised man, to this downtrodden human being, to this man in the depth of distress, everything is the same: money, jewels, the memory of his youth and of Leah, his deceased wife, and his daughter – all this is his life. He knows of no life beyond his home and his family, beyond his house, his 'sober house', and beyond the money which he had earned for the sake of his home and his family. Therefore after the flight of his daughter he does not know what he should lament first. Solanio, who reports this situation to us, characterises Shylock's behaviour as 'a passion so confused' and tells us that the words uttered by Shylock were 'so strange, outrageous . . . !'

> My daughter! O my ducats! O my daughter!
> Fled with a Christian! O my Christian ducats!
> Justice, the law, my ducats, and my daughter! (Act 2, Scene 8)

Such is Solanio's report. The world sees Shylock as Solanio describes him.

Iago, Edmund, Richard III and the King in Hamlet argue in a monologue about themselves in retrospect. Unlike these Shakespearean heroes, Shylock is not heard in a monologue. We see him only as one who reacts to the world. The world forced him into the money business, the world robbed him of money and home, the world despised him, when he progressed from feudal into bourgeois economy. The world mocked him in his suffering. The world, the hostile world, has made Shylock. But behind the Shylock whom the sins of the world have made into what he is, behind the Shylock whom the world abhors, is Shylock the man. If this man is a monster, he is a monster in the sense in which the Servant of God is one:

> He had no beauty, no majesty to draw our eyes, no grace to make us delight in him; his form, disfigured, lost all the likeness of man, his beauty changed beyond human semblance. He was despised, he shrank from the sight of men, tormented and humbled by suffering; we despised him, we held him of no account, a thing from which men turn away their eyes. Yet . . . the Lord laid upon him the guilt of us all. (Isaiah 53: 2,3,6)

Gustav Landauer writes in his book on Shakespeare that he has seen productions of *The Merchant of Venice* in which the actors added to the play a genuine interpretation of their own. Shylock returns to his empty house with a lamp in his hand. We only see the light, the house is in total darkness. The light moves from the ground floor to the top, from one room to the next: the old man searches in vain for his daughter. But in his mad search, in the light flickering in the darkness, we get Shakespeare's message: behold, a Jew, robbed by the Christians of his beloved child!

Shylock is forced to become a Christian. Baptism or death: that was the Christian alternative for Jews throughout the Middle Ages. Jessica, too, becomes a Christian. But her conversion is according to the rules of a new age in which Christian culture, not the Christian church, makes Christians different from Jews. Lorenzo teaches Jessica that art assists man in becoming a Christian. When Jessica contradicts her Christian tutor Lorenzo with the words 'I am never merry, when I hear sweet music', she is still the Jewish girl, the daughter of her puritanical father. He has warned her before:

Let not the sound of shallow fopp'ry enter
My sober house. (Act 2, Scene 5)

But Lorenzo is constant in his lesson about Christianity. 'Sit Jessica', he says, and begins with a hymn on music, which converts the wild gentiles into gentle men.

Since naught so stockish, hard, and full of rage,
But music for the time doth change his nature.
The man that hath no music in himself,
Nor is not mov'd with concord of sweet sounds,
Is fit for treasons, stratagems, and spoils;
The motions of his spirit are dull as night,
And his affections dark as Erebus:
Let no such man be trusted. (Act 5, Scene 1)

He means: do not trust the Jews. The whole cosmos – according to Lorenzo – proves the truth of the Christian faith.

Sit Jessica. Look how the floor of heaven
Is thick inlaid with patens of bright gold:
There's not the smallest orb which thou behold'st
But in his motion like an angel sings,
Still quiring to the young-eyed cherubins;
Such harmony is in immortal souls;
But whilst this muddy vesture of decay
Doth grossly close it in, we cannot hear it.

'Patens' are the small flat dishes used in Holy Communion. In using this word, Lorenzo finds the image of God in culture. Jessica, made fit for Belmont, enters not merely a civilisation new to her, she enters Christianity. She forgets the message of the 'Hear, O Israel', which says that no civilisation, no culture is identical with the holiness and absoluteness of the One God. Jessica becomes a Christian: a new form of baptism is presented to us by Shakespeare.

Yet Belmont is not what the medieval Christian church was. It is a place of Christian civilisation. Therefore Jessica's future remains in the balance. She may or may not become converted to the Christian faith. Shakespeare is not definite about this; he leaves the situation open to either possibility. The Christian faith of Lorenzo – man in his 'muddy vesture of decay' – is Manichean Christianity, and therefore irreconcilable with everything Jessica has received from her Jewish past.

On her return Portia greets the light coming from the little candle in her hall with the words:

> How far that little candle throws his beams!
> So shines a good deed in a naughty world.

With this sentiment she proves to be near to the world of the puritanical Jews. Belmont is, after all, not entirely Belgravia or Mayfair, not entirely Bloomsbury or Hampstead. Belmont too is a place on which the law has its hold. We can hope for Jessica. Jessica is of course pressed by Lorenzo to follow him into his faith. 'Come, Jessica!' But it remains open whether she follows him in true conversion, or whether she does it at all. Jessica, not really converted, Shylock, though robbed of his wealth, still alive – the Jews in the audience of Shakespeare's *Merchant of Venice* can leave after the fifth act and can still hope.

Heine saw it like this:

> Shakespeare would have written a satire against Christianity, if he had made it consist of characters who are enemies of Shylock, but who are hardly worthy to unlace his shoes. Antonio a weak creature without energy . . . Bassanio a fortune hunter . . . Lorenzo accomplice of a most infamous theft . . . the other noble Venetians do not seem to have any special antipathy to money, and when their poor friend is in difficulties, they have nothing for him but words.

When Heine saw the play performed in Drury Lane, he heard at the end of the fourth act a lady passionately crying out many times: 'The poor man is wronged!' Heine tells us: 'I have never been able to forget them, those great black eyes which wept for Shylock'.

Blessed are the eyes which weep for Shylock.

Part III

THE THIRD *CHURBAN*

Chapter 22

THE THIRD *CHURBAN*

In the year 586 before the Common Era the first Temple was destroyed. In the year 70 of the Common Era the second Temple was destroyed. In our history books we speak of the first *churban* (destruction) and of the second *churban*. The third *churban* took place in the years from 1933 to 1945. Six and a half million Jews were murdered.

We are the survivors of the third *churban*. Whatever else we are is of no importance in comparison with this crucial fact in our life.

We may be happy or unhappy, well-to-do or poor, we may be rich still with memories of the past or stripped bare of tradition like the children in the Displaced Persons camps who know only that they are of Jewish origin because it was for this they suffered persecution. We may be deeply rooted in the civilisation of our surroundings or we may be newcomers making ourselves known as foreigners with the first few words we utter. All these are minor differences amongst us Jews of this generation. There is a common badge which we all wear and which makes us a band of brothers and sisters singled out by God. We are the survivors of the third *churban*.

Dumbfounded and in agony we ask: What actually happened? The historian will try to explain what happened. He will show in detail how a sick civilisation collapsed and how this collapse involved the end of East European Jewry and the utter dissolution of continental Western Jewry. Perhaps it was a residue from the Middle Ages, still present in our own age, which poisoned the body of the European continent. A corpse can poison a living organism. Perhaps it was the rise of new generations which were only outwardly civilised and were in fact barbarians. These barbarians wanted to break out from what they felt to be the prison of civilisation. Perhaps the feudal civilisation of the Middle Ages, strengthened by the pagan legions of Prussia, revolted against the Protestant civilisation of the free democracies of the West.

The historian will analyse the past events of our time and offer us his findings. The historian is a retrospective prophet. He may do his best, but the way into the future remains full of risks. The biblical prophet looks back into the past like the historian but also gives guidance for the future. He speaks of the Judgment Day of God cleansing the land.

No man can be called righteous before God. But one thing can certainly be said of the six and a half million Jews who died. They were not the creators of, nor were they accountable for, that old, sick civilisation which was destroyed. They stand visibly for all the innocent who must die with the guilty when God's Judgment Day destroys the Wicked City. Even in their death, these six and a half million Jews fulfilled their holy mission.

We who have survived the Judgment Day ask what is our consolation, what is our duty, and what is our hope for the future.

Our own blood has been spilled; parents, brothers, sisters, friends have been foully murdered. Those who must live without consolation are embittered, and those who are embittered cannot build up new life.

There is only one consolation. We shall find it in our way to God. Only God can 'wipe away the tears from off all the faces, and the scandalous shame done to his people, he will extinguish it from off all the earth' (Isaiah 25:8). We, the survivors, must find our way to this God or we must drag on without consolation and therefore without the ability to live, still remaining the living victims of the catastrophe. Jewry has a religious future or none at all.

Those who survived and think and act as if their old background still exists will be condemned to walk through life as ghosts of a dead past. To be a survivor must mean something else. When a man loses everything, he is alone. Being alone, he has nothing unless he has God. A man who has found God has everything and he can progress to a new future. The good tidings of the Prophet of Consolation are not concerned with political or cultural prospects; the good tidings foretell that the people will stand again before God as in the great days of the past. The prophet says: 'Behold your God' (Isaiah 40:9).

The Day of Judgment which destroyed a past has its meaning for the future. We who have not been devoured by the wrath of judgment have one duty as survivors: we must change.

What is left in us from that past about which God has passed judgment must become changed. No one among us must remain merely the nineteenth-century Jew. God wants us to change. A man is not a man when he is a type.

East European Jewry was the heart of Jewry, from which life blood streamed to all its members. It was absolutely united with Western Jewry. East European Jewry looked to the West always. It had itself emigrated from the West in the eleventh and twelfth century. We had no political union connecting East European Jewry and Western Jewry. We did not need one. We were an historic unit closely knit together by the power of religion. This historic unit has been destroyed in the third *churban.* Jerusalem has been destroyed. The past from which we all come, whether Central or Eastern Europe was our home, is a religious past.

We shall have a future if it is a religious future. We must build Jerusalem again. This we cannot do if we remain what we were. We must not remain simply contemporaries of that catastrophe which devoured six and a half million Jews and left us alive. God sat in His judgment seat, and our old ideals and ideologies have been condemned. Whether we are Orthodox or Liberals or belong to the Reform Movement, whether we are Zionists or non-Zionists, we must not remain after the Day of Judgment what we were before.

Chapter 23

THE HUMAN IMAGINATION

I used the word *churban* for the first time in print in my book *The Jew-ish Mission* (1949). The first *churban* destroyed the Temple of Solomon, the second *churban* the Temple of Herod. The catastrophe of the expulsion from Spain or the massacre of Ukrainian Jews through the hordes of Chmelnicki was not called *churban* but *gezerah* (evil decree). The meaning of *churban* is a catastrophe which puts an end to an old era and creates a new one. This meaning is 'awesome', in the sense of the Hebrew word *nora*. The *churban* is a day of awe, of awe beyond human understanding. Having, like others, used the word *churban*, I began to see that it had a meaning which was not at once obvious but implicit and frightening: *churban* implied progress. The *Akedah* had the message that progress is possible without sacri-fice. The *churban*, on the other hand, is progress achieved through sacrifice.

What kind of progress can the third *churban* have created? Pon-dering about these questions in the pulpit, in fear and trembling, I preached that the Middle Ages have come to an end. Although my answer is the outcome of theological enquiry, it could first be given only in the form of a confessing sermon. Only in the exalted atmos-phere of the pulpit could I dare to say that *churban* and progress are connected. The Jewish people, although its Ashkenazi and Sephardi diaspora has become a world diaspora, now has its sole existence within the West; it is committed to a dialogue with the free democ-racies and is free to emancipate itself socially and culturally from all that which existed before the French Revolution. With this new com-mitment we can say farewell to our own Middle Ages. By preaching that *churban* and progress are connected, I was not saying anything more than the rabbis who preached that the Messiah to come was born on the day when Jerusalem was destroyed. One of them, in the apocalyptic exuberance of his comment on Amos's 'Day of the Lord' (Amos 5:18), even said: 'When the Messiah is to come, the House of Learning will be a place of fornication, Galilee will be devastated, people will wander from town to town but find no compassion, the wisdom of the rabbis will decay, the pious will be despised, chastity will not be found, and truth will be absent'.[1] What a terrible indictment of nineteenth century positivism, which viewed progress as a line leading upwards with mathematical necessity!

I am not satisfied with explaining this passage as meaning that things must become worse before they can become better. This passage is a warning against political messianism as it existed in the circles of Jewish and Christian zealots. But the profound meaning of this passage is really sensed in the following exposition: when man fails to provide a place for justice, civilisation decays and eventually collapses in an apocalyptic upheaval, and then historic change occurs like an earthquake or like any other catastrophe in nature.

The medieval society which had survived in Europe is crushed today. Hitler, Lenin and Stalin did what should have been done by kinder and wiser men but, alas, was not done by them. On the contrary, the old order had its defenders. We Jews could not do anything. The only outlet, emigration to America, was no longer open to large numbers of East European Jews after 1918.

East European Jewry was exterminated in the gas chambers. Two-thirds of the Jewish people survived Auschwitz, mainly because they were outside Hitler's reach. But after Auschwitz an East European Jewry no longer exists. Jews who left this pattern of life during the last two hundred years and entered the Western stage enriched the new world because they transferred what was best in the Middle Ages into the new era. Jews who have become westernised Jews are not secularised Jews. Jews are able to move from one historic time to another; it is nonsensical to speak of a secularised Jewry.

A church can become secularised. By being secularised the church gives free reign to her political components and is, in fact, a state outwardly displaying the insignia of a church. The gentiles hailing from the church, the secularised Christian gentiles, far from being innocent gentiles, become demonic gentiles, pagans who retained the principles of faith, sacrifice, obedience and hope, but with them served the Moloch. The secularised offspring of the medieval church practised medieval politics in the twentieth century. 'The SS were the Dominicans of the technical age' (Hochhuth), the

1. Mishnah, *Sotah* 9:15.

Führer-principle represented papal infallibility, Auschwitz was the place where the directors of the inquisition did their work in the midst of the twentieth century. The guilt of the Roman Catholic Church was that it was a medieval church in the twentieth century.

In the Middle Ages lord and vassal were bound together by the authoritarian principle. Fascism, rejecting democracy and choosing the authoritarian principle, was political medievalism. In the Middle Ages the hierarchical principle created a social pyramid in which not equality but inequality was the socially binding force. The man at the top was unique. The Caesar as pope or emperor made the Middle Ages the heir of Roman imperialism. In the Christian Middle Ages there was no place for the Jews; they were those who had killed Christ and who were, therefore, according to the Christian dogma providentially destined to be persecuted. Hitler could be viewed by the Vatican as a crusader. The change came late: a pope of the 1960s expunged the phrase *perfidiis Judaeis* from the Easter liturgy. The Middle Ages ended as late as that. Nazism was the last chapter of the Middle Ages. Jews and Christians are driven to reform lest their historic role dies with the dying Middle Ages.

The reform visualised now by all Christian churches demands first of all the rejection of the doctrine which regards the Jew as an anti-Christian. Jews are non-Christians whom Christians have to acknowledge in their importance for themselves. That Jesus had a Jewish mother is a philosemitic statement, but carries weight only within a dialogue in which both partners accept Christian imagery. The Jew does not do this; he has done for two thousand years what the Protestant Rudolf Bultmann began to do only recently: he has 'demythologized' the New Testament images. In this gentile world in which they are bidden by God to live as a dispersed people, Jews have a history for which the Servant of God texts of the Book of Isaiah provide the pattern. In Auschwitz, I say in my sermons – and only in sermons it is appropriate to make such a statement – Jews suffered vicarious death for the sins of mankind. It says in the liturgy of the synagogue, in reference to the first and second *churban,* albeit centuries after the event: 'because of our sins'. After Auschwitz Jews need not say this. Can any martyr be a more innocent sin-offering than those murdered in Auschwitz? The millions who died in Auschwitz died because of the sins of others. Jews and non-Jews died in Auschwitz, but the Jew-hatred which Hitler inherited from the medieval church made Auschwitz the twentieth century Calvary of the Jewish people.

The fact that a liberal pope expunged an offensive phrase about the Jews from a Christian liturgy should not be reported in a condescending way. It is a small matter and should only be a beginning.

The reform through which the church will emancipate herself from her medieval blindness with regard to the synagogue will have to mean much more. Judaism is the seed, and Judah Hallevi and Maimonides taught that out of this seed grows the tree, the church. The Golgotha of modern mankind is Auschwitz. The Cross, the Roman gallows, was replaced by the gas chamber. The gentiles, it seems, must first be terrified by the blood of the sacrificed scapegoat to have the mercy of God revealed to them and become converted, become baptised gentiles, become Christians.

We deceive ourselves when we plan for the future without admitting that it leads away from all our yesterdays. The frame of our mind is shaped by two events for which there is no comparison in the whole past of mankind's history: Auschwitz and Hiroshima. After Auschwitz the human imagination is not what it was before. After Auschwitz a new era begins which will either lead away from everything which led to Auschwitz or continue in the vein of Auschwitz.

Kant said after the French Revolution: 'The world is no longer what it was before'. After Auschwitz and Hiroshima we must face a hitherto unknown element of human existence. We have looked into an abyss which we know now to be very close to us. We can only save mankind through a greater charity and a greater responsibility than has been shown so far by civilised man. The globe itself, populated with numerous races, must become our concern. The whole earth can be devastated by the bomb, and entire races can be wiped out by barbarism. Only the biblical view of the world as the creation of God and every human being as created in the image of God can save us from the catastrophe looming on the horizon of a civilisation alienated from God, the creator of heaven and earth.

Chapter 24

THE 'TRAGEDY' OF AUSCHWITZ

'Comfort ye, comfort ye my people, saith your God' (Isaiah 40:1). It is now eighteen years since 1945, when with the end of the war Auschwitz, Belsen, Theresienstadt, Dachau and other places of horror revealed the undeniable truth about the crimes perpetrated by Germans. For those who still needed convincing there was the Eichmann Trial. Now the world knows. But what is the reaction of the world? And what is our own reaction? Our duty on today's Sabbath of Consolation is clearly expressed to us in the first verse of our prophetic lesson: 'Comfort ye, comfort ye my people!' Can we obey his commandment? Are we able to give comfort?

An understandable reaction would be to speak of tragedy. But surely the right word is monstrosity. We must distinguish between tragedy and monstrosity. Many have seen human history as a history of continuous tragedy. To talk of tragedy is to make excuses: nothing could be done; historic necessity made the cruel event inevitable; man looked on and could do nothing, in short, it was a tragedy. Nobody is responsible, the guilty are guiltless, it was just a tragedy.

If this is what tragedy means, then the death of the six million martyrs should not be called a tragedy but a monstrosity. Implicit in the concept of tragedy is an apology for the cruel event. Pilate washing his hands is only the obedient servant of the Caesar: he was doing his duty. But where no apology, no excuse is admissible, where no bystander can wash his hands, shrug his shoulders, and walk away without being condemned, it is no tragedy, but a monstrosity that has occurred. The death of the six million Jewish martyrs was a monstrosity.

When we speak of monstrosity, we can still speak of holy

martyrdom. The Jews always represent mankind, in life and in death. The way in which the six million Jews died was the way in which everyone has died on the battlefields of history. The Irish who died in the great famine – they died as people die who are starved to death, they died like the inmates of Belsen. The intellectuals who made the French Revolution possible and afterwards died on the guillotine died a bitter death; they died innocently. Millions of soldiers died in the two world wars; they died like the Servant of whom Isaiah says: 'He opened not his mouth; as a lamb that is led to the slaughter and as a sheep that before the shearers is dumb; yea, he opened not his mouth' (Isaiah 52:7). All this is monstrous. Monstrosity is the word here, not tragedy. The Jewish martyrdom, the monstrous fact of six million murdered victims, makes mankind's suffering truly visible. Their death is an accusation. Their death was not necessary: it was a crime. Their death was the doing of guilty men. The Christian symbol of the Cross speaks of tragedy. Human suffering is seen as an inevitable fate. It is not called monstrous when man hurts man every day, when man kills man in war; it is called the consequence of original sin, it is called the tragic side of life. Jewish teaching declares: tragedy is unneccessary. Jewish teaching does not know anything about so-called original sin. It is monstrous that man, destined by God to live in happiness and blessing, should suffer, suffer at the hand of his fellow man.

The Christian story of the crucifixion is told in the New Testament with the splendour of a great epic, with the poetic beauty of a classical Greek tragedy. Inspired by the New Testament, painters, sculptors and musicians have devoted their art to the crucifixion story. Eventually the man hanging on the cross became the 'gentle Jesus', a handsome young man with a spotlessly clean white robe gathering little children around him. The children are not frightened, but delighted. You could see this *schmaltz* in the recent Hollywood production of Ben Hur in which the New Testament was certainly distorted, but also truly expressed.

Children and normal adults are horrified and terror-stricken when they see pictures of the inmates of Auschwitz, degraded, dehumanised creatures in thin, dirty pyjamas, reminding us of the Servant of God as portrayed in the book of Isaiah. Christianity presented the man on the cross as a glorified persecuted tragic hero and obscured the fact that he was a Jew hanging on a Roman gallows. Christianity made this pagan, cruel monstrosity respectable, representing it through the symbol of the Cross as the Christian tragedy. The world knows now what history represents when it is nothing but the history of the sole kingdom of the all-powerful state. Mankind now knows that a man who is permitted to regard himself as subject to original sin will soon cease to be human. The Cross, as the poetic symbol of suffering, hides the truth. Auschwitz is the truth, the truth which reveals such monstrosity that the word tragedy becomes a white-washing lie. Now mankind cannot but face the truth. The Irish who perished in the great famine perished in their Auschwitz. The young boys who died in 1914 in the mud of Passchendaele died in their Auschwitz. The soldiers who died at the Somme and at Verdun in the First World War died in their Auschwitz. The soldiers, airmen and sailors of the Second World War, the Russian prisoners who were starved to death in Germany, the Russian peasants who were destroyed like useless cattle by Stalin, the men, women and children who died in the air raids, the victims of Hiroshima and of the air raid on Dresden, they all died in their Auschwitz. They died because what happened was a monstrosity: to call it a tragedy is to attempt to lie with the help of poetry. The Cross did not prevent the greatest carnage of history from happening: what happened happened while the Cross was the sign of respectability, while the Star of David was the sign of the outcast. The Cross was the smug symbol of a religion which lived in concordat with Hitler. Auschwitz is the uncompro-mising *ecce homo*: behold the suffering of man. Auschwitz cries out that mankind is threatened by monstrosity when man ceases to be what the Jew is: the messenger and witness of God.

'Comfort ye, comfort ye, my people!' We are entitled to say that we are true to our Jewish mission to be 'a light to the gentiles'. When Christians marched in Hitler's army, when non-German Christians were for a long time reluctant to regard Fascism as an evil, we Jews had clean hands. Our Auschwitz, our loss of six million martyrs, tells the truth, which mankind cannot but remember. All suffering which man has to bear in this valley of tears called history is monstrous. Historians and artists, and Christians with them, mince their words when they present human suffering as a tragedy surrounded by and fulfilled in human glory. What man suffers is monstrous. Against tragedy, you may say, there is no remedy, as there is no remedy against fate. But to fight against monstrosity is meaningful for every-one who is honest, sane, and not misguided by the excuse that orig-inal sin makes the fight of the honest and sane futile. Those who died in Auschwitz demand action from the survivors. Mankind can be redeemed. 'Comfort ye, comfort ye, my people'.

Chapter 25

THE END OF THE MIDDLE AGES

The prophetic lesson of our fifth Sabbath of Consolation is again taken from the last part of the Book of Isaiah, in which a prophet whose name we do not know speaks to us. But we know the historic circumstances of his time. The destruction of Jerusalem and the subsequent disappointment when the entire Jewish people was unable to return to the former homeland are the facts of the immediate past, and the prophet has them in his mind. And yet he has a message which announces great joy. As a true biblical prophet, he is not a traditionalist. The man who walks with God always has a new way before him. The joyful message of this prophet speaks of a return, not of a return to a past chapter of history, not even of the desired return to the beloved land of the forefathers, but of the return of God to his people. God returns, and in his mercy and love brings joy, progress, and expansion.

> Enlarge the place of thy tent,
> And let them stretch forth the curtains of thy habitations, spare not:
> lengthen thy cords,
> and strengthen thy stakes.
> For thou shalt spread abroad on the right hand and on the left.
> (Isaiah 54:2,3)

In all this joy, in all this happiness, the memory of the years of suffering and destruction is not forgotten but seen in a new light. Measured against the mercy of God, these years were only 'a small moment', 'a little wrath', in the words of the prophet.

> For a small moment have I forsaken thee;
> But with great compassion will I gather thee;
> In a little wrath I hid my face from thee for a moment;

But with everlasting kindness will I have compassion on thee
Saith the Lord, thy redeemer.

(Isaiah 54:7,8)

We too, must regard the years 1933–1945, the years of tribulation,
persecution and martyrdom as 'a small moment'. We too, must see
God, as the prophet does, as merciful, in spite of Hitler, in spite of
the concentration camps, in spite of the six million Jewish martyrs.
We must see our *churban* as the prophet sees the first *churban*: as 'a little wrath'. The first *churban,* the destruction of Jerusalem at the hand
of Nebuchadnezzar, the second *churban,* the destruction of Jerusalem
in the year 70 by Rome, and the third *churban,* the destruction suffered by Jewry in the years 1933–1945, these catastrophes are 'a
small moment', 'a little wrath', measured against the eternal love
which God showers on his people.

After every *churban,* the Jewish people made a decisive progress
and mankind progressed with us. After the first *churban* we became
the people of the Diaspora, proving to the gentiles that a people can
exist without the heathen attachment to its land. After the second
churban, after the loss of the Temple, we made worship dependent on
the spoken word alone. After the third *churban,* that of our own time,
the Jewish Diaspora is no longer limited to the Ashkenazi and
Sephardi regions, but has become a world Diaspora. The medieval
organisation outside which God was not supposed to be found has
been destroyed. You can be a Jew outside the *din,* outside the religious organisation as defined in the codes. The Middle Ages have
come to an end. It is the same for us as it is for the Christians. They
can be Christian outside the Roman Church: at last we can all be citizens living in freedom. That is the blessed end of the Middle Ages,
the end of the Empires, through the rise of democracy.

The end of the Middle Ages was overdue. After World War I the
West had the opportunity of bringing freedom, land reform and the
blessings of the industrial revolution to the East European countries,
from the Baltic States down to Roumania. Nothing was done. British
officials accepted invitations to go hunting and shooting from the
aristocrats of these countries. The feudal system remained. The
allied soldiers of World War I had died in vain. Then Hitler came.
He, the nihilist, did what the progressives should have done but
failed to do, he destroyed the Middle Ages, but he did so by destroy-
ing the old Europe. The sins of a stagnant Europe, the sins of an iso-
lationist America, the sins of the democracies failing to progress
towards the solution of the new problems gave birth to Hitler. Of
Nebuchadnezzar, the destroyer of Jerusalem, the word of God in the
book of Jeremiah says 'Nebuchadnezzar, my servant' (Jeremiah
27:6). Of Ashur who destroyed Samaria, Isaiah says that God himself

called him to come. Would it shock you if I were to imitate this prophetic style and formulate the phrase 'Hitler, my servant'?

In the Book of Job, Satan is there among the servants and messengers of God. Hitler was an instrument, in itself unworthy and contemptible. But God used this instrument to cleanse, to purify, to punish a sinful world. The six million Jews died an innocent death; they died because of the sins of others. Western man must, in repentance, say of the Jew what Isaiah says of the Servant of God: 'Surely, our diseases he did bear, and our pain he carried... He was wounded because of our transgressions, he was crushed because of our iniquities' (Isaiah 53:4, 5). Jewish martyrdom explains the meaning which the Cross can retain better than medieval Christian dogma ever did.

After 1945, when Jews surviving in the free countries realised the whole abyss of the catastrophe, we had only Job's submission as our answer to the horrible event. We could only say what he said: 'I lay my hands upon my mouth, I have nothing to say'. We shall go on saying this when we ponder about the fact that God permitted what happened to happen. But from Job's submission we have to proceed to the prophet of our Sabbath of Consolation. In today's lesson, Isaiah 54:1–10, the message of great joy comes to us. It is joy about the progress which leads away from ruins. It is joy about the miracle in which God renews the world. Eighteen years after the end of the era of Auschwitz, the welcome to the new era inspires us with hope and joy.

The end of the Middle Ages also means the end of the Jewish Middle Ages. It is not merely small isolated groups of our people but the whole of the Jewish people that is now westernised. We march with the Western nations. We can progress. Religiously we emancipate ourselves from the dictate of the *din*, from a medievally enforced supervision of our religious life. Politically we can dismiss the medieval mentality which separated one community from another with walls and towers, making Zionism necessary. We remain loyal to the citizens of Israel: they need us, and we shall not fail them. But we now realise that our Holy Land is not a country on the shores of the Mediterranean. We now realise that our Holy Land is mankind's future. Mankind's future and nothing else is our goal. As Jews we serve mankind. Our exodus from the Middle Ages is assured. We re-enter history in the joy of still having the privilege of serving the old mission, in the joyful knowledge that the unchanging and unending kindness of God accompanies us.

> For the mountains may depart,
> And the hills be removed;
> But my kindness shall not depart from thee,
> Neither shall my covenant of peace be removed,
> Saith the Lord that hath compassion on thee.
>
> (Isaiah 54:10)

Chapter 26

THE DAY OF THE LORD

It is now nineteen years after the end of the war, and one may ask why it is only now and not much earlier that people all over the world look for an explanation of the madness in which six million Jews died as martyrs. This delay concerns us Jews, too. It takes time to recover after a blow.

It is psychologically understandable that the Jewish answer to Auschwitz is only slowly forthcoming. Jewish and non-Jewish historians have carefully sifted the facts; we know in every gruesome detail what happened. But the religious question remains: why could all this happen in a world in which Jews worship God as the Redeemer from Pharaonic oppression? Why were the six million Jewish martyrs not redeemed by him whom we worship as the Redeemer? Sodom was destroyed because ten righteous people were not to be found in the whole city. If Hitler's Reich was a Sodom, or, to go further, if the whole world inside and outside Germany in the age of Hitler was a Sodom which produced Hitler in common guilt, the six million Jews who perished were certainly innocent people, not guilty of the general decay which had infested our civilisation. Why did six million Jews have to die in the destruction of the Sodom of our time, when God was willing to save the biblical Sodom with the vicarious presence of only ten righteous people? Auschwitz and the Germans is one thing; the Germans as a nation will have to live with the memory of Auschwitz. Auschwitz and the surviving Jews is another thing. It concerns our religious strength and understanding. We who mourn the six million martyrs have, in the way of our forefathers, to carry on worshipping God, the Redeemer of His people.

At the Eichmann Trial in Jerusalem a Hungarian Jewish witness spoke of the impossibility for Jews of escaping from the net of the Gestapo even in the last months of the war. Ninety-nine per cent of the people could not escape. Of the remaining one per cent who tried to escape, half were captured and killed. Where could they have gone, the Hungarian Jew exclaimed, where could they have fled? The witness brings back to our mind the passage from the Book of Amos which we read today:

> Woe unto you that desire the day of the Lord!
> Wherefore would ye have the day of the Lord?
> It is darkness, and not light.
> As if a man did flee from a lion,
> And a bear met him,
> And went into a house and leaned his hand on the wall
> And a serpent bit him.
>
> (Amos 5:18,19)

These verses illustrate well how a Jew could not help feeling in the whole realm of Hitler's Europe. But why speak here of the Day of the Lord, as Amos does?

From the days when I taught at the classes of my congregation I remember an intelligent boy with whom I read prophetic texts. The lad was terrified about the injunctions and accusations raised by the prophets against the Jewish people. The boy was bewildered and full of protest. Surely, he said, we were not as bad as that. This youngster was quite right, absolutely right. In view of the approaching catastrophe of the destruction of the State of David, and in view of the catastrophe after it happened, the prophets made the people face it in the way of their teaching: no accusation against God! Interpret the national catastrophe as the work of God's judgement, as the Day of the Lord, as Amos says.

Can you see the day of Auschwitz as the day of judgement? Who was condemned on this day of judgement? Not the six million Jewish martyrs! A whole chapter of history which produced Hitler was condemned. It produced him with the necessity in which evil creates evil. What were the evils of the Hitler era? I may be very inadequate in enumerating them, but I give you my list: unemployment of millions, American isolationism, the clinging to vested interests by the old French and English ruling classes, the feudalism in the East European countries, cruel zealotry and hatred in the political arena everywhere, a petrified conservativism in politics, both left and right, and also in religion. My list may be ill-arranged and wrong in various respects; when all is said it is the German people who made the Hitler era possible. It is not my task to give an historical analysis of the pre-Hitler western civilisation. But it is my task to search our conscience and to ask whether you and I are prepared to say that we, as Jews, were inevitably involved in the stagnation which took place after 1918 and long before. It is my duty to teach what the prophets taught.

When the catastrophe came and the Davidic chapter of history came to an end with the destruction of Jerusalem and Samaria, the prophets said: it is *our* God who did it, the God of Israel. It was his judgement over the past. It was 'the Day of the Lord'. In saying this the prophets found the formula for survival. When Samaria, the capital of Israel, was destroyed in 722 BCE, the Jewish people, who had suffered grievously, had with the help of their prophets – as we read in our Hebrew Bible – the religious strength to celebrate God's victory over an evil, decadent chapter of history and to confess as suffering victims, with no co-operation with the real leaders, their share in the sins of the condemned age. Therefore they survived and progressed hopefully to the next chapter of history.

We are now living in the post-Auschwitz era, and we look back to the pre-Auschwitz era. It was what Amos calls 'the Day of Lord' which created the division into a condemned past and a new era. Before Auschwitz there were various ideologies of political messianism, in which many thought they could shape the pattern of the future; they thought they could make history in the way they arranged their front gardens. They thought that they themselves and they alone could do it. They looked forward into the future, which they regarded as a happy playground for their creative enterprise, forgetting the Creator, the maker of man and of history. The Day of the Lord came: it was darkness and not light, it was a day of judgement which destroyed the pride of man and taught him his utter dependence on God. The six million who died innocently died because no man is an island, because everyone is responsible for everyone else. The righteous are responsible for the sinners. The innocent who died in Auschwitz, not for the sake of their own sins but because of the sins of others, atone for evil; they are the sacrifice which is brought to the altar and which God acknowledges favourably. The six million, the dead of Auschwitz and of other places of horror, are Jews whom our modern civilisation has to canonise as holy martyrs; they died as sacrificial lambs because of the sins inherent in western civilisation. Their death purged western civilisation so that it can again become a place where men can live, do justly, love mercy, and walk humbly with God.

Auschwitz closes a past for everyone – for us Jews, of course, too. There are people amongst us who preach the same doctrines and talk in the same old ideologies and party slogans which are familiar to us from pre-Auschwitz days. These people of yesterday offend our martyrs, they ignore their sacrifice. The Day of the Lord, as a day of judgment, condemns the past. But in doing so, it opens the door to a new future. The martyr dies to give us, the remnant, an atoned future, a new day, wonderful like every morning in which God renews his creation. The end of the Book of Amos is an exalted perspective into a happy future. Man can leave the past behind him and progress into the new chapter of the future.

Chapter 27

THE LAST WILL AND TESTAMENT OF EAST EUROPEAN JEWRY

Since the days of Moses Mendelssohn East European Jewry was closely connected with German Jewry, and looked towards the West. Every gifted student of the Talmudical high school looked to the Western university as the holy Zion which he was desirous to enter. If he could not do so, he read the books of the Western philosophers with zeal and with no small capacity for grasping what was going on in the world of freedom outside his feudal East European prison.

Germany Jewry, for its part, never forsook its brethren in Eastern Europe. The word *Ostjuden,* when spoken by German Jews, was not an indication of unkindness. That Germany was not a country fit for immigration was not the fault of the German Jews. They were themselves partly East European Jews by origin: the Polish province of Posen had been incorporated into Germany by Frederick the Great. Faithful fellowship with the East European Jew was always alive in the German Jew. We must even speak of a romantic love which he felt for his brethren in Eastern Europe. All this is on record in a whole literature from Heinrich Heine's *Journey to Poland* up to Arnold Zweig's and Hermann Struck's *The Face of the East European Jew* and to Franz Rosenzweig's enthusiastic letters which he sent home in World War I from Poland. Rosenzweig's experience there in a *shtibl* (prayer room) shaped his view of what a synagogue service ought to be.

Rosenzweig said 'We can run away from the law but we cannot change it'. Zunz said: 'As long as the Talmud is in force, nothing can be done'.[1] Both Franz Rosenzweig and Leopold Zunz made their statements, the one about Jewish law, the other about Talmudic studies, out of loyalty to East European Jewry. They felt: we here in Germany – which they regarded as belonging to the civilised world – can easily do away with the medieval pattern of Jewish life and still remain Jews; what about East European Jewry living under the conditions of the Middle Ages? These conditions, the two men felt, would make Reform Judaism create a rift between themselves and their brethren to whom they wished to be loyal. Such consideration no longer applies after Auschwitz. The habitat of the whole of the Jewish people is now in the West. Unless the West reaches Russian Jewry and the Jewries of the Satellite countries, they will become the lost tribes of twentieth-century Jewry.

East European Jewry is no longer. Neither is German Jewry. It is understandable that *Landsmannschaften* gather to share memories and to warm their hearts with pictures of what was once their very life. It is not merely for emotional reasons, however, that we turn back and treasure what can be preserved of the past. There is a duty which drives the historian to his work. We heard from survivors that Dubnow, before he was murdered by the Nazis, repeatedly admonished those around him with the words: *niederschreiben, alles niederschreiben* (write it down, write everything down!). The old historian died with the hope that history books would do what the prayer of the Jew beseeches God to do: 'Remember O Lord, remember what Amalek has done to me!' The remnant of the Jewish people is well aware of the duty to honour the memory of the six million martyrs by calling on the historians to let mankind know what has happened. If the historians write as Jews who know what Judaism stands for, they will write with the knowledge that holy history is not only in the Bible, but happens in our times too.

We must soberly refrain from a nostalgic criticism which clings to names and institutions of the past, and forgets that the exhibits of a museum are dead and cannot be brought to life. To call an American high school a 'yeshivah' is childish. The East European yeshivah is not transportable. We cannot build Gothic cathedrals in the twentieth century. Study of the Talmud has to become an academic enterprise in rabbinical seminaries and at universities. Scholars trained in historical criticism and comparative religion and capable of distinguishing between the various forms of law must take over from those who lived an ascetic life as students of the Talmud. In the Talmud the

---

1. Zunz should have said: 'As long as the concept of a Sacred Law similar to the Islamic concept of Sharia is in force, nothing can be done'. Anyway, this sentence of Zunz is a random remark in a letter to a friend which only recently came to light. Zunz never said anything like that in public.

spirit of the prophets and the spirit of Roman law is alive. Roman law brought civilisation into barbaric lands conquered by the Roman Empire. The rabbis changed Roman law, and made it a 'law of mercy'. Yet legal procedure and rule by law was the common principle for rabbi and Roman lawyer. In the last centuries of the Roman Empire the Roman lawyer was often a Syrian and therefore no linguistic barrier existed between him and the rabbi. But the East European yeshivah-trained rabbi no longer breathes the air of the free cities of the Roman Empire. The more the post-Maimonidean codifiers guided him, the more he moved into a world similar to that of the Islamic *ulema*, dispensing the sacred law to their rural clientele. Legal casuistry became an instrument of torture which had the same effect on the mind as the whip on the Christian flagellant. East European 'rabbinism' – to quote the term used by Zunz and Dubnow – is different from the world of our classical rabbis, who speak to us in Mishnah and Talmud.

Here are two examples of the decline which East European medieval surroundings inflicted on Jewish life:

The Maharam, that is Rabbi Meir (died 1616), head of the Yeshivah in Lublin, was the author of halachic responsa still quoted by Orthodox rabbis today. But what kind of a person was this rabbi? We come to know his personality by quoting the following sample of his legal work: 'Is a woman guilty of adultery if the circumstances are such that the intercourse took place with the devil who appeared to the woman as the apparition of (a) her husband, (b) the Polish *pan* (squire)?' In very long and subtle discussions, the Maharam investigates whether this case should be dealt with according to the laws concerning adultery or sodomy. In each case the consequence for the woman would be different. The result of the long, hairsplitting legal definitions has, after all, a happy ending: the woman is an adulteress only if adultery has been committed with a living person. Intercourse with a ghost who appears in human form cannot rob the husband of his honour, and the woman is therefore not an adulteress.

Rabbi Aryeh Loeb, head of the Yeshivah of Minsk, and subsequently rabbi in Metz (1776) is another example of the decline of Jewish learning. This rabbi is known under the name *Shaagat Aryeh* (Roaring of the Lion), the title of the book in which he discourses at length on how a left-handed man should put on his *tefillin*. The rabbi's exposition of scholastic sophistry was learned by heart by thirteen-year-old boys who recited it in their public oration *(derashah)* on the day of their Bar Mitsvah. In the name of religious instruction mental acrobatics were forced on these children who had to find their way through a labyrinth of sentences in which the terms 'left side', 'left hand', 'right hand' and 'right side' were constantly interchanged. Rabbis of the type of *Shaagat Aryeh* were numerous in Lithuania and in other parts of Eastern Europe.

East European Jewry emancipated itself from the barbarism of the East European Middle Ages by accepting the message of Moses Mendelssohn. The *Haskalah*, the Western enlightenment movement, penetrated East European thinking in great measure. Politically very little could be done. The Tsar in the Kremlin and the feudal lord in town and country prevented any political self-emancipation. The only practical remedy was emigration to America, and this stopped almost entirely after 1918. But books came from the West, and were eagerly read by the East European Jewish intelligentsia. They did not know that the West had declined after 1918 until it reached the level of decadence in men of the type of Neville Chamberlain. East European Jewry, like German Jewry, believed in the West. They were not granted the blessing of seeing the new rise of the West and the final destruction of Hitler's barbaric representation of the Middle Ages.

Loyalty to what East European Jewry once was is misunderstood by those in our midst who, preaching Orthodoxy and fundamentalism, try to continue to wear the 'gown woven in the Orient'. East European Jewry had begun to hate the 'gown' of Roman Catholic–Islamic civilisation forced on them by their oppressors. Any Orthodoxy is anti-Western. When the West awakened and reasserted itself in the *filioque* dispute and severed its link with Byzantium, the Byzantine Church called itself Orthodox. The West is founded on the belief in progress. In his heart, in his thinking, in his hope, the East European Jew was a Western man turning away from the Middle Ages. The East European Jews perished, murdered by Hitler. We are the loyal executors of their will when we teach and preach a progressive Judaism which is able to renew the Judaism of our prophets and classical rabbis.

Chapter 28

FATHERS AND SONS

Jews and Christians are both committed to history, but the commitment in each case is different. The Jew stands in history as the creature of God, as the whole man. After the first *churban,* after the first destruction of the Temple of Jerusalem, the Jewish people approached the prophet Ezekiel with a radical proposition. They suggested building a temple in Babylon. Their argument was: we are without a country or state of our own. History has cast us out from the community of nations. Their suggestion: 'Let us build another temple' meant: 'Let us become a Jewish church: let us become a religious organisation.' What they meant becomes clear from Ezekiel's answer. He said No, and he said it in these words: 'And I passed by thee, and I saw thee weltering in thy blood, and I said unto thee: "In thy blood live!" Yea, I said unto thee: "In thy blood live!"' (Ezekiel 16:6).

After the first *churban* the Jewish people was a people without a state and without a country and therefore different from the gentiles. Yet it was told by its prophet to live in history as the gentiles do. The commandment 'Live in thy blood!' means: live as creatures of God, live as the Jewish people, do not live the spiritual life in which man the creator cuts himself off from creation. Live as a people, but live as the people of God. It was different at the second *churban.* After the dissolution of the Maccabean state a part of the Jewish people, the first Christians, stopped living as a people and began to live as members of a church. Spirit, not blood, makes the Christian: spirit, a turning away from the human situation, a leap of man, the creature, into a superhuman situation.

Changes in history are made by sons who revolt against their fathers. The Old Testament repeats again and again the phrase 'from generation to generation'. Abraham leaves his father's house and becomes a stranger in a foreign land. He does not revolt against his father.[1] In the New Testament the phrase 'unto your children's children' does not occur a single time. The Christian church begins as a revolt of sons against their fathers. Since this beginning Christians have a choice between two attitudes to the Jews: to love them as their begetters or to hate them as those whom the church has to fight so that the spirit should prevail over the blood, the church, the second creation, over Creation. The Christian church, no longer aware of her roots in Judaism, will see the Jew as Antichrist and speak of the crucifixion as the murder of the Son. During World War I, Richard Aldington, in his poem 'The Blood of the Young Men', expressed the feeling which was central to the other war poets, especially Owen and Sassoon, that young men are sacrificed in large numbers for the good of those at home:

> Old men, you will grow stronger and healthier
> With broad red cheeks and clear hard eyes –
> Are not your meat and drink the choicest?
> Blood of the young, dear flesh of the young men.

The man on the Cross is a young man. Christianity won through its message, 'Somebody must die that others may live.' It prevailed against the cult of Mithras through its appeal to the Roman soldiers who fought the endless wars of the Roman Empire. The Roman sculptor of 'The Dying Gaul' bestows a bliss on the dying soldier which is spiritual and divested of all heroic self-assertion. Eventually the West created in the tomb of the Unknown Warrior a modern equivalent to the Cross on which the crucified body of a young man represents all the sons who die a sacrificial death on the battlefield.

On every Armistice Day when the Last Post is sounded the whole nation unites in silent devotion with those who pay their homage at the tomb of the Unknown Warrior. In this silence the Christian tenet of the Resurrection gives hope to those who have lost their dear ones in the battles of two world wars. The Jew has the promise of his prophet: 'He maketh death to vanish in life eternal; And the Lord will wipe away the tears from off all faces: And the shame of his people will he remove from off all the earth' (Isaiah 25:8).

The second *churban* was Rome's destruction of Jerusalem, which led to the separation of Christianity from Judaism. The same separation took place during the Holocaust of 1933–1945, now called the third *churban*. During these terrible years a Marcionite Christianity

---

1. The Midrash which tells the story of young Abraham smashing the idols of his father is of late date.

without connection with Judaism looked on while an antisemitism resembling nothing in history eventually culminated in the father-murder of Auschwitz. When Christianity withdraws into the realm of the spirit and disobeys or does not even understand Ezekiel's commandment 'In thy blood live', man, the creature of God, is abandoned, his blood is shed in the Christian cruelty which leaves history and does not interfere in the dominion of the gentiles.

Auschwitz happened in Christendom; it is the Christian scandal. Auschwitz is the third *churban* which the Jewish people suffered for the sake of mankind. Auschwitz is a commentary on the second *churban,* which led to the separation of Christianity from Judaism. Auschwitz proves that Golgotha is partly patricide. The Cross should show a murdered father, not a murdered son. A father was killed by his son. The Jew is the father, the Christian the son.

The Jewish–Christian dialogue which is now in progress is, indeed, an epoch making event. But this dialogue is idle talk if the subject of Auschwitz is excluded. Who is responsible for Auschwitz? 'Surely,' an Asian intellectual said to a missionary, 'Hitler was a Christian'. The explanation that Hitler was a secularised Christian, a heathen, will not satisfy the Asian observer of European affairs. Only in Christian lands is the secular opposed to the spiritual. Only there does the unremitting tension between gentile and Christian exist. Only there can secularised Christians in their passion for a 'second creation' become guilty of a demoniac destruction of the creation – only there, not in the lands of the Buddha. It was in a Christian country, not in the lands of the Buddha, that Hitler and those who followed him were born and bred.

The church established in history, the visible church, as the Christians call her, is a secular institution. All secular institutions carry with them the mark of original sin. Secular history never has the innocence which is the glory of men, beasts and things in the world created by God. The Jew is in history as a man created by God. The history of how man, the image of God, came into being cannot be recorded. He is there, as the miracle of the existence of the world is there, daily with us, but always transcending our understanding and only fittingly described in the liturgical praise of the Psalmist. Whereas the Jew is within history as the world created by God is within history, the church for its part is a product of history, and as such it carries the burden of original sin. The original sin of the Christian church is her separation from Judaism. Auschwitz proved that the original sin of the historical church can re-create the conditions which once led to the Marcionite separation of Christianity from Judaism.

Antisemitism is of Christian origin. We know next to nothing about the historical details of the first separation of Christianity from Judaism. But we do know the history of the Christian church, and we also know what happened in Auschwitz. Those who had once received the word of God from the Jews deserted the Jews. The two thousand year old Jew-hatred led to modern antisemitism and eventually to Auschwitz. In the beginning of Christianity Jewish sons tore themselves away from their Jewish fathers. When sons rebel against their fathers, the terrible sin of patricide looms over the divided family. The guilt of the beginning of Christianity repeated itself at Auschwitz. Christian sons revolted against their Jewish fathers: patricide was committed again. Auschwitz is the monument of a *judenrein*, de-Judaised Christianity.

Judaism, the first monotheistic religion, appears in history like the miracle of the starry firmament arising out of the darkness and shining in mighty splendour. Christianity participates to a smaller degree in this miracle. We see the chapters of Jewish Christianity and of gentile Christianity preparing for the entry of the Christian church. But her real beginning lies in the darkness where no historian can recognise any contours and where the Christian believer is thrown back on his faith which alone can tell him what happened. What happened? A schism? Judah Hallevi rejects this suggestion. He has the parable of the seed and the tree, Christianity being the tree which grows from the holy seed of Judaism. Where the Christian church does not accept the truth of this parable, she is thrown back to the time before she had rejected the Marcionite heresy, which sees Jew and Christian as enemies. The son who is an enemy of his father is a potential patricide. After the Middle Ages the dominant force on the stage of history is no longer a church but a Christian world. The post-medieval Christian world gave birth to the Christian antisemite, whom no Christian dogma tamed in his fury. This makes the guilt of the post-medieval church even greater than that of the medieval church, which was great enough. The patricide of Auschwitz throws light on the beginning of Christianity when its separation from Judaism took place. What happened then? We know now: sons rose against their fathers; patricide took place.

It has been said of Franz Kafka that he described the appalling situation of the concentration camps in his novels long before the soil of Europe was fouled with them. Something similar can be said of Freud. The post-medieval modern church had become a Marcionite church, a church entirely cut off from Judaism and therefore no longer the 'tree' grown from the 'holy seed'. The Nazis found a de-judaised Christianity on the scene and only drew a radical conclusion from what already existed. Freud sensed this situation and spoke of it in his own way, as a child of his times, as a believer in science holding all the organised religions around him in contempt.

Relying on Robertson Smith's *The Religion of the Semites* Freud explained the origin of civilisation as a revolt of sons against 'the old male leader of the horde'. All the world told Freud that Robertson Smith's facts were unproved. Freud would not budge. What he could not defend as scientific fact he called his 'intuition', and he never gave up what his intuition had conveyed to him. The way in which Freud was wrong is obvious but negligible. What is important is the way in which he was right.

Freud, like Franz Rosenzweig and Kafka, saw history around him as motivated by Christian thought and, therefore, as the continuous revolt of sons against fathers. Freud did not use the word 'herd', which would have placed this group in pre-history. He used the word 'horde' for the group at the beginning of history which used violence as means of action.

The history of states begins with an act of violence. The state dispenses justice, but before it is in a position to do so, it has to establish itself, and this is done with the help of violence. Justice and power are the two pillars of the state. Every state begins with an act of overthrowing a predecessor. The Greek cities invented myths to hide this gruesome beginning. Christianity did justice to the memory of a guilt by teaching the doctrine of original sin as characteristic of all gentiles, who become creative in history as founders of cities and states. The guilt of the gentiles in politics is also incurred by the makers of culture. Every artist commits the sin of aspiring as a mere man to be what God is, a creator. He neglects the ways and duties of the creature of God. 'The true artist will let his wife starve, his children go barefoot, his mother drudge for his living, sooner than work at anything but his art' (G. B. Shaw).

Any Jewish preacher speaking about 'Jewish warmth' will find his congregation in full agreement with him. On the other hand, Kafka speaks about 'Christian coldness'. Graham Greene in his novel *The Power and the Glory* shows Mexico under communism, when Roman Catholic clergy were forced to marry to evade persecution. One such priest, having found his way back into the church, meets his child, now, with a Roman Catholic priest as father, a fatherless child. Graham Greene shows the whole tragedy of the situation. 'Why have I not got a father like the other children,' the little one says. The priest is deeply moved but can do nothing. A world cuts him off from his own flesh and blood. It is the spiritual world to which he belongs as a Christian priest. A father in spirit cannot allow himself to be a father in the flesh – an example of the Christian coldness produced by the rise from the secular to the spiritual.

He who follows Christ must leave father and mother, brother and sister.

Freud discovered the whole man. He rejected the Platonic dichotomy between mind and body and the Christian dichotomy between spiritual and secular, and saw man, even in his highest flights of thought and imagination, as rooted in the subconscious depth of the creation. In this Freud is a great Jew. His theory of the male leader of the horde killed by his sons reflects history motivated by Christian teaching. The spiritual/secular division is, from the point of view of the 'mothers', seen as a cold denial of human happiness. And every son revolting against his father will justify the patricide of Christian history by saying 'one has to love God more than one's father'. What Freud thought to be the explanation of primitive history is in fact the explanation of Christian history. Freud, absolutely unversed in theology, is all the more convincing as his theory is based on observation. He observed the whole man, man rooted in the creation. He also observed contemporary history with clinical exactitude, and therefore discovered the patricide in Christian civilisation. 'The pious', as he termed them, were the Christians, and in antisemitic Vienna the Christians were his enemies. Kafka 'saw' a concentration camp before it existed, Freud 'saw' Auschwitz before the world knew the name of this place of patricide.

With his story of patricide, of the murder of the male leader of the horde, Freud discovered a fact which he observed clearly but failed to understand. He discovered a guilt characteristic of a history under Christian influence. Where the Christian tension between spiritual and secular breaks up and leaves a secular history without spiritual influence, secular history begins with guilt, the consequence of which cannot be eradicated by future events. Freud discovered the guilt complex, guilt as a sickness of the mind. The guilt complex is different from real guilt, from authentic guilt for which man is responsible before society and God. Besides the guilt complex and authentic guilt a third guilt exists, which Freud also discovered and which he described in his story of patricide. The third guilt is 'built in' in history, and is recognised by Christian theology as original sin. It is the guilt of the first step which man makes when being creative without God. Man, the creature of God, assuming the role of his maker, burdens himself with guilt. This guilt becomes a burden like the guilt complex, and it has its vengeance like authentic guilt, but it is different from both. Original sin is the guilt in history where the Christian gentile interrupts the course of the created world by making a new beginning. How can man as creator avoid becoming a rebel against God who alone is creator? This question means: how can original sin be avoided? This is the Christian question, and Christianity offers the answer in its doctrine of redemption. It speaks of redemption, and redemption is more than forgiveness, it makes undone what has been done. Such redemption, Christianity teaches, is achieved through the sacrifice of a ransom.

On the Jewish Day of Atonement the Jew says before God: 'I have sinned'. He does not say 'I am a sinner', in the way the Christian does. The Jew confesses 'I have sinned', and the Jewish liturgy answers with the word of God: 'I have forgiven.' On the Day of Atonement the Jew confesses his sins in all humility, he prays *'with* the sinners'. Although man has been created in possession of a 'pure soul', he is drawn into the contest of good and evil. Every man falls into the trap of sin. This does not make man a sinner who is a fallen angel through original sin. Christianity sees him as a sinner through no personal fault but through a creation to which the biblical attribute 'very good' would not be applicable. Paul Tillich once said, in a Jewish–Christian dialogue: 'I have met Jews who were very good people. But there is one fault which they all have: they have no sense of sin'. What Tillich should have said is: 'they do not understand the meaning of original sin'. Men who remain rooted in creation while being active in history do not understand why the resort to original sin is needed.

The Christian, with his confession 'I am a sinner', wants more than God's forgiveness. He wants God to change an existing situation. The Christian hope is redemption from a sin which burdens every Christian but which he has committed without any chance of avoiding it. Every Christian is born a gentile and aspires through faith in the only Christian, Christ, to rise to a spiritual existence. No Christian regards himself as born a Christian. He can become one by leaving his gentile status behind, by becoming a 'new Adam', integrated into the 'second creation' and therefore freed from original sin. The statement 'the Jew is born a Jew' means: man born of woman can meet God. Creation is without the blemish of original sin.

An action can be forgiven, but the man who has broken away from his status as a creature of God needs more than forgiveness, he needs redemption, that redemption which the Gospels preach as their good tidings. It is a redemption achieved through a sacrifice. In the Old Testament God holds Abraham back from slaughtering Isaac; in the New Testament Isaac is sacrificed. The blood of the scapegoat redeems others from their sin, from the sin which cannot be forgiven and which needs redemption. The Christ of the Gospels is not the only scapegoat. Christ, the one scapegoat, stands for many scapegoats, for the hecatombs of sacrifices which history devours: soldiers, martyrs, Jews. Golgotha repeats itself on thousands of battlefields, in the permanent revolution of Christian history, in Auschwitz. The scapegoat is killed. Judaism, the faith of the prophets in which Abraham does not sacrifice Isaac, is a faith without a scapegoat. A Christianity not rooted in Judaism will see the death of a scapegoat, the death of soldiers, martyrs and Jews, in a spiritual light, and, in the context of the Gospels, as unavoidable. Jew and Christian preach good tidings for man's future, they proclaim the possibility of progress. But Christian dogma sees progress as unavoidably connected with heroism and martyrdom in war and revolution. The Jew believes in a peaceful way of progress. *Pax* was the message to the fratricidal gentiles of the Roman Empire. *Shalom,* peace for mankind seen as a family, is a message to Jew, Christian and gentile.

Herder, one of the leading German Romantics, said that each nation has its great hour in history. In its 'great hour' a nation rises in creative power to the moment which is different from the ever identical stream of human birth, life, and death and also different from the eternal cycle of the stars and the seasons. What happens in the 'great hour' is history; it is performed by masses of men, but the masses act as if they were not many but were a single actor. After the 'great hour' nothing is as it was before.

1914 was Europe's 'great hour': the flower of the manhood of the European nations went in selfless submission and in exalted spirit to the Golgotha of their battlefields. 1918 proved to be only an armistice, and when in 1945 the liberation arrived, the *churban* of Auschwitz, Treblinka, and Belsen became known to the world. Heroism and martyrdom were near to each other. To distinguish between them appeared to be wrong. In each case human beings had been sacrificed. Soldiers and Jews had been killed, they were – in Christian language – crucified. In the language of Isaiah 53 the Christian gentiles can speak sentences which portray the Jewish inmate of the concentration camps:

> as one from whom men hide their face:
> He was despised, and we esteemed him not.
> Surely our diseases he did bear, and our pains he carried.

1914 cannot be explained only by referring to nationalism, imperialism, patriotism, diplomatic shortsightedness and the lack of imagination on the part of the military. In the songs of the youngsters and in the sorrows of the adults there was a rising above everyday life, a readiness for sacrifice, and therefore there was something holy, something spiritual, in those who marched away. Sacrifice is holy. Martyrs need not look, or be, as they were depicted by the less gifted painters of the Middle Ages. Martyrs can be of the ordinary kind. A soldier is a soldier. He smokes his pipe, enjoys a drink and likes a joke. But the soldier's march to his 'great hour' often turns out to be his crucifixion. 1914 was the great hour which put an end to the world of the fathers. The sons died and their death was the end of Europe's world of the fathers. The Middle Ages, still preserved in many pockets of resistance, collapsed in ruins. This is what happened in the years 1914–1945. The Eastern European bearded Jews represented the old European world of the fathers, destined to die. They died, but not in battle; they died by murder. It was a patricide of six millions.

We know very little about the exact moment in history when Christianity became separated from Judaism. Crucifixions often occurred in Roman Palestine and everywhere in the Roman Empire. But we do know the events of the years 1914–1945. The 'great hour' of those years was a revolution in the midst of which we are still living. Sons went new ways. In all the capitals of Europe, in the villages and in the hamlets, the sons marched away in August 1914 with an enthusiasm which today is difficult to understand, unless we remember what the heart of the young is like. It is full of love, but not that love which binds human being to human being. It is something else. It is a love burning to render the greatest sacrifice. The sons marched away filled with sacrificial love. They marched towards an altar. They marched as crusaders determined to fight infidels and to conquer the holy city.

Golgotha, the story of the crucifixion, is not recorded in a way which allows us to sort out in neat detail: here is the father, here is the son. In the carnage of battle it is not like that either. The dead are fathers, and the dead are sons. But the Gospels seem to adopt a position which they assume to be accurate. On the Cross hangs a son. Why a son? Was it not the son who rebelled against the father? Was not the deicide in which a man with the image of God in himself was killed *patricide?* Should not the man on the Cross be a bearded patriarch of the kind which the Germans mocked, murdered and tortured in Poland? In the Orthodox Church icons portray a bearded Christ who is no longer young. This is strange only to the western mind; it reminds us that father and son are one, and that the tragedy of the one is connected with the tragedy of the other.

The Tomb of the Unknown Warrior, that modern form of the symbol of the Cross, commemorates the dead of two world wars. When a man is killed, deicide occurs. The Christian symbol of the God killed by man cannot but remind Christians of the Jews who perished, because Christians shouted 'Kill the Jews!' It is a Christian story which tells of people shouting their antisemitic 'Crucify him, crucify him!' This story repeated itself in Auschwitz and the other camps which the Germans built, as the Romans erected the Cross when they set out to kill.

Chapter 29

APOCALYPSE AND *CHURBAN*

When Auschwitz is now called an 'apocalyptic event', Christian terminology is being used. The New Testament Apocalypse belongs to the type of writing which is nowadays called underground literature. The enigmatic phraseology is necessitated by the impossibility of speaking freely in a time of persecution. To speak of the 'Apocalypse of Auschwitz' puts the early Christians living in an anti-Christian Roman period on the same level as the Jews under Nazi terror. 'The Four Horsemen of the Apocalypse' who were given 'power over a quarter of the earth, with the right to kill by sword and by famine, by pestilence and wild beasts' (Revelation 6:8), did indeed ride through the world from the Atlantic coast of France up to North Africa and Southern Russia. Those who carried out these killings on a massive scale 'worshipped the beast also, and chanted, Who is like the Beast? Who can fight against it?' The beast was allowed to mouth bombast and blasphemy and was given the right to reign. 'It opened its mouth in blasphemy against God, reviling his name and his heavenly dwelling. It was also allowed to wage war on God's people' (13:4–7).

Apocalypse is the Greek word for revelation. John sees God on his throne, and near him 'the lamb'. The lamb, the animal sacrificed on the altars of Jerusalem, represents Christ in a Christian exegesis of a verse from the Servant of God texts: 'He is brought as a lamb to the slaughter' (Isaiah 53:7). If the ashes of those buried in Auschwitz were not those of Jews, Christian sentiment would find it appropriate to erect a huge cross at Auschwitz as a fitting memorial. But it cannot be done.[1] Auschwitz means six million Jewish martyrs, and

1. [Ironically, in view of what Maybaum says here, a huge cross *was* subsequently erected by Christians at Auschwitz!]

Christians must stand in awe in the face of a martyrdom in which Jews, not Christians, were the main sufferers and in which Christians are forced to search their consciences and to ask whether they are not implicated in what happened.

The New Testament Apocalypse, or 'Revelation of St John', sees revelation in the framework of a catastrophe taking place in history. How do Jews, on the other hand, connect history with revelation? We have pointed out that according to the Hebrew Bible the creation of the world is the content of revelation. Christian doctrine, however, sees revelation taking place at a distinct point in history. This doctrine makes history all-important, to such a degree that the world, created by God, and God, the Creator, can move into the background of Christian consciousness. The Redeemer is worshipped, the Creator forgotten. The Son is more important than the Father for Christian faith, especially for a faith uprooted from Judaism.

The whole Jewish people today must see itself as the survivors of Auschwitz. Everyone today is a survivor. Western man is a survivor of World Wars I and II. The survivors rub their eyes and are surprised to be alive. They ask: what happened? They ask: what is history? What does history convey to us? Must it convey something, or must it convey nothing? What is the condition under which history can convey something to man?

Moses Mendelssohn is usually seen as the first Jew to enter the postmedieval chapter of the Jewish people. His statement 'history bores me'[2] can be taken as expressing the approach of the Enlightenment which saw past history, especially the Middle Ages, as a dark age, now, at last, moving forward into the age of reason. But Mendelssohn need not necessarily be understood in this way. Perhaps he is in harmony with the Psalmist's attitude towards the gentiles: 'He that sitteth in heaven laugheth, the Lord hath them in derision' (Psalm 2:4). The Psalmist remains passionately interested in history and expresses his contempt, not of history, but of those in history who rebel against God.

Mendelssohn's lack of interest in history represents the attitude of superiority which the European Jew in the Middle Ages displayed towards his surroundings. Outside his ghetto he did not see the 'Christian West', he only saw power politics, bloodshed, brutality and drunkenness.

The Romantic period led, especially in Germany, to the century of the great historians. Jews, too, turned to history and investigated their past. The Jewish historians regarded their work as capable of leading to a gentile rehabilitation of the Jewish people. As soon as

2. See Cassirer, *Die Idee der Religion bei Lessing und Mendelssohn, Festgabe zum zehnjähri-gen Bestehen der Akademie für die Wissenschaft des Judentums* (Berlin, 1929), p.32.

the world realises the holiness of the Jewish past, it was said, the miserable state of the oppressed Jewish people will be seen as injustice and relieved by the civilised nations. The historians will achieve Jewish emancipation. What German Jews called *Wissenschaft des Judentums* was mostly the work of historians; *their* craft was *Wissenschaft* (science, learning). Splendid results were achieved in the century of the *Wissenschaft des Judentums*. Above all, the thought that history is a progressive process filled the Jewish generations between Mendelssohn and 1914 with an optimism which was identified with the very faith of the prophets and the classical rabbis.

This optimism was shattered by the apocalyptic event of the Great War. When events are viewed as apocalyptic, the historian is no longer the person to deal with them. Consequently a critical attitude to the historian made itself felt. He was accused of having become a mere chronicler of meaningless events. 'Tomorrow and tomorrow and tomorrow, a tale told by an idiot, signifying nothing.' Nihilism crept into the hearts of those who had believed in the stability of the contemporary historical world. Death and nothingness stared into their faces, and death and nothingness became the problem of those thinkers who were called existentialists. What was common to them was despair. Sartre's nihilism is, above all, the hangover after the Nazi invasion of France. Sartre's existentialism has its roots in those years of despair, frustration, humiliation and disgust. Heidegger's existentialism had similar reasons. With him it was the defeat of Germany after 1918 which preceded the publication of his main work *Sein und Zeit* (Being and Time) in 1926. Six years earlier Franz Rosenzweig had written his *Stern der Erlösung*. He had written the first notes of this work as a soldier at the front. Nevertheless his message was one of hope and not of despair. The ways in which Franz Rosenzweig belongs to and remains apart from the philosophical school of existentialism have to be carefully considered.

With the exception of Rosenzweig, all the existentialist thinkers from Pascal and Kierkegaard to Heidegger are 'philosophers of despair'. Pascal is the first to feel deeply the loss of the belief in a created world and its replacement by Newtonian–Cartesian 'nature'. He speaks of 'this remote corner of nature' in which man 'should regard himself as lost', he speaks of 'the little prison cell in which man finds himself lodged, I mean the (visible) universe'.[3] But still, Pascal remains faithful to the 'God of Abraham, Isaac and Jacob'. Kierkegaard does not end up in nihilism either. He remains a Christian. He even significantly criticises Hegel, in whose system historical necessity, understood as political necessity, had obliterated the

3. *Pensées,* ed. Brunschvig, p.72.

uniqueness of man. But Pascal and Kierkegaard are not the teachers and forerunners of Sartre. Sartre is like Heidegger, who is entirely a nihilist. In 1933 he addressed the students of Freiburg University as its Chancellor, not in his academic robes, but in S.-A. uniform. When at that time he met his philosophical mentor of many years, Edmund Husserl, he passed the old Jewish sage without greeting him. He may have later deplored the speech which he delivered in 1933, yet he stands in the history of philosophy as the German philosopher in S.-A. uniform. His whole philosophical writings justify this picture as congenial to the philosopher of nihilism who severed all his links with the Christian faith.

Heidegger shares with the German romantics a constant reference to death. There is a romanticism in England, in France, and in Germany, but only in Germany is romanticism preoccupied with death. No nation has pondered over death as much as the German. Clemenceau, who knew the Germans very well although he did not love them, said: 'In the soul of the Germans . . . there is a lack of understanding of what life really is, of life's charm and greatness. How these people love death! One has only to read their poets: everywhere you find the reference to death.' Heidegger, the German existentialist, sees death in the centre of human existence; he defines life as 'running towards death'. How different is Franz Rosenzweig who writes: 'When death unmasks himself in your last hour, he will say to you: "Don't you know me, I am your brother!"' Rosenzweig finishes his great work *The Star of Redemption* with the words: 'Where does the way lead us? Don't you know? It leads into life', and according to his directions to the printers 'life' is to be written in capital letters: LIFE.

Fichte and Hegel led to Heidegger. These two German thinkers regarded themselves and were regarded by others as bringing the spirit of Greece to the German people. This was another way under the prevailing circumstances of expressing the fact that their philosophy cut itself off more and more from Christian roots. In their search for revelation these thinkers look exclusively to history, to man alone, to man without God. In this they resemble the Gnostics of old. Gnosticism was the 'hellenisation of Christianity' (in Harnack's phrase) and post-Kantian German philosophy achieved a hellenisation of the German people. Instead of 'hellenisation' we can also say 'paganisation'. The so-called German philosophy of idealism was a philosophy of history which, like Gnosticism, looked exclusive to Promethean man as the sole creator of history. This was the German heresy, born in the studies of the German philosophers and leading to Nietzsche's nihilism, proclaiming 'God is dead'. A god constructed by the philosophers is a 'dead god'. A god who is only a god of history and not also the creator of the universe becomes a 'dead god'.

Who once has lost
What thou has lost stands nowhere still,

said Nietzsche to modern man, whose universe was no longer creation, but only 'nature', physical nature, and, above all, man-made history.

In the civilised West outside Germany the question 'Can it happen here?' is often asked. It is more revealing to understand why it was bound to happen in Germany. The entire post-Kantian philosophy lost its connection with the West, with Hume and Locke, whom Kant had carefully studied. Fichte, Schopenhauer, Hegel and Nietzsche are the leading philosophers of what in Germany was called 'German idealism' and what in historical perspective is better called German 'Gnosticism'. Faust is the fatherless man, and he is the German Prometheus who inspired the post-Kantian philosophers. Faust, the Ego without family and fellow man, becomes in Fichte's and Schopenhauer's solipsism the Atlas of Homeric mythology and the maker of history. Goethe's 'way to the mothers', his reverence of nature as the Great Mother, was a rebellion against the father. The rabbis of the Hellenistic age and the Church of that time recognised the danger of Gnosticism. Nobody, or too few, rejected German Gnosticism, with its Marcionite anti-Jewishness. Hitler came. It was bound to happen.

Where history is emancipated from the world created by God and becomes a process without a transcendent realm beyond man, the door is open to nihilism. The philosophy of history of Fichte and Hegel was bound to lead to the nihilism of Heidegger. In a letter written on April 12th 1926, Goebbels defined nihilism as 'the courage to destroy, to crush those things which were once holy to us, such as tradition, education, friendship and human love'. Auschwitz is the monument of German nihilism. German university professors had educated German youth to see in the history of the German nation a self-sufficient 'absolute'. When this history faced its disaster in 1918, the believers in a holy German history were left with nothing. The way to nihilism was open.

German post-Kantian idealistic philosophy generated that nihilism which eventually led to Auschwitz. The Germans were taught from school to the grave to seek edification entirely in history. Victories and battles, revolutionary and conservative enactments, in fact human acts alone, were seen as the creators of history. History was reduced to visible facts, and what invisibly moves history from outside, from a sphere transcending history, was not considered.

Where man makes himself the Atlas of history, the breakdown is bound to follow. Nietzsche with his 'God is dead' merely diagnosed the end-result of the German philosophy of history. When man looks only to history to find revelation and blasphemously calls the world a creation of the human Ego, of man's *Erzeugung* (production), as Fichte does, or when he sees the world as 'World as Will and Imagination', the title of Schopenhauer's main work, he encounters in history a non-Ego. A non-Ego created by mere abstraction, the *via negativa* of the materialist, is a nothing. This nothing must be identified in one way or another and was eventually seen as something cruel, as Moloch. This was the way of German philosophy leading to Hitler and Goebbels. German philosophy was unable to halt the invasion of Germany by the Austrian Nazi ideology.

Fichte and Hegel still thought of themselves as 'Greeks'. They were Greeks not like Plato but like the Christian Gnostic Marcion. In speaking of an Absolute they still thought they were speaking of the demiurge of Greek philosophy. But they soon moved away from the demiurge of an ordered cosmos. A cosmos with an immanent logos was associated in Pharisaic Palestine with the Jewish teaching of a world created by God. But a philosophically-constructed Absolute is a nothing. This Absolute may be thought of as a transcendent being, but it has lost the characteristic of that transcendence with which the God of the Hebrew Bible is associated. No *nomos* emanates from this philosophical transcendence, no law for the world and none for human action. To quote Heidegger's interpretation of Nietzsche: 'The phrase "God is dead" means that the supra-sensible world is without effective force'.[4] Hans Jonas confessed that Heidegger's philosophy was the key which unlocked the closed door which had for so long barred his way to an understanding of Gnosticism. In antiquity Gnosticism rejected the testimony of the universe pointing to a benevolent creator. The Gospel of Marcion shows the gnostic contempt for a 'Jewish God', i.e. for a creator-God. 'Turning up their noses, the utterly shameless Marcionites take to tearing down the work of the Creator: "Indeed," they say, "a grand production, and worthy of its god, is this world!"'.[5]

German nihilism was radically different even from Gnosticism. German antisemitism is also different from Marcion's anti-Jewishness, from his rejection of the Old Testament. Marcion's Gnosticism was a Christian heresy, but it was still Christian. The German nihilism of the Nazis was a revolt against two thousand years of Christianity. German nihilism makes the German Siegfried more responsible for Auschwitz than the rest of the Western world in the

4. *Holzwege*, p. 200.
5. Tertullian, *Against Marcion*, 1.13.

nineteenth century. The West to some degree also confessed a Christianity of the Marcionite pattern, forgetting the Creator as against the Redeemer and blind to the rightful place of the Jew in a Christian civilisation.

After the defeat of Hitler, Georges Bernanos wrote the following remarkable letter to Karl Barth:

> Nothing is left to us, I think, except to pray for Germany silently and from the depth of our soul. We must pray for Germany which, though defeated, has not yet arrived at the end of her destiny. Perhaps it is a wonderful sign of her destiny that she is given freedom, to suffer her terrible experience to the bitter end. May it please God to let Germany suffer, in her soul and in her flesh, according to the measure of her unlimited ability to suffer. May it please God that Germany repent entirely and abundantly, even beyond human strength. When she has paid for her guilt in the cry of her heart seeking expiation, may she also atone for our sins and gain expiation for the victorious nations who are not worthy to be her judges.

These wonderful words were written by a Frenchman to a Swiss at a time when Germany was in ruins. That seems long ago, today. Today Germany is the country of the economic miracle, and a new generation has grown up which wants to forget and to be acquitted of the verdict which the older generation had to accept. This new generation may say: 'The fathers have eaten sour grapes, why should the children's teeth be set on edge?' (Ezekiel 18:2).

Mankind is an indivisible whole. The Western nations, as Bernanos implies and as the Germans now readily repeat, are implicated in the German guilt. The whole Christian West stands accused in the face of Auschwitz. But it should not be overlooked that the philosophy of nihilism had its stronghold in Germany and followed as a logical consequence from preceding German history. The deification of the state and the assumption of revelation within culture, within the various forms of art, was the German blasphemy.

Adolf Harnack (1851–1930), the renowned German church historian, himself a liberal and in his private life not an antisemite, displayed all the animosities of Marcion against the Old Testament. Like Marcion he praised the New Testament as the Gospel of Redemption and decried the value of the Old Testament. He made his choice of what he liked and what he disliked in the Old Testament – and he disliked certain essential parts of it.

In view of the close relationship between the Apocalypse of John and the gnostic book *The Gospel of Marcion* it appears quite appropriate for Christians today to speak of the 'apocalyptic event' of Auschwitz. In the Apocalypse of John 'apocalypse' means revelation, but revelation in which history reveals Moloch. Adolf Hitler, hailed by Germans as the Redeemer, turned out to be the Moloch, bringing death and destruction. A history in which man alone is the Promethean agent, a history in which man and not God who created heaven and earth is the Lord of history, leads to catastrophe. We Jews can therefore agree when Auschwitz is called an apocalyptic event, an event revealing Moloch in history. In Nazi Germany the Moloch was a reality.

It is time for the pinpricks and superficialities of the Christian apologists who speak of the 'Moloch in Yahve' and censure him for demanding Abraham's son as sacrifice to stop. The death of the six million in Auschwitz, of the many more millions which the age of Auschwitz devoured in violence and cruelty, can be understood by the Christian as the price to be paid for the Christian doctrine of original sin, or as the sacrifice which has to be rendered in a history under the sign of the 'lamb', under the sign of the 'crucified son'. For the Jew every war is an unnecessary war, progress in history and faithfulness to God are possible without the sacrifice of Isaac. In a Christian understanding of history Isaac is sacrificed on the altar of God. In the Christian understanding any progress, including the progress from Hitler and Stalin towards an age which is once again human and ruled by man's fear of God, inevitably involves the shedding of the martyr's blood.

True, the martyrs are dead. So far the Christian exegesis of Genesis 22, the Christian view of the encounter of Abraham with God, is correct. Jewish exegesis, on the other hand, sees this encounter as a trial. It is the temptation of Abraham. Abraham is 'tested'. Thus it says in the first verse of this chapter, which no man can ever read and remain calm. Breathless, and with his heart beating, the reader hears God saying: '"Abraham"; and he said: "here am I". And he said: "Take now thy son, whom thou lovest, even Isaac, and get thee into the land of Moriah; and offer him there for a burnt-offering upon one of the mountains which I will tell thee of"' (Genesis 22:1,2). The commandment 'Thou shalt love the Lord thy God with all thine heart, and with all thy soul and with all thy might', and the commandment to Abraham, 'give me what is more precious to you than your own life', are one and the same. But what is really demanded from Abraham – and herein lies the difference between the Jewish and the Christian exegesis – is Abraham's *readiness* to offer the sacrifice; the sacrifice itself is not demanded – a fact which was not known beforehand. Abraham could only be truly tested when the sacrifice was demanded in absolute seriousness.

The Jewish martyrs of the third *churban* have gone. They have gone like the millions of others sacrificed on the altar of the Nazi Moloch. But after the third *churban* the surviving Jewish people is still on trial; every Jew is tested in his faithfulness to the God of his fathers. Auschwitz proved the utter political weakness of the Jewish people. Every Jew who remains a faithful Jew after Auschwitz is Abraham steadfast amid the uncertainty whether God will decide to accept or not to accept the sacrifice. After Auschwitz, Jews who believe in God, the just and merciful, pass the test in which they are tried today, as Abraham was tried before them. Jews must see the third *churban*, as their ancestors saw the first and the second *churban*, as a victory of God. *Churban* is not only the destruction of the old order, it is also progress into a new chapter of history. We, the Jewish people after Auschwitz, make this statement and proclaim the victory of God. In doing so we are in a state of mind which we often witness in the Psalmist: he cries out against his predicament and yet rejoices in the victory of God.

The first *churban*, the destruction of the Temple of Solomon – let us repeat the often-reiterated lesson of Jewish history – made the Jewish people a people of the Diaspora. For the first time mankind had in its midst a people without a land and without a state and yet pursuing a mission in history, a holy mission. The second *churban*, the destruction of the Temple of Herod, signified the end of the Maccabean State and established the synagogue in the Mediterranean world. For the first time mankind saw a form of worship in which no blood was shed: prayers took the place of sacrifice; worship was constituted by the spoken word alone. The third *churban*, the *churban* of our time, also destroyed a holy Jerusalem: the religio-cultural unity of the Ashkenazi and Sephardi Diaspora in Europe and North Africa, the medieval unity created by the rabbinic interpretation of the Jewish law. The medieval frame of the Jewish people is destroyed; after the third *churban* it must either live as a westernised Jewry or disappear from the scene of history. What has been destroyed had lasted as long as the Roman Empire, which finally went down with the end of the Hapsburg, Hohenzollern, Tsarist and Ottoman empires. Their end and the end of rabbinic law have the same historical reason: the end of the Middle Ages. The interpretation of Jewish Law remained unchanged from the days of the Mishnah to the third *churban*. The medieval civilisation, Jewish, Christian, Islamic, is over. The Jewish Middle Ages lasted longest. After the third *churban* the attire woven in the Middle Ages is no longer appropriate for the Jewish people. Those of us who insist on wearing the kaftan and the Polish fur hat in the twentieth century are like those who nostalgically look back to the times when feudal lords prevented a sensible land reform and the liberation of the peasants in Eastern Europe. But the thousand year old tyranny of the Germans over the Slavs has come to an end. It began with the man-hunt of the

Prussian Templars, who behaved as the S.S. did later, and it ended with the Oder-Neisse line. The Slavs are free. We Jews do not wish to remain Ashkenazim, medieval German Jews, or Sephardim, Jews of the Islamic cultural pattern. We look forward to our new duties as westernised Jews.

To be hopeful or not to be hopeful after the third *churban* – this is the test by which the Jewish people are tried. After Auschwitz it would be natural for Jews to be full of despair. After Auschwitz it would be natural for the Jew to fail in the temptation in which Abraham was tried. We could even say: it would be human for the Jews after Auschwitz to stop being the people which brings the good tidings of the just and merciful God to mankind. By seeing the *churban* not only as an apocalyptic catastrophe, but as the awesome work of God who leads mankind forward, we overcome despair and begin to hope. We ask: what kind of progress after the third *churban?* Where is the victory of God which can be celebrated today, as we celebrated God's victory after the first and the second *churban?* We need not go into details. Hope, if specified, becomes calculation rather than hope. But we can specify the progress which will follow the third *churban* by saying: the Diaspora of the Jewish people, now a people of the post-medieval Western world, will become a world diaspora.

Parallel to the widening of the Jewish Diaspora to a world diaspora is the world diaspora of Christianity. Asia has opened itself to the West, and Christianity will prove itself as the 'eternal youth movement', as the rising of the world of the sons against the world of the fathers. It will, as the eternal mission to the gentiles, convert the Buddhists and rejuvenate Asia.

When Jew and Christian speak to each other in peace, the world has peace. They are, of course, different from each other. We Jews see history realistically. We remember Auschwitz. History is not yet redeemed. With this view we differ from the Christians. The Jew worshipping in his family and testifying in the world to God as the creator of the world, and the Christian worshipping the Redeemer and rejoicing in the world, assumed to be redeemed, are as different from each other as Jew and Gentile are different, and yet they are as near to each other as fathers and sons. It is in the peace prevailing between fathers and sons that the peace of the world grows.

A fatherless generation becomes a generation of cruel zealots, rejecting peace and choosing war. It hails a Messiah and forgets that within history every Messiah is a false Messiah. 'Historic revelation', belief turning to history alone, leads towards an apocalyptic situation: a man who believes in a utopia round the corner is crushed by history, and the many involved in such history perish.

The Cross is the symbol of final messianic redemption. It can also point to the apocalyptic disorder in which zealot sons rise against their fathers on their way through history. The Prophets warned the people: 'The Day of the Lord? It is darkness, not light' (Amos 5:19). The Rabbis warned them, too: 'The Messiah? – I do not want to see him'.[6] Freud warned our own generation: 'The new era is hastened in through patricide'. A cross at Auschwitz would proclaim that what happened was patricide.

Both *churban* and Apocalypse express Jeremiah's terrifying words: 'For death is come up into our windows, it is entered into our palaces, to cut off the children from the street, and the young men from the broad places' (Jeremiah 9:20). But there is a difference, which prompted the Rabbis to exclude books inspired by apocalyptic vision from Holy Scripture. In the Apocalypse of John there is an impostor, a Satan, and he is a false Messiah. This dualism is not overcome by the belief in a true Messiah. The true Messiah exorcises the false Messiah. With the Cross Christianity condemns all the Hitlers of history: this is the glory of Christianity. The choice between the true and the false Messiah remains: this is the predicament of Christianity. A cross at Auschwitz would proclaim the victory over Hitler. But with the word *churban* the Jew looks only to God and to nobody else. The mourning Jew visiting Auschwitz as a pilgrim says *Kaddish,* the prayer praising the Kingdom of God. In this prayer, which is said by a Jew at a graveside, he is alone with his God who is God alone. *Churban,* any catastrophe in history, does not contradict the oneness of God, does not curtail his justice and mercy. In the *churban* no reference to Satan is implied; the visionary of the Apocalypse does not cease to wrestle with him.

Mark 13:12, usually called the 'little Apocalypse', reads: 'Brother will betray brother to death, and the father his child; children will turn against their parents and send them to their death.' In the Talmud we find a similar saying: 'It has been taught: Rabbi Nehorai said: In the generation when the Messiah comes, young men will insult the old, and old men will stand before the young (to give them honour); daughters will rise up against their mothers, and daughters-in-law against their mothers-in-law. The people shall be dog-faced, and a son will not be abashed in his father's presence.'[7] But Mark has this advice for the Christian community: 'Those who are in Judaea must take to the hills' (13:14). Christians are involved in the apocalyptic catastrophe as individuals. The Jewish people are exposed to the *churban* as a people. Christians stand with one foot in the gentile camp. Jews are totally exposed.

6. Babylonian Talmud, *Sanhedrin* 98ᵃ.
7. Babylonian Talmud, *Sanhedrin* 97ᵃ.

The phrase 'when the Messiah comes' is not biblical. Demythologised it means: with the breakdown of the old order the new one will arrive. 'The Day of the Lord' is a biblical phrase. The Apocalypse refers only to hopeless catastrophe. The concept of *churban* points also to the renewed and purified order, once again in God's creation. 'When the Temple was destroyed, the Messiah was born', was the rabbinic consolation after the second *churban*.

In the rational age of Freud, evil forces, which are recognised by the religions as morally wicked, were only observed elements of the unconscious seeking blindly for outlets. Freud observed the hatred between the various nationalities of the decaying Austrian Empire. He observed 'fraternal hatreds'. But, being a Jew, Freud was more occupied with the hatred of the son against the father. The Hungarians who hated the Slovaks, the German-speaking Austrians who hated the Czechs, were all involved in fratricidal strife. Patricide compared with fratricide lies even deeper in the subconscious layer of the mind. The antisemite in his hatred of the Jew hated not a living human being but a phantom, a figment of his imagination. The fantasy Jew of the antisemite is unconsciously seen as the 'bad' son, the rebellious son full of murderous wishes towards the father, and also as the 'bad' father, the potential torturer, castrator and killer of the son. In the midst of a rational age belief in evil spirits arose as it did in the age of which the above quoted words of the 'little Apocalypse' and of Rabbi Nehorai spoke. An exclusively rational age is not protected against insanity. Freud could heal individual patients. He could not heal his age: he was part of it.

The history of our age has led to an apocalyptic catastrophe. Is there a meaning in the apocalyptic event? Guilt inherent in an age cries to heaven like the blood of Abel killed by Cain. There is a tradition within the Book of Genesis which makes Cain a city-builder; his descendants develop the various arts and crafts of a civilised community. Another tradition in the Book of Genesis describes Abel as the founder of a different kind of community, one not burdened with guilt. An age need not end in apocalyptic disorder. If history remains connected with the world of the patriarchs, of fathers as they live in all ages, man can look forward with hope. On the other hand, when history is reduced to a youth movement, men, young and old, are without any protection against dark powers, against the ruthless assault of irrational forces. Men who are creative in history need not be cut off from the world of the fathers as described in the Book of Genesis. The goal of mankind's progress is not the horror of the apocalyptic end but the eternal return to the holy beginning. Father and son 'both walking together' (Genesis 22:6) are on the path which leads on to those chapters of history in which blessing is showered on mankind.

Part IV

ZION

Chapter 30

ZEAL

We read at the opening of this week's portion of the Law, 'And the Lord spoke unto Moses, saying, Phineas, the son of Eleazar, the son of Aaron the priest, hath turned my wrath away from the children of Israel, in that he was very zealous for my sake among them' (Numbers 25:10).

What does the word 'zealous' mean? It is the same Hebrew word that occurs in the second commandment, 'I the Lord thy God am a jealous God' (Exodus 20:5). Both words in English derive from the same Greek root *zelos*, and jealous, in this sense, is defined as 'watchfully tenacious of one's own or another's rights', so that the two words are synonymous.

The jealous God has and demands jealous, zealous servants, like Elijah, who, as he reviews his life's work and his lonely path fraught with suffering, in which he had always stood firm for God's cause, exclaims: 'I have been very jealous for the Lord God of Hosts.'

This zealousness, this jealousness, means hazarding one's all for God. It is the unsparing, unconditional, uncompromising standing up to the world for God's sake. This zeal is something spiritual. But it is also something passionate. Think of Moses in his anger at the sight of the golden calf, casting the Tables of the Law out of his hands and breaking them, a man full of human wrath and human passion, yet as such a prophet. Spirit becomes passion. Faith becomes passion. Faith becomes ecstasy. Faith becomes impelling, impetuous activity, blazing forth out of ever-renewing flames. Our God, who is a jealous God, wants it so. To this God Elijah is faithful, and in his faithfulness he exclaims 'I have been very jealous for the Lord God of Hosts.'

Now we understand what this zeal is. 'Thou shalt love the Lord thy God with all thy heart, with all thy soul, with all thy might.' This being utterly and wholly for God – with all your heart, with all your soul, with all your might – that is zeal. Anyone who has come in contact with great Jews knows that zeal is a precious quality of a specifically Jewish character. Truth is not a dead conception. Truth is a power, through zealous love. It is only through a warm human heart that truth becomes a light in this world.

When we have learnt from the Bible everything that teaches us to understand zeal as the zeal of faith, as an ecstatic act of love, we must still add something more. The Talmud does not employ the term *Kanaim*, the Hebrew for 'zealots', in any appreciative sense. The zeal that leads to an act of love is religious, is Jewish. The zeal that leads to an act of violence is un-Jewish. The zeal that is the zeal of faith is Jewish; the zeal that leads to political fanaticism is un-Jewish. The word is used in the Talmud in the sense of political zealots, and they are intolerant, sinister and violent. The Talmud has another name for them as well, *Sicarii*, dagger men, assassins. They are the fanatics who, at the time when Rome confronted the Jewish commonwealth, were so un-Jewish and so impolitic as to imagine that what was possible for Rome was also possible for the Jewish people. It was not possible. Neither then nor now.

The idea of Jewish terrorism by which some young people in Palestine think they can improve the situation created by the White Paper[1] is un-Jewish and extremely dangerous for us. I had hoped that in speaking of Jewish terrorism I should have to deal only with the theoretical idea, never with Jewish terrorism as an actual fact. But the deplorable events of the past week force me to confess that we must now face something more than a theory, and though the acts of terrorism committed are few and we pray they may not grow in number, we must definitely speak of Jewish terrorism in Palestine as a reality that exists.

It is hardly necessary to insist on the folly of attempting to put pressure on Britain by such means. But we are concerned not only with the political perversity of a Jewish policy of violence, but also with the fact that it is entirely contrary to every principle of Judaism,

---

1. [The MacDonald White Paper of 17 May 1939 embodied a fundamental change in the attitude of the British Government towards Zionist aspirations in Palestine. Stating clearly that it was not British policy that Palestine should become a Jewish State, the White Paper curtailed Jewish immigration (precisely at a time of acute concern for the Jews of Central and Eastern Europe), and severely limited the transfer of Arab property to Jews. The White Paper was regarded by the Zionist movement as the final betrayal of Britain's obligations to the Jewish people, and was followed by acts of violence against the British Mandatary authorities.]

to all its ideas and its faith. *The Jew is zealous in love, in faith, and in good deeds.* The zealots whom the Talmud repudiates and considers un-Jewish want to be zealous through hatred and strife. The zealots, both in olden times and now, distort Judaism and inflict terrible harm on the Jewish people. We cannot have any partial acceptance of violence. When we realise that the Jewish people cannot survive in a world of violence, we must at all times and everywhere repudiate violence as a weapon, even where violence appears – for it can be only apparently so – to be a means of bringing about some momentary advantage. The gentile nations may have the palm and the sword as the emblems of their political life. Only the palm of peace can be the appropriate emblem of the political life of the Jewish people. We must never forget that the Zionist greeting is *shalom.* And *shalom* means peace.

The admirable behaviour of Palestine Jewry does not put this sacred Zionist greeting to shame. Only a few hotheads and fools, dangerous fools at that, seek to reproduce today the type of the old zealot and so recreate the dangerous situation which resulted in the destruction of the Jewish commonwealth in Palestine in the Hellenistic age.

Almost everyone of us has children, relatives or friends in Palestine today, and when we write to them we should all add a few lines in our letters stressing the importance of *havlaga*, that attitude of restraint which in a world that lauds violence as a means of conducting politics repudiates violence as a means of conducting Jewish politics. We are no impotent pacifist theorists, our aim is not to shirk military service. Jews fought at the front in the last war and fought well. Wherever we share as free people in the destiny of the nation in whose midst we live, the Jew has proved himself a valiant soldier. And the Roll of Honour on which we have proudly inscribed the names of those Jews who have shed their blood for their fatherland includes also the names of the brave men in Palestine who today stand at their posts in defence of Jewish settlement and Jewish labour against Arab terrorism. But we are Jews, and we continue to be Jews in our political life, too. If we were to think or act differently, it would mean for us annihilation and spiritual emptiness. For those Jews who would apply violence in Palestine for the supposed good of Jewry we have only the repudiation of the Talmud, which describes them as zealots. The zealot in politics is an un-Jewish figure. The dream of the Jewish state is for the most part a dream of unpolitical Jews who have little comprehension of the meaning of a state.

Theodor Herzl, who coined the term 'Jewish state', was certainly not a man without political understanding. He knew well what politics mean. But he lived in a liberal era that had no idea of the demonic aspect of the state. Even the state that is founded on justice has its roots in the demonic. For the state is the administration of force. The Jewish people is the people which has no force. God willed it so. The Jewish zealot, the political zealot who wants the establishment of a Jewish structure of force and power for the achievement of Jewish aims in Palestine, who seeks to build up a Jewish state in one form or another, repudiates the Jewish mission of the chosen people. This requires of us that we should serve as priests, that we should, without possessing power, realise justice. But where a state uses its power to realise justice we serve it as citizens of Jewish faith. To the credit of modern Jewry the Jew as a zealot – successfully combated by Zionism – is a solitary appearance, but the Jew as a loyal citizen is the rule. We Jews serve the states of Christendom in their struggle for civilisation, for, humanity, for justice.

Yet the zealot may be a Jewish figure, so much so that he becomes an example. Wherever zeal converts faith into glowing conviction, to a belief so firm that no defeat can shake it, the result is a Jewish attitude of mind. The life of a man like the Jewish philosopher Hermann Cohen was aglow right through with a sacred fire such as glowed in Elijah who, at the end of his life, could exclaim, 'I have been very jealous for the Lord God of Hosts' (1Kings 19:10). Hermann Cohen turned the little university town of Marburg into a German Athens. Marburg and Hermann Cohen became identified in the mind of every intellectual person in Germany, Jew or Christian. As a German philosopher, as the man who gave new life to Kantian philosophy, Hermann Cohen believed that he could prove through the success of his work that antisemitism, this monster in the field of the civilised nations of the world, could be finally kept within bounds by the progressive spirit of the time. For Hermann Cohen expected that the spirit of this pre-1914 era, the spirit of political liberalism, would bring about the fulfilment of his Messianic hopes: peace between the nations of the world and harmonious relations between them and Israel. Hermann Cohen had to carry both these hopes to their grave in his old age. The war refuted his optimistic faith in the coming victory of reason, and Ludendorff's antisemitism showed him that antisemitism could be not merely a mob ideology but also the official programme of a political leader. Hermann Cohen was accustomed to dismiss the ingratitude that ignored his great achievements for Germany with the bitter remark: 'But they will give me a marvellous funeral'. He believed that all who represent intellectual Germany would come and stand by his grave and deliver grateful speeches paying tribute to him as the man who had renewed Kantian philosophy, and would emphasise that this observant religious Jew was a great German. He was also mistaken in this. It is true that he was given a marvellous funeral. The grateful Jewish people bore its great son to his grave. Gratefully they paid reverence to the memory of this great Jewish thinker. Beside these sorrowing Jews stood a group of Christians, no official delegation of any significance. Yet even so, a comfort and a consolation at such a time, because of their community of fellowship with the Jews.

Hermann Cohen had devoted the last years of his life to the exposition of the Jewish faith; with his philosophically trained mind he had expounded the ideas of Judaism in the language of the time. Franz Rosenzweig, one of his outstanding pupils and his equal as a thinker, has left us a revealing picture of the noble zealot Hermann Cohen. 'I hope I shall still live to see the days of the Messiah,' Hermann Cohen once remarked to Rosenzweig. Rosenzweig, startled by this extravagant expression of faith, yet unwilling to remonstrate with his old teacher, ventured to suggest: 'Yes, perhaps in hundreds of years' time.' Hermann Cohen, who was a very old man, did not hear distinctly, and thought Rosenzweig had said, 'In a hundred years' time.' 'No!' he exclaimed, 'don't say in a hundred years' time. Say fifty years.' This is not naiveté, it is zealousness. Those who know Hermann Cohen's life and writings will bear me out. It is a glowing conviction defying all onslaughts and not to be rebuffed by any reverses, like that which all his life animated Elijah who, at the end of his life could exclaim, 'I have been very jealous for the Lord God of Hosts'.

We read at the opening of this week's portion of the Law, 'And the Lord spoke unto Moses, saying, Phineas, the son of Eleazar, the son of Aaron the priest hath turned my wrath away from the children of Israel, in that he was very zealous for my sake among them'. To turn away God's wrath from this world must surely be mankind's supreme task today, when we realise, horror-struck, how low we have sunk in our cultural life, how the descent to barbarism has become the characteristic feature of our epoch. Israel's suffering in this period shows us clearly what has come upon mankind as a whole. Mankind has suffered a terrible reverse. The barometer of our suffering proclaims it to all. If we are to surmount these bitter times we must have genuine zeal, the zeal of love, faith and good deeds. There are many hardships in the story of a human life as there are in the history of mankind. Zealous faith is the only faith that stands firm. May God strengthen Israel and all men in this zeal.

Chapter 31

POLITICAL IDEALISM

We Jews, fascinated by political idealism, will discover that our Jewish distinction between holy and profane is no longer applicable in the political realm. What is real is either holy or profane. But the world of politics makes us face the non-real, the ideal sphere of the various political myths. Attracted by these myths – in Zionism the myths of nation and state – we shall unexpectedly become involved in the dilemma ideal/material, and eventually in the Christian dilemma of spiritual/secular.

A Jewish state presents us with a secular world, which we call secular Judaism. The Christians' point of view is that a secular world can become spiritualised. With Zionism lending spiritual splendour to the political values of secular Judaism, we are implicated in a Christian dilemma; we are drifting towards an assimilation to Christianity, and, so far, without experience where it will lead to. A whole Jewish generation is educated to pay homage to what is not Judaism.

The hero-soldier dying for the state stands in his self-denial at the point where Christianity can begin to preach. Christianity, pointing to the crucified Messiah, has a message for the political sector of human life, where the iron rule prevails that somebody must die that others can live. In our admiration for heroism displayed now so splendidly in Israel, we are challenged by something which is great and noble, and yet not Jewish. That it is not un-Jewish either shows only that hard thinking will be necessary in this newest process of our assimilation to Christian idealism.

The death of the soldier is a noble tragedy. Dare we say: It is *kiddush hashem* (sanctification of the name of God)? Dare we use this expression in regard to the gallant Jewish youth who died fighting the Arabs? Did they only die for a state? We speak of *kiddush hashem* where a man dies for God. The death of our six and a half million brothers who lost their lives in the years 1933–1945 was *kiddush hashem*.

We Jews may be fascinated by the nobility of Greek pagan idealism surrounding the soldier who dies defending his fatherland. We may and we do respect the faith which sees the death of the soldier in the light of the New Testament story of the crucified Messiah. We may admit that political life with its unavoidable tragedy needs to be raised into a non-political and truly religious sphere. But we have to know what is Judaism, what is pagan idealism and what is Christianity. We have to know that Judaism is the message of the good life; this message says that a life in which tragedy is avoided is, through the mercy of God, possible, that it is not ignoble, that it miraculously exists again and again. As Jews we must preach Judaism. We shall adopt the philosophy and practice of idealism in politics and culture; we shall not ignore Christian spirituality and we understand it as implicit in Judaism. But idealism and Christian spirituality are not Judaism.

Calling those who conceived the idea of a Jewish state 'non-religious' Jews does not get us far. It only tells us what these Jews are not. But if we say that they are idealists, we make a positive observation which can be enlarged and eventually fully elucidated.

To say that idealism and Judaism are not the same is very important, but it is not enough. We have to say also that under certain conditions which have to be carefully investigated a synthesis of Judaism and idealism is possible. We have proof in our history, in the Hellenistic chapter of history and in the history of nineteenth-century Jewry, that Western idealism and Judaism are capable of becoming combined in a creative synthesis.

The justification of idealism lies in the fact that it is the philosophy of a man who is in the middle of a job. As long as the Messiah is still to come, man is in the middle of a job. The world is finished and glorious, as the Psalmist repeatedly proclaims. But man has his hands full: he must feed the hungry, house the homeless, educate the primitive. The workman has a plan according to which he proceeds; the ideal is the plan for the work which must be done. The Jew may say: idealism as method is justified, but as faith it is noble paganism and needs the Christian corrective. Those who build states may do something beneficial, justifying even heavy costs, but those who worship the state are idol worshippers. Those who spread culture are doing a necessary work of education, but those of us who make culture, even Jewish culture, a substitute for faith in God have strayed away from Judaism.

Idealism is a fine flower growing out of the soil of despair. Leo Baeck once spoke to me about a Hebrew writer whom he had as his guest at his Sabbath table in Berlin. When grace was said, this man, who came from Eastern Europe, where Jews were suffering and living without freedom, refused to join in the prayer; he remained silent and bit his lips rather than say the responses required by tradition from those around the table. This despair explains and justifies the Jewish idealism which eventually led to a Jewish state.

The ideal can be a political ideal or it can be the ideal of beauty and harmony inspiring the artist. To the Jew the ideal is still part of reality. We Jews are not deceived by the might and splendours of Olympus. It is the merit of Karl Marx to have shown the dark earth in every ideal. Like the prophets jeering at those who in their idols manufacture their gods, Karl Marx showed that the ideal world is a superstructure above human interests. The gods of idealism are man-made gods. But this is not the whole story. To recognise the ideal as earth-born power is a necessary analysis of what pretends to be superhuman. After that, the task of creating order out of chaos is still there. This task is done by Western man. He is the idealist who builds up his state and through culture creates a world-wide society of men and women who read books and appreciate the works of the artists.

Marx, with his apocalyptic hope that the state would wither away after the proletarian revolution, was blind to the mission of the state. The state did not wither away in the land where Marxist ideology was made the ruling dogma; there the most totalitarian state was established. Everywhere in the world new states came into existence. Israel, this holy name of a people who are subject to no one but the king of the world, is now the name of a state. The state cannot confer the brotherhood to which we aspire in our Jewish congregation; the fellowship of man for which we hope and work is conceived by the prophet as a fellowship of families and not of states. But this cannot prevent us from being citizens of a state. We must only be reminded from time to time that the attribute 'Jewish' is due to our messianism. A Jewish state cannot and must not mean anything else than a state of Jews, and not a state embodying Judaism. This, no state can do; the kingdom of God is not a state.

Of course, the Jewish state is a secular state. What else should it be? A state which becomes spiritualised is a church; a state seen as terrestrially holy is a caliphate. Jews can only serve the secular state. The state need not be a pagan institution. It is not so much through a Jewish state but through a 'Jewish' youth movement that Jewish life is in danger of becoming Jewish paganism.

In the German pagan *Wandervogel* the boyish idealist set the standard which the adults eventually accepted. The romanticism of the youth movement protested against rational society, which means civilisation, and fed on the unconscious layer of the mind. The unconscious, given permission to dominate man, is barbarism as distinct from humanism. In imagination the artist awakens the unconscious and makes it articulate; but ordinary man, swayed by the forces of instinct and the unconscious and without a way through creative activity, loses his human dignity and equilibrium. The youth movement became the most dangerous revolt against the city civilisation of the West: life was declared as a fine thing in itself, not in need of a code or machines; what is needed, we were told, are fine bodies and freedom from the town.

The malaise of German youth before and after World War I influenced the Zionist youth movement, in fact it influenced Zionism. What Huizinga calls 'puerilism' penetrated Jewish life. The *hora* may be a Russian or an Arab dance – it is of no importance to know. But it is important to know whether these *hora*-dancing Jewish youths, like the German youths with their ceremonial fire dancing and singing, prefer instinct to reason. Youth led by youth, youth living exclusively on political ideologies, is pagan, whether in Israel or Germany. When the festivals of the Jewish calendar are celebrated not in synagogue and home but in the streets, with torch processions and folk dances, with theatrical bombast reminiscent of Richard Wagner's staging of religion in Bayreuth, it is clear which way this is leading. The prophet speaks about those 'who served their gods upon high mountains and upon the hills, and under every tree' (Deuteronomy 12:2), and sees them as heathens.

A totalitarianism without visible dictatorship is possible, and establishes itself inevitably when political values are the only ones offered to a generation. This kind of totalitarianism threatens us, in Israel and everywhere. The Jewish politician aspiring to be a teacher deprives us of the Jewish content of our life. The replacement of the rabbi by the politician, and the fact that youth is led by youth, transforms the *kehillah,* our Jewish congregation, into a political body, it transforms our Jewish people into a gentile nation, and the Torah, our holy law and doctrine, into myth and ideology.

The argument that political freedom is freedom of political creation is a fallacy. The most precious gift of political freedom is the freedom to withdraw from politics and have a private sphere. The Zionist propagandist sees human dignity only in the man who can unfold his activity in political creation. He sees, therefore, only a decision between political independence and existence as a pariah. But only a very small minority of the vast populations of the free countries of the West have the opportunity to be active themselves in political creative work. They delegate their rights to a political élite, and they devote themselves to doing their daily work, which has nothing to do with political action. Democracy gives all its citizens responsibility in the political sphere, but does not and must not uproot all its citizens from the private sector of life to transplant them entirely into the political arena. A state cannot be a home.

The Zionist misinterprets the whole of Jewish history as a long chapter of slavery, and he proves it, especially, with a distorted picture of Jewry in the Middle Ages. The truth is different. In the centuries preceding the Crusades, Jews had political and economic freedom in Southern France and in the Rhineland, to speak only of the Christian West, unsurpassed even in the liberal nineteenth century. This freedom remained theirs when, under the pressure of the Crusades, they emigrated to Eastern Europe.

In the European Middle Ages the Jew had the freedom to stand outside the totalitarian political and spiritual system. He alone had that privilege, which, although attended by deadly dangers and often leading to martyrdom, must always be seen as such. Sir Isaiah Berlin reads modern totalitarianism into the whole past and speaks of the slavery which, he says, existed 'for the Jewish community for two thousand years'.[1] This statement, typical of every Zionist from Herzl to Ben-Gurion, betrays a misunderstanding both of Judaism and the details of Jewish history. It is a statement of the same calibre as the one which asserts that we prayed for two thousand years for Zion, implying that Zion and the modern Jewish state are identical. But how are we to explain to the Jew who professes the political idealism of the Zionist Romantic what Zion means, has meant, and will mean? Idealism is a religion without God, without hope, without joy and without mercy: it is a religion aspiring to and rejoicing in the spectacle of tragic heroism and is, therefore, far from Jewish messianism. But the word 'Zion' receives its meaning from Jewish messianism alone. In a Judaism without God, Zion may mean anything, but not what it meant for two thousand years.

The history of the Jewish past was state history for only two short periods. The Davidian and the Maccabean states did not last long. But the end of these states did not mean the end of the Jewish people. The message of the Jewish people, important for the whole of mankind, and unknown to pagan antiquity, is the good tidings that man can have human dignity outside the state. The man who does not command need not be a slave. In a society which is nothing but political, created entirely by the politician without the priest at his

1. In *A Hebrew University Garland,* edited by Norman Bentwich (London, 1952).

side, a man is either a master or a slave. The priest is neither; he is free and prepared to obey where he sees that the ruler has a vocation and commands for the sake of justice. But the vocation of the priest is to bless and not to rule.

We Jews serve the Western state; we are satisfied that the State of Israel will remain this type of state. We can give our best in its service, as citizens of the State of Israel or of any state in the Western world. The family, not the state, is the reality which makes us realise that the Kingdom of God is not a mere utopia. The family is the visible pattern of things to come when God is king over all the earth. For that day, prophet and Psalmist do not envisage states or churches, nor a union of states or churches. They speak of God as king alone, and of mankind as a union of families.

Our hearts are with the guardians of the Western state, who safeguard its freedom. We see the glory of the soldiers who defended freedom at Thermopylae and in the Battle of Britain, and we see the glory of those who defended the Yishuv from extermination by the Arabs. We praise Greek, English, American and Jewish heroes as Maccabees.

Our own Maccabean chapter, which reveals the splendour of political idealism, is a Jewish chapter. The priests of the God of Abraham, Isaac and Jacob can, if need be, wield the sword. In its aloofness from the state, Jewish priesthood neither takes the point of view of the conscientious objector nor does it stand for anarchism; the pacifists who 'abjure' violence can only do so because others are committing violence on their behalf. But the Maccabean chapter is the history of the emergency, it is history confronting the exception and not the rule. For the Jewish way of life the example is set by Abraham, who went out into the world to build house and altar and went without the sword. The way of Abraham is the holy way; it is the way into the whole world, into every country: everywhere houses and altars must be built and the swords beaten into ploughshares.

Outside the State of Israel Jews possess their nonpolitical sphere in which they establish their Jewish home, their Jewish congregation, their Jewish social life connecting family with family. In Israel the Jew lives in a political sphere as a Jew. We outside the State of Israel also live in a political sphere, but not as Jews. Jewish boys serve as soldiers in the citizen armies of the Western world. So do the boys in Israel. But there the spirit of the soldier must permeate the whole life, or they are lost in the political danger which is always imminent. We are loyal citizens in England, America, everywhere, but nobody demands from us in the free world of the West that citizenship be our religion. In Israel it is demanded.

For the Zionist the State of Israel is the highest aim in life. This gospel is preached to the Israeli citizen. The young State of Israel has not yet achieved security, and cannot be safe if its citizens regard the family as more important to them than the state. Judaism is never and nowhere easy. I am open to grave misunderstanding when I say, it is easier to be a Jew outside the State of Israel than in the State of Israel. The conditions of the Diaspora are more favourable to the fostering of privacy and independence, which one has when left alone by the state.

As long as Zionism was far off from its goal and a Jewish state out of reach, the Zionists ferociously criticised the modern Jew for complacently dividing his world into two neatly separated halves: his citizenship and his Jewish religion. At that time the Zionists saw the loss incurred by this division. Judaism, the power making the Jew, was reduced to a religion.

Religion may be the liberal's word for church, it may mean the church in its secular manifestation. Religion may be a myth, a philosophy, an ideology or a superstition. The world is full of religions. In Biblical times prophetic monotheism emptied Palestine of the gods, in Hellenistic times it emptied the Greco-Roman world of the gods. Prophetic monotheism is a force that could free our whole world, now ripe for Western civilisation, from the tyranny of various religions. God, not the religions, is the message of the prophets. Every local religion is a false religion. The Jew, at least, must face the world with his whole personality, not being in one respect a citizen and in another a man with his religion. He must not have a dual loyalty: God and the State. God, and nobody besides him, must be his faith.

With the prophetic fire burning within it, Judaism is more than a denomination. A Jew is a Jew not merely in synagogue worship and ritual; he is a Jew in his contributions to all the sectors of life. The Zionist critic saw certain aspects of Jewish life becoming weakened. Have the *Deutsche Staatsbürger jüdischen Glaubens* (German citizens of the Jewish faith), have 'the Englishmen of the Jewish persuasion' sold their birthright of prophetic Judaism for the mess of pottage of citizenship? Were they what German Zionists contemptuously called *'Religionsjuden'*, Jews who narrowed Judaism to a denomination and withdrew it into a separate corner of life? But today, when the State of Israel as a Western state has the duty of separating state and religion, the same question must be formulated differently. The question now is whether the 'Israeli of the Jewish persuasion' will make his appearance, a Jew who is partly a Jew, and partly – and probably in greater part – an Israeli citizen?

Looking back into the history of Jewry after the Emancipation, which bestowed on the Jew the dignity of citizenship, it can be said that the modern Jew could avoid the pitfalls of the new situation. The Jew remained a Jew as a citizen, too. We Jews can serve the state without losing our Judaism. But will this be possible in the different and more difficult circumstances prevailing in the State of Israel? How shall we, in the State of Israel, and indeed everywhere in the Western world, avoid the impact of the state on our Judaism? Will a Jewish state, will the noble determination of the Western Jew to be a citizen, force us to accept a division between a spiritual and a secular sphere and thus to speak Christian language? We can give a negative answer when we see clearly the difference between Jew and Christian as citizens of the state. This negative answer can dispel our fear of an assimilation which brings Jews into proximity to the church while they think they are only citizens of the state.

The state splits human reality into a political and a private sphere. The political sphere makes man into an idealist who puts the cause of collective man higher than the cause of private man. Christianity questions the idealist: 'Where do you get the evidence that your ideal is not an illusion?' And it offers to provide him with the evidence he needs. The ideal world is not an illusion when it is verified in history, even if only in a single case. Christianity provides this single case. Patriotism, the soldier's death in battle, the flag, collective honour, all political values and also all the values revealed to artist and lover, all of them alike meaningless to the nihilist, are guaranteed as meaningful by Christianity. If it was true once that in a human being God and man were one and that this human being defied the laws of nature in regard to birth and death, every ideal receives meaning from this single case. It is not an illusion: every human being can defy nature and can conquer as an idealist. The Christian narrative of the Crucifixion and Resurrection gives the idealist what he needs, something which is not there in his own world. In his creative action the idealist aspires to be like God; he receives from outside idealism the help that saves him from despair, *hubris* and insanity. Christianity lets the idealist enter Jerusalem, the world of the prophets, from which he was so far away. Looking with eyes enlightened by the biblical prophets, Christianity interprets history to the idealist and shows it as a scene open to the help of God, who is just and merciful.

The Jew, becoming a citizen, inherits the dualism created by the state, the dualism between the ideal and the material. Thus he becomes involved in the Christian dilemma of healing this dualism through the distinction spiritual/secular. But the Jew does not need the outside help offered by Christianity. The world of the Jew is the one and indivisible world, seen as the creation of God. It is a world with eternity within it. 'Eternal life has he planted in our midst.' The

Jew serves the ideals of the political pantheon because they are, or insofar as they are, part and parcel of reality. The Christian serves these ideals because he is inspired by the Christian narrative that tells of the precedent in which reality was defied. The Christian idealist is engaged in an *imitatio Christi,* the Jewish idealist is inspired by the possibility that in the political realm, too, he has the opportunity to fulfil the commandment 'Love thy neighbour as thyself'.

Chapter 32

DIASPORA

The Jews belong to a people which lives dispersed among the nations. State and church cannot create walls around a people which lives in a diaspora. The State of Israel must not be allowed to create a type of Jew who is predominantly shaped by the influences issuing from the state. A Jew shaped by the state is a Jewish gentile. A dual loyalty can become the problem of the Israeli Jew, proud of and happy with his Jewish state. The late Chief Rabbi Dr Hertz was afraid of this dual loyalty and distinguished between *Ha-tikvah* Jews and *Shema-Yisrael* Jews.[1] In our loyalty to the Jewish people in Israel we demand that it should not lose the characteristics acquired in the Diaspora. There the Jew is alone with his God, as is the prophet. No creed, no faith in the Pauline sense, binds him to God. God does not let him go, and this makes him a Jew.

   Prophetic Judaism is not merely a list of doctrines, summarized as the 'faith of the prophets'. Nor is it the justification of various utopian programmes and of messianic movements in which a generation expresses the hope for its future. The most adequate way of understanding prophetic Judaism is to realize how different the Jew is from all those who live in the closed society of Christianity or Islam. Nowadays the demand to live in an open society has been acknowledged as the condition of freedom. But those who demand an open society as the truly human form of social existence hardly think of the open society in which the Jewish people has lived during its two-thousand-year-old dispersion. The Jewish people has lived under the conditions which a prophet has to endure. Prophetic Judaism is

1. [I.e. national and religious Jews. *Ha-tikvah* is the Zionist national anthem and *Shema-Yisrael* ('Hear O Israel') is the Jewish declaration of faith.]

Jewish life shaped not by creed but by the conditions of the Diaspora. Jewish life is created by the same force which makes a prophet a prophet. Between God and prophet there is no mediator. Belief has to be upheld, law has to be obeyed, but neither belief nor law is the bond which chains the prophet to God. God takes hold of a man – that is the fate of a prophet. The notion of 'prophetic religion' is a contradiction in terms.

God takes hold of the Jew, has him in his grip. This is achieved by Jewish existence in Diaspora conditions. The end of the Diaspora would be the end of prophetic Judaism. This end would mean the disappearance of the Jew, with his right and his role to stand aloof, to remain separate from the Christian and the Muslim and from all the nations of the world. The joy and elation which have pervaded all sections of the Jewish people since the establishment of a Western Jewish state in the land of the prophets must not blind one to the fact that the Jewish people must remain what it was: a people of the Diaspora. Moses could exclaim: 'I wish that all the Lord's people were prophets and that the Lord would confer His spirit on them all!' (Numbers 11:29). The prayer of Moses demands a great deal, but not the impossible. Yet it is to expect the impossible to suppose that a Jewish state should become free from the division of its citizens into ruler and ruled, into organizer and organized, into those above and those below. The dichotomy which political existence inflicts on man does not permit him to be a whole man. Christian faith and Muslim law are the historical attempts to solve this dichotomy, which does not arise for the individual Jew in the Jewish Diaspora. The Jew speaks to God as a whole man, and this dialogue, as it has lasted in the past millennia, will not break up in the millennia to come. The State of Israel is not outside, but part of, the Diaspora. To carry the yoke of the kingdom of God means to carry the yoke of the *galut* (exile). Living under the conditions of the Diaspora, the Jew carries the yoke of the kingdom of God. The rise of the State of Israel may wipe away the tears which we shed over the holocaust, but it is not a messianic event. We must distinguish between the true messiah and the false messiah. In regard to political messianism we always were and will always remain unbelievers. The difficulties Israel faces are not those of a really sovereign state but those of a Diaspora people, sorely dependent on world powers. Israel's present situation is a microcosm of that of mankind.

Jewish life under the conditions of the Diaspora rules out both national and denominational unification of the Jewish people. The Zionist acknowledges the impossibility of a national unity of Diaspora Jewry and therefore thinks little of the positive role which the Diaspora is called upon to fulfil. The ingathering of the exiles, as

Jewish nationalists understand it, would be the desired end of the Diaspora and would make the Jewish people similar to the gentiles: one nation on one and the same soil. Besides being utopian in a most sterile way, this hope sidesteps the prophetic vision of the one world, of the one mankind. 'Gather in the exiles' is the messianic prayer for integration of all nations into one mankind under the kingship of God. The exiles who turn to God with the prayer for the ingathering of the exiles are men in fear of men, men lacking freedom. The exiles crave to return to God's peace, to *shalom*. The Jewish people with its messianic prayer for the redemption of the exiles is like the priest who prays for mankind. In the Diaspora we are without the protection of the nation state, we are entirely thrown upon God. He is our shield, or we are lost. This is the prophetic situation of every Jew, be he a simple small shopkeeper or a luminary of science or art. The Diaspora makes the Jew. This is how the election of God works.

Chapter 33

HELP ISRAEL

'And he said, make a path, make a path, clear the way, take up the stumbling block out of the way of my people' (Isaiah 57:14). This is the message of our prophetic lesson today. The prophet who is the author of this message lived in Babylon and he hoped that the fall of the Assyrian and the rise of the Persian government would mean the end of the Diaspora, would mean that the Jewish people in its entirety would return to the homeland and become again what it had been in the days of David: a people no longer dispersed but united through its ancestral soil. This prophet changed his view in later years and learned that existence under the conditions of the Diaspora, far from being a danger to Jewish religious life, is a necessity; it enables us to be what we have to be, servants of God for the sake of mankind. He added a second message to the earlier one: he announced that to preach of the return to Zion is not the whole of the holy vocation; the mission is 'to be a light of the gentiles' (Isaiah 49:6) so that the whole world should know God and worship him.

We are a generation which has had the same experience. After the establishment of the State of Israel many of us believed it was the solution of the Jewish question. There is a Jewish state, now all will be well. We only have to work for it. 'Make a path, make a path, clear the way, take up the stumbling block out of the way of my people.' We did our duty. The financial contribution of the Diaspora to Israel proved that our people was capable of making sacrifices. It was also our good fortune that the German reparations became a source of great material assistance. And yet, we see today that the State of Israel is not the end of the Diaspora. The State of Israel is one of the various settlements of the Jewish world Diaspora. We see today that the Jewish people remains what it was for two thousand years: a people of the Diaspora, a people denied the unity which political and national cohesion gives to the gentiles. God wills it, and say ye all: 'So be it'.

Before I continue I want to make one thing quite clear: it is true that the romantic dream of a miraculous end of the Diaspora, of a return of the whole of the Jewish people from all the four corners of the world to the tiny State of Israel, has now come to an end, as every dream must come to an end in the sober light of day. But this does not put an end to our commitment to the citizens of the State of Israel, to our kith and kin there, to the two million Israelis who live and toil and fight on the soil which is the only ground under their feet. 'Make a path, make a path, clear the way, take up the stumbling block out of the way of my people.' Help Israel! Help them as they try to progress with so many stumbling blocks in their way. The economic predicament, political parties with outworn nineteenth-century programmes, an Orthodox minority empowered by the government to suppress the religious freedom of the majority, the problem of the Arab refugees, politically exploited by Arab leaders – of all these troubles you may not notice anything when you board your El Al flight and spend a fortnight in Israel in hotels which can compete with the best hotels in England and America. The tourist sees an impressive and colourful panorama. The sight of Jews engaged in agriculture seems to the tourist like a bucolic scene from a rococo painting, with shepherds and shepherdesses living in Hollywood happiness. The tourist enjoys a scene which is a harsh reality to those engaged in it. A most distressing element of this reality is the dissolution of the family unit in the *kibbutzim*, a hang-over from the days of the pioneers which today can be seen as a tragedy.

Against whom do I speak? Against the misleading advertisements in the Zionist press, against the silly talk of the fund-raisers, against Israeli politicians who refuse to discard the fictitious world of nineteenth-century Zionism. God forbid that I should say a single word which could be interpreted as directed against the Israeli citizens themselves. They all work harder than you do and gain less reward than you. I want to bring the Israelis near to your heart, to remind you of their difficulties and urge you: 'Make a path, make a path, clear the way, take up the stumbling block out of the way of my people'. Help Israel, not by being Zionists – Zionism as a political programme is dead – but by being truly Jews. Help Israel by strengthening the Jewish Diaspora. The immigrants who arrive in Israel today are not Zionists; they are fugitives from totalitarian countries. Rabbi Dr Joachim Prinz, the President of the American section of the World Jewish Congress, made this statement: 'Zionism is dead – long live the Jewish people.' I think I can improve on this formula. I say: 'Zionism is dead. Help Israel!' Israel needs a strong Diaspora, strong through Jewish religion, coming forth from the free Western Diaspora.

Recently I interviewed a young Israeli woman to find out whether she is fit to teach at my religion classes. At such interviews I ask the young Israelis one question : Do you believe in God? That settles it. We do not teach the Hebrew language alone. We do that certainly with great energy and according to modern methods. But we teach Judaism. We teach the prayerbook, Jewish rituals, the minutiae of the Jewish calendar, Jewish history understood as holy history and not as secular history. This young Israeli woman of my last interview, a mother of two young children with a husband working at the Israeli embassy, said to me: 'I kindle the lights on Friday evening, but I do not say any prayers'. We in Anglo-Jewry also have our atheists and agnostics, but they do us a great favour, they drift away from the Jewish community and have not yet tried to build up a so-called Jewish life on the basis of atheism and agnosticism. But in Israel they do. These are the dangerous stumbling blocks in the way of our brothers and sisters in Israel. On the one hand there is in Israel an Orthodoxy of the medieval anti-Western pattern, on the other hand there is agnosticism and atheism, to which, admittedly, the whole Western world is prone if not checked by the Jewish heritage. Israel needs a Judaism emancipated from medievalism, and you help Israel by making your Judaism, faithfully re-interpreted in the language of today, a strong force in world Jewry. 'Make a path, make a path, clear the way, take up the stumbling block out of the way of my people.'

What Israel needs is peace. Let us silence the talk of politicians and fund-raisers who speak of borders which are not negotiable. They complain about borders which are unnatural. But the world is full of unnatural borders, and people consent to them for centuries for the sake of peace. Give money for Israel, as you did before, but make it clear where you stand. We Jews have no other programme but peace. In this dangerous world conflict between East and West the only contribution we have to make is the contribution which God-believing Jews have always made: we pray for peace. Power is no deterrent against power. Power is self-destructive. Mankind has only one escape from tyranny, whether that coming from Russia or that coming from other quarters: a religious revival. Agnosticism is with us in the West, as it is in Russia. Belief in God must truly be 'the light of the gentiles'. This light leads mankind to peace. Let us serve mankind by being God-believing Jews, a people who have a political programme which is at the same time a spiritual programme, because this programme is *shalom,* peace.

BIBLIOGRAPHY

Leo Baeck, *Judaism and Christianity*, translated with an introduction by Walter Kaufmann. Philadelphia, 1958.

Steven T. Katz, *Post-Holocaust Dialogues: Critical Studies in Modern Jewish Thought.* New York/London, 1983.

Nicholas de Lange, 'Ignaz Maybaum (1897–1976) and his attitude to Zionism', in Brian D. Fox, ed., *Tradition, Transition and Transmission. Jubilee Volume in honor of Dr I. O. Lehman* (Cincinnati, 1983), pp. 93–107.

Dow Marmur, 'Holocaust as Progress: Reflections on the Thought of Ignaz Maybaum', in Mary Jo Leddy and Mary Ann Hinsdale, eds, *Faith That Transforms. Essays in Honor of Gregory Baum* (New York/Mahwah, 1987), pp. 8–15.

Dow Marmur, ed., *A Genuine Search. God, Torah, Israel–A Reform Perspective. Essays in Memory of Ignaz Maybaum* (London 1979).

Ignaz Maybaum, *Man and Catastrophe. Sermons preached at the Refugees' Services of the United Synagogue, London.* Translated from the German by Joseph Leftwich, with a Foreword by His Grace the Archbishop of York. London, n.d. [1941].

Ignaz Maybaum, *Synagogue and Society. Jewish–Christian Collaboration in the Defence of Western Civilisation.* Translated from the German MS by Joseph Leftwich. London, 1944.

Ignaz Maybaum, *The Jewish Home.* London, n.d. [1945].

Ignaz Maybaum, *The Jewish Mission.* London, n.d. [1949].

Ignaz Maybaum, *Jewish Existence.* London, 1960.

Ignaz Maybaum, *The Faith of the Jewish Diaspora.* London, 1962.

Ignaz Maybaum, *The Face of God After Auschwitz.* Amsterdam, 1965.

Ignaz Maybaum, *Creation and Guilt. A Theological Assessment of Freud's Father-Son Conflict.* London, 1969.

Ignaz Maybaum, *Trialogue Between Jew, Christian and Muslim.* London, 1973.

Ignaz Maybaum, *Happiness Outside the State.* Stocksfield, Northumberland, 1980.

Eugen Rosenstock-Huessy, ed., *Judaism Despite Christianity.* Tuscaloosa, Alabama, 1969.

Franz Rosenzweig, *The Star of Redemption*, translated from the Second Edition of 1930 by William W. Hallo. New York, 1970/London 1971.

Richard L. Rubenstein, *After Auschwitz* (second edition). Baltimore/London, 1992.

A. Steinberg, ed., *Simon Dubnow: The Man and His Work*. London, 1963.

SOURCES OF EXTRACTS

The 'Tragedy' of Auschwitz: A sermon preached on August 3rd, 1963. *The Faith of God After Auschwitz,* pp. 46–9.

The End of the Middle Ages: A sermon preached on August 31st, 1963. *The Faith of God After Auschwitz,* pp. 65–8.

The Day of the Lord: A sermon preached on January 11th 1964. *The Faith of God After Auschwitz,* pp. 81–4.

The Last Will and Testament of East European Jewry: *The Faith of God After Auschwitz,* pp. 247–52.

Fathers and Sons: *Creation and Guilt,* pp. 90–103.

Apocalypse and *Churban: Creation and Guilt,* pp. 104–122.

Zeal: A sermon preached at Hampstead Synagogue, London, July 8th, 1939. *Man and Catastrophe,* pp. 51–60.

Political Idealism: *Jewish Existence,* pp. 83–101.

Diaspora: *Happiness Outside the State,* pp. 35–9.

Help Israel: A sermon preached on September 20, 1961 (the Day of Atonement). *The Faith of the Jewish Diaspora,* pp. 219–22.

BIBLICAL INDEX

INDEX OF PERSONS